By Gracious Permission of
Her Majesty Queen Elizabeth II
and
Her Majesty Queen Elizabeth the Queen Mother

BIRDS and FLOWERS *of the* CASTLE of MEY *and* BALMORAL

James Alder

Prefaces
Sir Yehudi Menuhin
and
Viscount Ridley

Botanical Text
Jennifer and Paddy Woods

Published by Northumbria University Press

Trinity Building, Newcastle upon Tyne NE1 8ST, UK

Birds and Flowers of the Castle of Mey by James Alder was originally published by James Alder, 90 Whinfell Road, Darras Hall, Ponteland, Northumberland, UK and printed by Oakley Press PLC, Bristol, UK as a limited edition in 1993.

Birds and Flowers of Balmoral by James Alder was originally published by James Alder, 90 Whinfell Road, Darras Hall, Ponteland, Northumberland, UK, and printed by Jackson Wilson Ltd, Leeds, UK as a limited edition in 1997.

British Library Cataloguing in Publication Data. A Catalogue record for this book is available from the British Library.

ISBN 1-904794-01-7

Designed by External Relations, Northumbria University

Printed by The Amadeus Press, Ezra House, West 26 Business Park, Cleckheaton, West Yorkshire BD19 4TQ.

FOREWORD by Sean Figgis

James Alder counts among his heroes and greatest influences the celebrated Northumbrian engraver Thomas Bewick, and upon reflection, there are some notable similarities in the careers of the two artists, both of whom were born by the banks of the River Tyne.

At the age of fourteen Bewick was apprenticed as an engraver in Newcastle. Alder began his apprenticeship, aged fifteen, in the art department of Newcastle's local newspaper, the *Evening Chronicle*. Later he was to set up in business with his brother as a commercial artist, echoing Bewick, who had entered a partnership around 150 years earlier, engraving inscriptions and decorations for clients.

This new single edition of James Alder's two magnificent volumes, *Birds and Flowers of the Castle of Mey, and Birds and Flowers of Balmoral* provides us with another remarkable coincidence. Alder's series of beautiful, intricate illustrations, capture the essence of our bird population in a way that provides, for a contemporary audience, what Bewick achieved at the turn of the nineteenth century with his two volume *History of British Birds*. The publication of this collection places Alder firmly alongside Bewick as a master in the art of depicting birds in their natural environment.

It was Alder's mother who first noticed and encouraged her son's precocious talent for drawing. However, his remarkable ability with pencil and paper lay undeveloped until the age of 13, when a drawing he had made was shown to the Headmaster of his school.

The following day, Alder recalls with the same sense of wonder he must have felt at the time, 'I was presented with a leather case containing a complete set of drawing materials such as I never even knew existed'. Perhaps even more significantly, he was given encouragement and time to draw, and subsequently, a scholarship to attend art classes at Kings College in Newcastle.

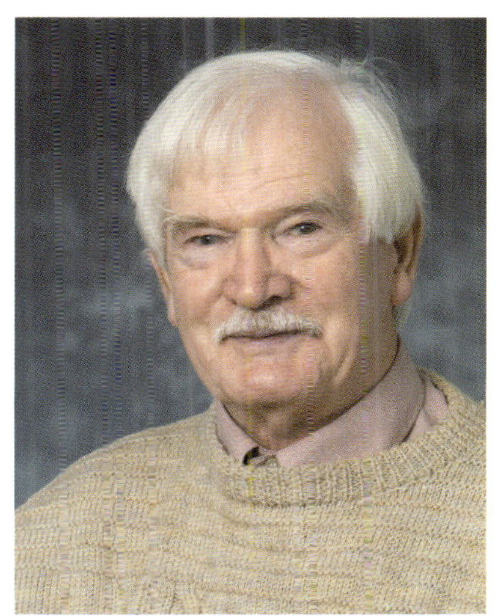

The artist James Alder

His love of nature soon took him into the depths of Northumbria with his note-book, sketching animals, birds and plants. He learned to be patient, to become part of the scene he was observing. He was discovering what he now describes as 'the inseparability of the birds from the process of observation and the process of drawing'.

Alder developed his skills as an illustrator and columnist, earning a well deserved reputation and a loyal following. He was invited in the mid 1980s to contribute designs for a local creative project The Northumbria Quilt, now in the Bowes Museum, depicting local scenes, with a border of birds and animals. 'I had the privilege', he recalls, 'of presenting a print of the quilt to the Queen Mother for her signature and approval'.

Her approval was enthusiastic, and it was from this beginning that the project to produce a limited edition book for the Queen Mother was born. *Birds and Flowers of the Castle of Mey* was so successful that a second commission was soon forthcoming, this time from Her Majesty the Queen, and the subsequent volume, *Birds and Flowers of Balmoral* was produced.

These two limited edition collections have been brought together in this new single volume with permission, gratefully acknowledged, from the Royal Household It has enabled Northumbria University Press to make available, to a much wider public, James Alder's meticulous and essentially personal vision of our northern bird population, in beautiful drawings accompanied by Alder's own commentary.

This is a book to be enjoyed, treasured and, like Bewick's *History of British Birds*, handed down to future generations as a valuable addition to the culture of these islands.

CONTENTS

BIRDS and FLOWERS of the CASTLE of MEY

CONTENTS

BIRDS and FLOWERS of BALMORAL

By Gracious Permission of
Her Majesty Queen Elizabeth the Queen Mother

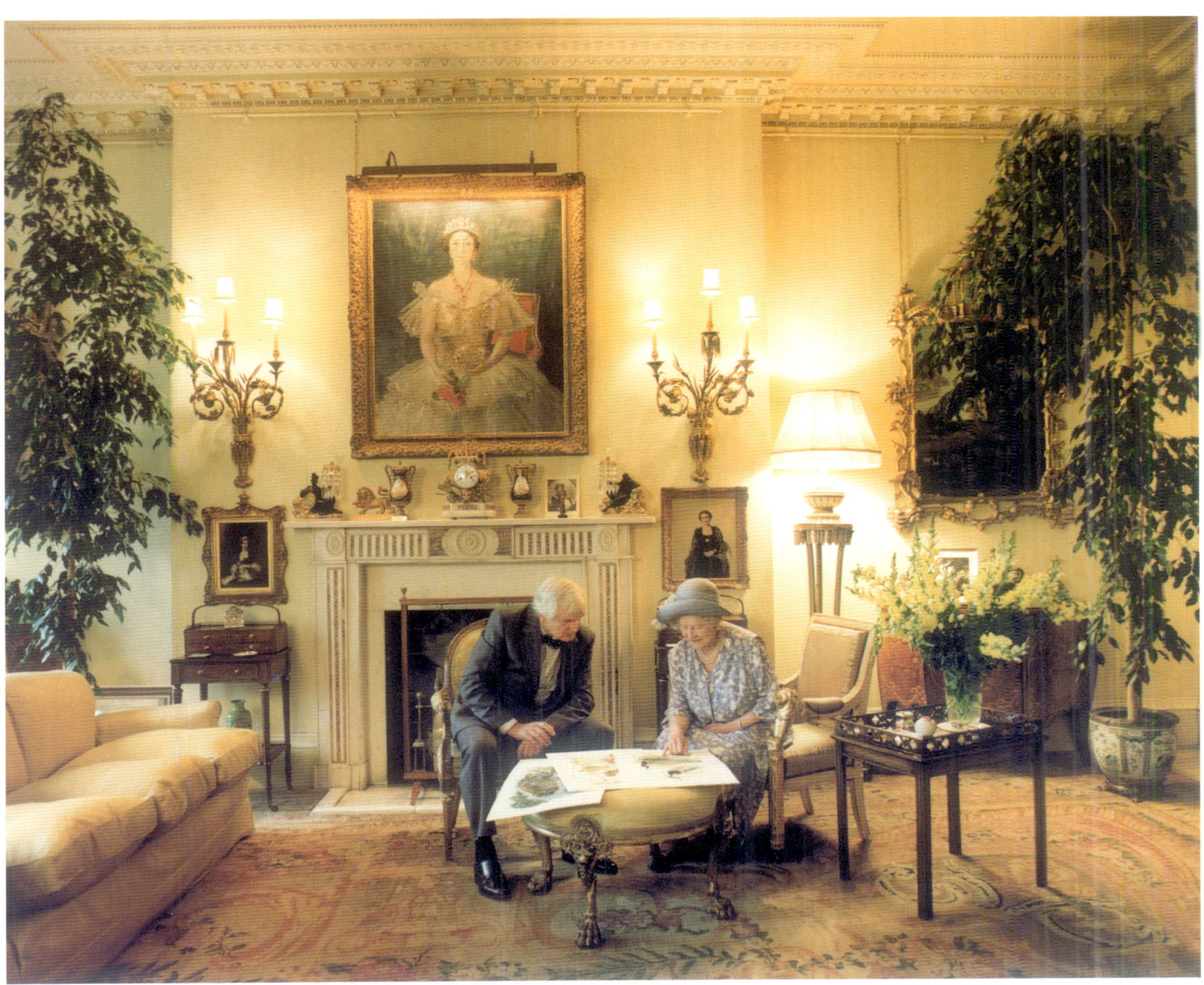

Her Majesty the Queen Mother and James Alder in the drawing room, Clarence House.
Photo: Malcolm Crowthers

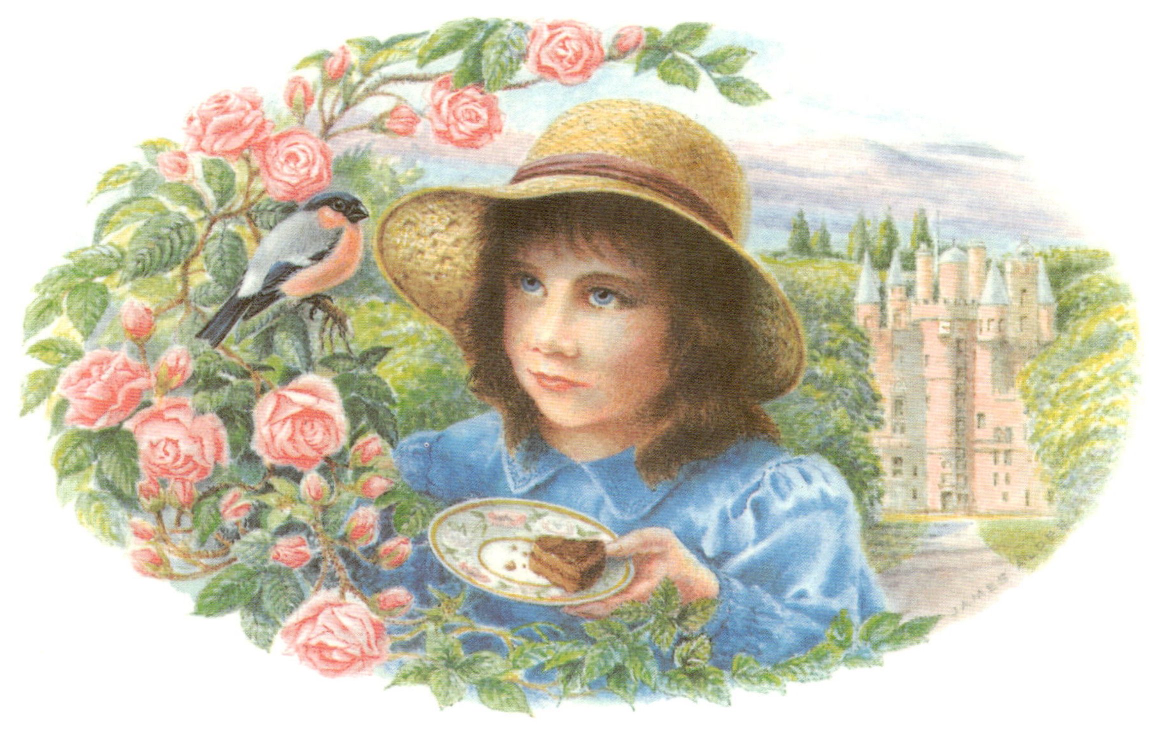

The young Elizabeth taming the bullfinch at Glamis.

BIRDS and FLOWERS
of the
CASTLE of MEY

by

James Alder

Preface by Sir Yehudi Menuhin

Botanical Text by Jennifer and Paddy Woods

PREFACE

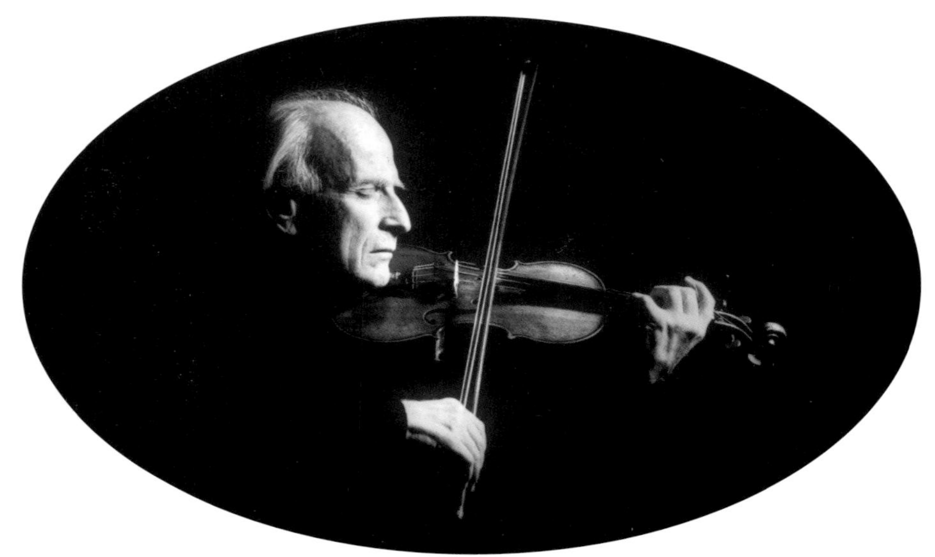

Photo: Malcolm Crowthers

Nov. 11, 1991

As I have the privilege of contributing a few words to this most splendid book, I feel it is an occasion to recognize that these beautiful drawings are not only a feast for the eye but a reminder of our companions among the myriad voices of life – and as a modest warbler myself on my violin, albeit earthbound, I feel a kinship with the haunting and expressive sounds evoked by James Alder's exquisite artistry.

Birds and music are a suitable tribute to Her Majesty Queen Elizabeth the Queen Mother, for she has, by example, by Her love and concern, protected and encouraged both human beings and nature to complement each other in their highest expression.

Birdsong is one of the most elusive and enchanting of nature's gifts to mankind and surely closest to the heart of all musicians.

Plato said "music is a moral law, it gives wings to the mind, soul to the universe, flight to the imagination, charm to sadness, life to everything."

I feel that this sentiment must have lain in the heart of Her Majesty when she conceived the idea of this magnificent book.

Yehudi Menuhin

Sir Yehudi Menuhin

INTRODUCTION by James Alder

In her delightful book 'The Gardens of Queen Elizabeth the Queen Mother', the Marchioness of Salisbury has written an evocative local and botanical account of this magic place, although mentioning the birds but briefly. In this book 'Birds and Flowers of the Castle of Mey', illustrated and written especially for Her Majesty the Queen Mother, the flowers and trees are seen as a setting for the birds, although I hope that the plants have not been neglected in their drawing. I have left their text associated with the plates, in the more able hands of my friends and fellow conservationists, Paddy and Jennifer Woods of the Royal Botanic Garden, Edinburgh.

Despite the many privileges of an Audience with Her Majesty in Clarence House and Birkhall, and the warmth of her welcome to the Castle of Mey and its environs, when the Queen Mother has shown the keenest and most generous interest in every aspect of the book's development, I can make no claim to be an 'authority' on 'The World's First Lady'. Our pleasant conversations, that treated of birds and flowers, of gardening and wilder landscapes, created a world of its own, from which I readily drew inspiration.

My first meeting with Her Majesty was in Durham Cathedral in 1988. I had been involved with other craftspeople in the design of a 'Northumbrian Quilt' which showed cathedrals and castles surrounded by a green 'ruched' border, representing the hills and valleys of Northumbria, among which the beasts, birds and flowers were embroidered and hidden. This was on display in the cathedral, and I had the honour to present to the Queen Mother a framed print of the quilt, number one of an edition, sold to make funds for the church. Her searching gaze was not to be deceived by the ruse of hiding the flora and fauna in the border. 'This is lovely', she said 'but what a pity there is not more information about the beautiful creatures embroidered here.' The desired information was in fact located on the back of the frame and she was delighted.

Some ten months later, in April 1989, I again encountered the same powers of observation. I had produced a leather-bound, gold and silver illuminated book containing the names of the owners of the limited-edition prints, with a special, heavily-gilded page of flowers and insects and a singing willow warbler, which her Majesty was to sign. Every manuscripted name was carefully read, people and personalities remembered! Turning back to the special page she was to sign, Her Majesty said, 'What if I make a blot on this beautiful page?', 'Ma'am', I replied, 'I have taken the liberty of bringing with me several pieces of the same paper…' 'And', she said enthusiastically, 'I will sign one of the spares, and you will cut out the spoiled part and replace it. That *is* thoughtful – now I have confidence.' Of course, the Queen Mother signed the page first time, exactly balanced!

Later that year, when the 'Birds and Flowers' book was first considered, I suggested to Her Majesty that I should first prepare two sample watercolours for her consideration. A reconnaissance of Mey and its adjacent shores and countryside became necessary.

After the Queen Mother and her staff left Mey in October, I drove the four hundred or so miles north to Caithness where road signs increasingly reminded me of ancient Viking occupation. At the Castle of Mey I met Sandy and June Webster, who take care of the castle and its grounds. When relaxing from her duties, June proves to be a fine craftswoman, as are many of the ladies of Caithness, producing exquisite crochet works, some requiring years of patient industry. Sandy, often faced with strong, cold winds and rainstorms, tries to keep a 'tidy' garden. Her Majesty first approving, he constantly experiments with plant species and varieties offered, it seems, almost sacrificially to the powerful selective forces of this breathtaking land. 'The gales still throw my cabbages over the wall,' he says, with dry philosophy. Here, where remnants of the defeated Armada tried to navigate these treacherous reaches, the great Atlantic tides surge from the west between the sharp edge of Scotland and Orkney, and clash with the cold North Sea, elbowing its way westwards through the Bores of Duncansby.

Rarely are the clouds unspectacular as their masses are wedged upwards by the northern islands: the quiet dawns are lark-lauded, and the sunsets marvellous in their dying.

The brave little castle, first seen almost derelict by the Queen Mother in 1952, and later restored with loving care, lies but three hundred yards or so from the shore. Hoy and Orkney are framed through her garden gate, and Scapa Flow, where great fleets anchored, lies hidden by distant misty headlands. Well-managed fields to each side of the castle, pasturing prize sheep and cattle, slope gently towards the sea, ending in flower-spangled dunes and turf and rock embankments. Here is a small bay, fronted by parallel reefs which break the waves, a haven for many species of shore birds and duck. A little to the east, two man-made ponds which empty into the bay, via a small stream, are edged with marsh marigolds, celandine and yellow flag. Wild duck nest here and the quaint dabchick, while the plumed heron stalks its eels and frogs. Further to the east, but still within easy walking distance along rabbit-cropped turf paths, are great impenetrable sweeps of gorse. Flaming gold in sunlight or shade against clean blue skies, the colours are almost too much to bear. Pipits, larks, twite and stonechats find sanctuary here.

A tiny disused haven miraculously appears, approached by a perilously descending, slippery turf path. Two towering walls of stratified lichen-encrusted rock embrace a leaden sea and create a natural amphitheatre, which echoes with sound. Gossiping fulmars squat on ledges garlanded in sea-pink and campion, and rock doves 'coo' from secret caverns. Above, there is drama. A tiercel peregrine emerges from the wings and a pair of breeding ravens, ragged in flight, hurl themselves at the aristocrat of the air who chatters angrily as the ravens harry him. He is no match for their black fury and exits while chuckling harshly, they insolently victory-roll to celebrate retreat. The grey seals, which were reclining on the broken pier like tired senators, had slipped quietly into the sea and were submerged. The cantrip northern islanders will still tell you 'sing a song to them and you will enchant them'... so I did. A favourite, 'The Waters of the Tyne', I sang to them, and they slowly re-appeared: but only their disembodied black-glassy-and-bald heads with huge sad eyes that watched my departure.

These are the wild pageants that the Queen Mother will have encountered and observed for forty years and many more. It would be near here, as she walked along a turf path near the sea that she encountered a 'bonxie', the great skua. 'It stood over a baby rabbit. It had such a fierce and wicked look... and when it launched at me, or so it seemed, I turned and beat a hasty retreat!' she recounted. Wise caution, because a knock on the head from the feet of a three-and-a-half pound skua *is* painful!

To the west, Dunnet Head can be seen from the castle turrets. A mighty, hunch-backed giant, caped in indigo, that plunges a full three hundred feet into the deep water, it is the most northerly point of mainland Britain. It is the home of gannets and puffins, kittiwakes and fulmars, guillemots and razorbills and, of course, the lordly peregrine. The landward slopes, frequently drenched in sea spray, yet grow orchids and Scottish primroses. To the foot of the slopes are small lochs, fish-filled, the haunt of the red-throated diver whose 'jizz', if you cannot spot the red throat on a dull day, is the unmistakable up-tilted beak. I have described the invented word 'jizz' to the joy of note-taking American birdwatchers, as 'a lifetime of bird-watching distilled to a split-second of understanding!' Rather like Whistler's famous reply, 'How long did it take me to paint the picture... all my lifetime, madam!' Snipe nest here, and the dapper wheatears, as well as that little swashbuckler, the merlin, which may be watched pursuing its favourite prey, the common meadow and rock pipits. Notice that you will rarely see the merlin capture its prey first time – that's not the way with nature. Predator and prey must hone each other to a perfection that is never really attained by either!

In autumn the small rocky bays and sand-girt shores are landfalls for innumerable sea birds and rare visitors which arrive from Arctic tundras and forests. They cross the northern seas from Scandinavia, flop exhausted on treeless Shetland, refuel, and then make their leisurely way southwards down the island chain to the Orkneys and the shorter flight to mainland Scotland. How many tiny, unrecorded rarities have welcomed the sight of the Queen Mother's private wood by the shore, the only deciduous wood for miles?

For obvious reasons, the Queen Mother is not a pursuer of rarities! Her pleasure is found in the small birds, the common ones, to her never 'plain', which she encounters as they pursue their daily rounds in her garden or about her estates. Of course, she also finds the larger species attractive, especially where they reveal 'character'. The curlew, with its lovely bubbling song is a favourite, the puffins, which are both comical and economical – in spring they grow extra large and colourful beaks, necessary in courtship, and to carry the extra fish for their families later. The short-eared owls, rolling in flight as they search for voles, and the occasional hen harrier, gilded in evening sunlight are pure joy.

Her Majesty seems to be a protectionist rather than a conservationist, although no one can doubt she recognises the need for care of the apparently self-sufficient predators, and of the lands that nurture them.

While chatting over tea, a splendid old-fashioned ceremony, with homemade buttered scones, strawberry jam, a thickly layered chocolate cake and a huge brown British Rail teapot kept hot and full, I mentioned that I had at home a delightful ten-year-old bullfinch. He had been rescued after his baby brothers and sisters had been taken by a magpie. 'How strange', the Queen Mother replied, 'we had one when I was a little girl. He was an adult and wild, yet came to our little tea parties in the garden and took cake crumbs from a plate.'

Imagination stirred, we decided that a small vignette illustrating this would make a nice frontispiece for the book. Her Majesty lent me various photographs, showing her as a very small Lady Elizabeth Bowes-Lyon, from which to draw the portrait.

I studied these for days, nervous at a new challenge, while fascinated by the concentration in those fine blue eyes. Hats were firmly for heads, and must not obscure the vision! Unafraid, instinctively commanding without hauteur, naturally sympathetic and encouraging, those beautiful eyes were already set to conquer and inspire a future Queen's world.

Her Majesty's garden, exquisite by any standards, yet born of willpower against the elements; those private, quiet walks, when yellow-buntings flit before her, down scarlet and lichen-silvered hedges and shorebirds pipe softly by the waves, are surely a sublimation of the deep understanding the Queen Mother has shown all her years for life and humanity.

The Plates 1–25

PLATE 1 WRENS *(Troglodytes troglodytes)*

From its ancient origins in North America, via the Aleutian chain, Asia and Europe, again island hopping through Britain to St. Kilda and volcanic Iceland, this rusty, wee smidgen of a bird has virtually circumnavigated the Northern Hemisphere. On reaching Asia, the wren may have exploited its new world quickly, since it is now known that 'the wren of little quill' is capable of annual migrations of hundreds of miles.

The wren nests in the Queen Mother's garden by the sea, hunting spiders and insects in crevices, there, and on the stony foreshore, while varying its diet with sand hoppers caught along the wrack. Northwards across the waves to Orkney and Shetland, wrens are slightly bulkier, with longer wings. This conforms to 'Bergman's Rule' – the bulkier a given shape, the better the heat retention in colder environs. Eggs are larger for that reason, and have better hatching success.

Wrens are 'troglodytes', 'cave dwellers', apt because their nests are little caverns of woven grass and fern, sometimes filling out the larger caverns of deserted dipper nests that overhang the burns. The males, whose rapid songs are loud for their size, are polygamous, as I discovered the related dippers to be. Both species build several nests in their territories to varying standards of perfection, which after coy and excited showing by the males are inspected, accepted or rejected by critical females. Near the Castle of Mey the wrens will nest in heather by peaty hags and haunt the precipitous cliffs of Dunnet Head. In the far away Himalayas they survive as high as 15,000 feet, recalling Shakespeare's 'wrens make prey where eagles dare not perch'.

Plutarch first quoted Aesop's fable about the bird's choice of King. It was argued that the one flying highest should have the title. The eagle, powerful symbol of the East, seemed a certainty as it ascended above all except the tiny wren who, having hidden in the eagle's mantle feathers, flew out to rise above his exhausted competitor. Cunning won the day, and the Greeks whose history records not a little intrigue, celebrated the wren as 'King of the Birds'.

Until recent times, some western people of Britain and France have annually celebrated 'the King' by hunting him on St. Stephen's Day, perhaps even now in Ireland! He was harried down the hedgerows, caught and hung over a pole carried by boys and men who made him the butt of satire. 'We'll need a horse and cart to carry this one back...'

Sarcasm, ridicule, irony, diminishing the minute, satisfying for a day mans' need to reduce the great to manageable size. It may be coincidence – Stephen is the Greek name for crown or wreath.

ROSE 'Elizabeth of Glamis'

The Floribunda rose 'Elizabeth of Glamis' was introduced by the Irish grower McGredy in 1964 and soon became a favourite with its beautifully scented salmon pink flowers and dark green foliage. Unfortunately it is not completely hardy in the north and is susceptible to mildew and blackspot. David Austin, the famous rose breeder, recently has commentated 'this once popular rose is not much grown now as unlike the lady in honour of whom it was named its vigour diminished not long after its introduction.'

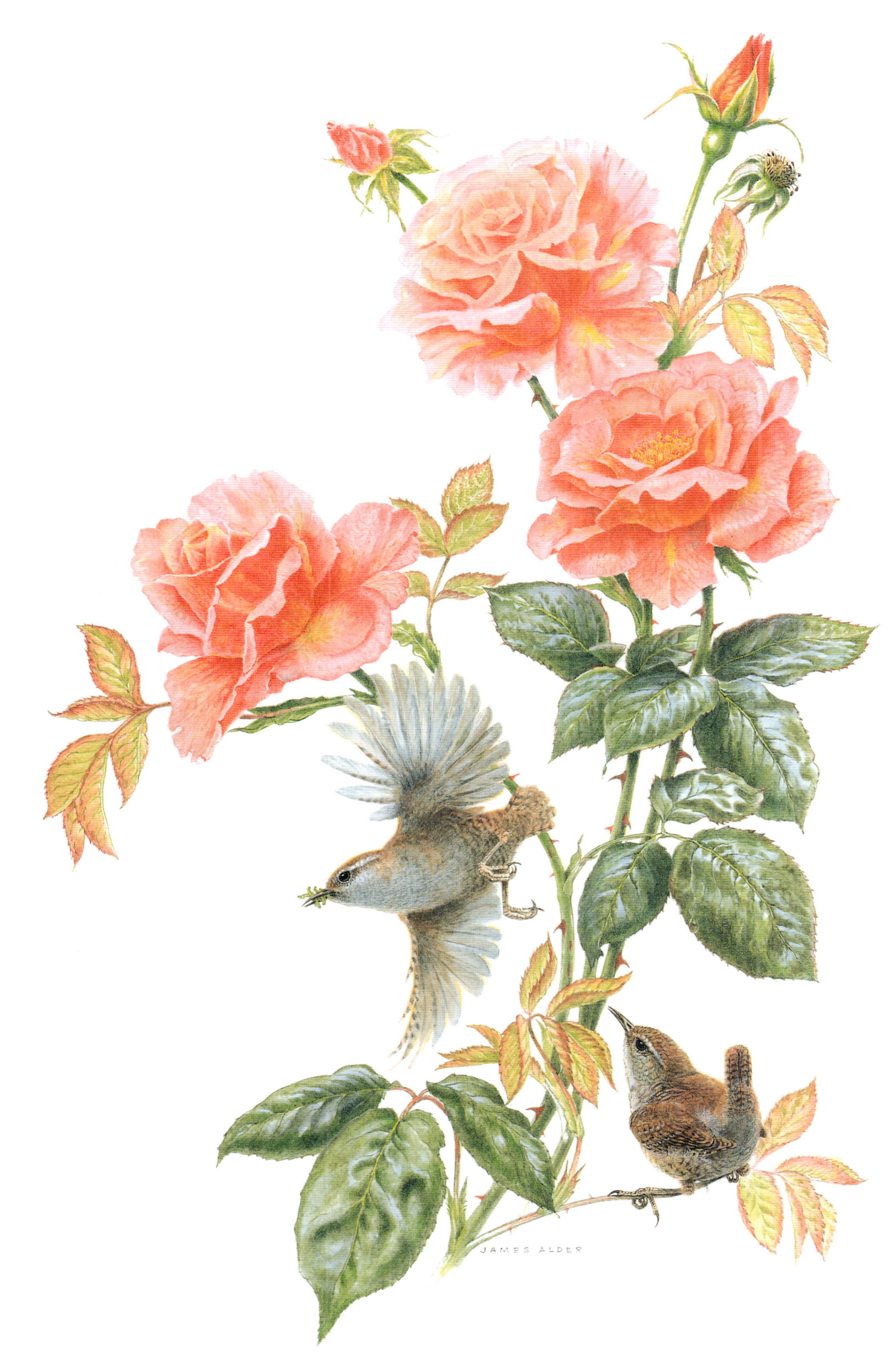
JAMES ALDER

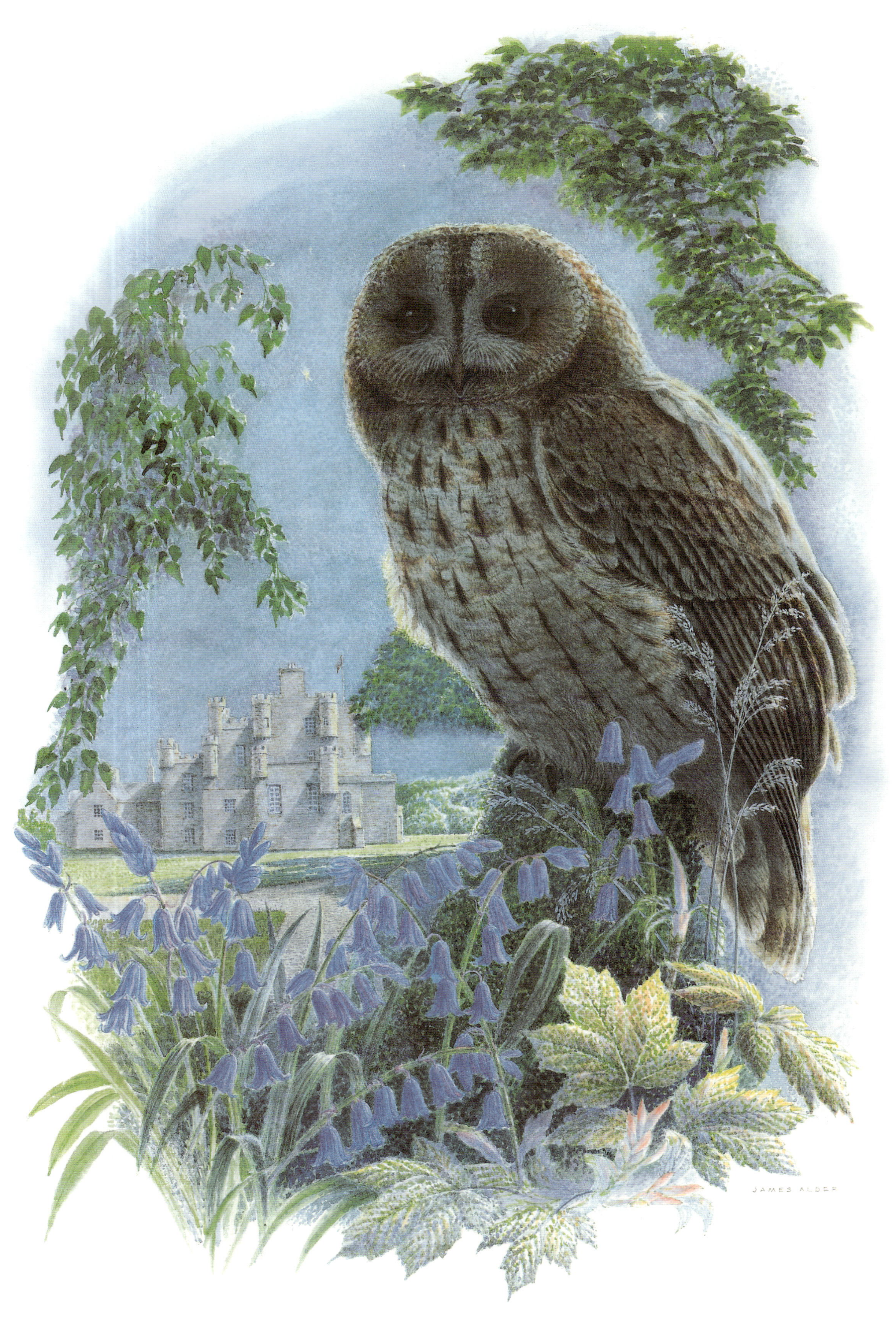
JAMES ALDER

TAWNY OWL *(Strix aluco)*

The almost completely nocturnal tawny owl is the best known of the British breeding owls – 'the one that hoots'. Traditionally, the hoolet nests in holes in trees, walls and niches, takes over disused nests of crow and magpie, and will even nest in heather or in a brackeny hillside. The 2–4 white eggs are laid at intervals of two or more days, incubation beginning at the first egg, producing a brood that is stepped at age and size. This is known as asynchronous hatching and is characteristic of many owl and hawk species.

Tawny owls have expansive tastes – wood mice, voles, rats, bats, rabbits, insects and earthworms, all are welcome, while small birds caught in roosts and occasionally at least, frogs and fish taken in shallow waters, list a diet that can hardly be called specialist.

Although these owls are well distributed in England, Wales and Scotland, they have never been recorded in Ireland, and despite their presence in Caithness they are not found in Orkney or Shetland. It has been suggested that they do not like crossing large areas of water, perhaps because they have a larger wing loading than other British owls. The tawny owl is relatively heavier, with a shorter rounded wing, a formula that suits a highly sedentary and fiercely territorial lifestyle.

In contrast, long-eared owls, recorded near the Castle of Mey, have light, smaller bodies with much longer wings, and they are widely distributed in Northern Ireland, where their food is wood mice and rats. Barn owls, whose breeding range extends north to Sutherland, have a wing loading formula similar to the long-eared owls and they too, with similar food preferences, breed in Ireland in numbers. Short-eared owls, however, with great powers of flight and the ability to migrate annually across the North Sea, are vole specialists. They don't visit Ireland simply because there are no voles there!

WILD HYACINTH
(Hyacinthoides non-scripta)

The wild hyacinth or English bluebell *Hyacinthoides non-scripta*, is essentially a plant of deciduous woodland which carpets the ground with a haze of blue in late spring. Where trees have been felled and bracken has crept in masses of bluebells can linger on, an attractive contrast to the bright light green of the young fronds. Seaside slopes and low hillsides are also favoured habitats. They are frequently cultivated and naturalised as at the Castle of Mey, where bluebells follow on from daffodils and celandines under the sycamore and ash, scenting the air with their delicate and unmistakable fragrance. Purplish-blue bell-shaped flowers hang along one side of a gracefully curving stem growing, along with the narrow leaves, to over a foot in height. By summer the papery seed pods are held erect and are filled with black shiny seeds.

PLATE 3

SKYLARK *(Alauda arvensis)*

The north-eastern triangle of Caithness is mainly wide, flat and open, with a topography of heather and heathland, bogland, arable and pastureland. Rising gently from its sea-sculptured northern shores in a series of slight undulations, the terrain is flanked right and left by the awesome three hundred foot high shoulders of Dunnet and Duncansby, which plunge suddenly downwards as if throwing all back into the sea.

This is a challenging country, which begets and is kind to its own special flora and fauna, and the skylark entirely reflects this in its song flight. Leaping from concealment among the bent, it begins to sing almost immediately, fluttering upwards, sometimes rising and falling, to become an almost invisible speck, poised at last on its own glorious cone of silver sound. Less poetically, it may adopt for its stage a moorland wall, or a lichened wooden gatepost, which I portray with a backdrop of the Pentland Firth, Hoy, and Mainland Orkney.

Despite its aspirations to sing at Heaven's Gate, the skylark is, inevitably, a ground nester. A slight depression in a tussock, lined neatly with course and fine grasses and hair, will do to hold the 3–5 eggs. Secret runnels in the grass may conceal the lark's movements as it approaches and leaves the nest. The unfledged young will leave this comfort earlier than hedge nesters, and fly after about ten days. Such precocity has survival value, since scattering gives the predator less chance of catching the whole brood.

The food of skylarks consists of insects and worms, seeds of weeds, corn and chickweed and leaves of clover and brassicas, a simple diet, which combined with their strong and persistent flight, make them birds of the great plains.

Over the centuries, their habitat may have been greatly extended by man's destruction of the forests. Skylarks are found throughout Europe, eastwards in its different races through Russia and the central plains of Asia, to China and Japan.

Surprisingly, the meaning of the scientific names of many bird species are difficult to trace, but I like to think that Linnaeus, who in his great work named the lark, meant it to read 'praising the heavens above the fields.'

SCOTTISH PRIMROSE *(Primula scotica)*

WILD PANSY *(Viola tricolor)*

There are not many species which are restricted to the British Isles. One of the few British endemic plants is the Scottish primrose, *Primula scotica* which is found only on the coasts of Sutherland and Caithness and on the neighbouring Orkney Islands. It grows in dampish places from sea level on dune slacks, on cliff pastures and on grassy heaths and, when nibbling rabbits allow it to flower freely, is a charming little plant with about ten flowers clustered on a short stalk which seldom reaches more than four inches in height. Each flower is purple with a yellow eye while the leaves which are held in a rosette at the foot of the stem are mealy underneath.

In contrast the wild pansy or heartsease, *Viola tricolor*, is widely distributed throughout Britain and Europe with a low growing rather fleshy leafed variant being recognised from coastal areas.

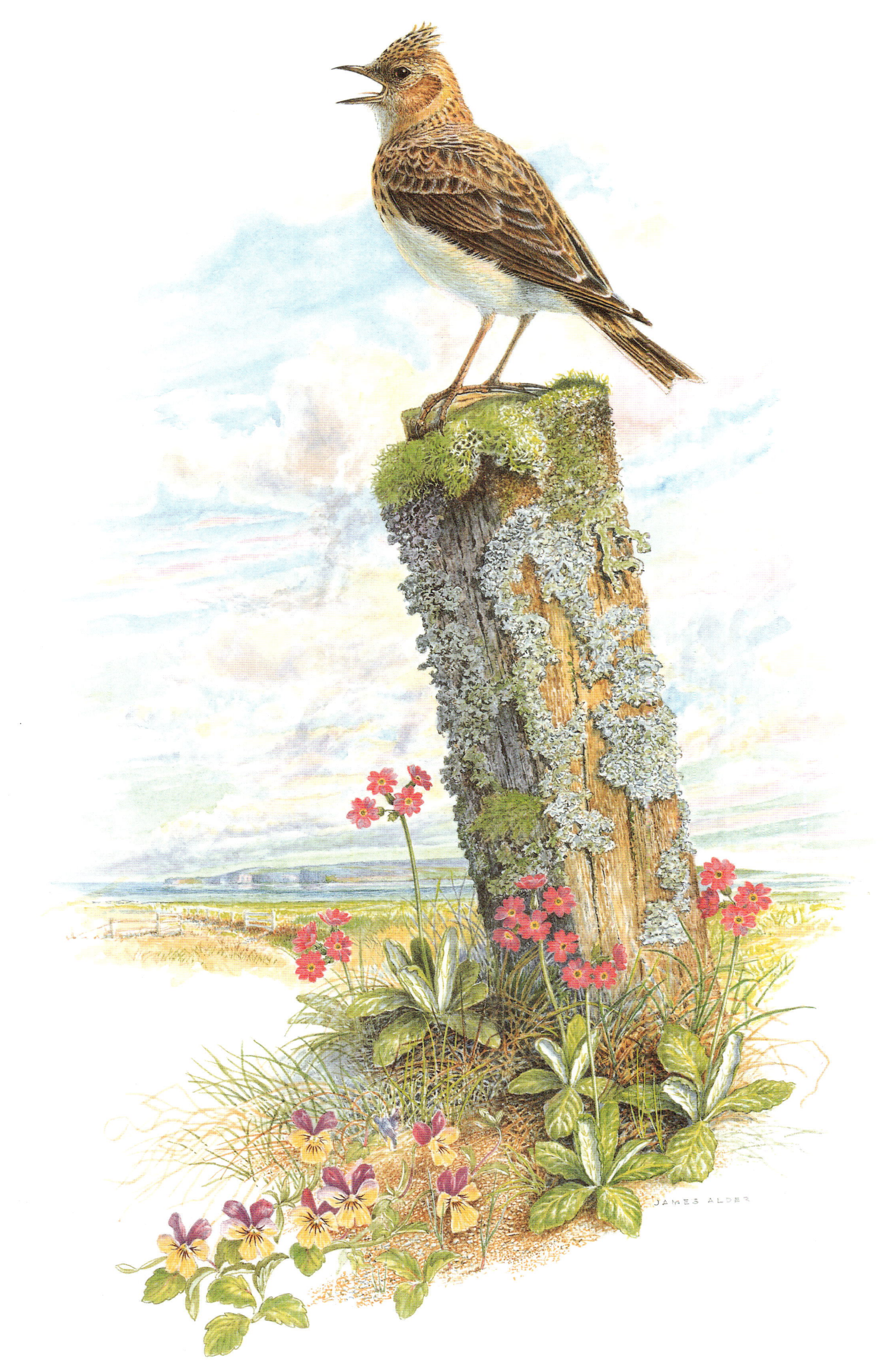
JAMES ALDER

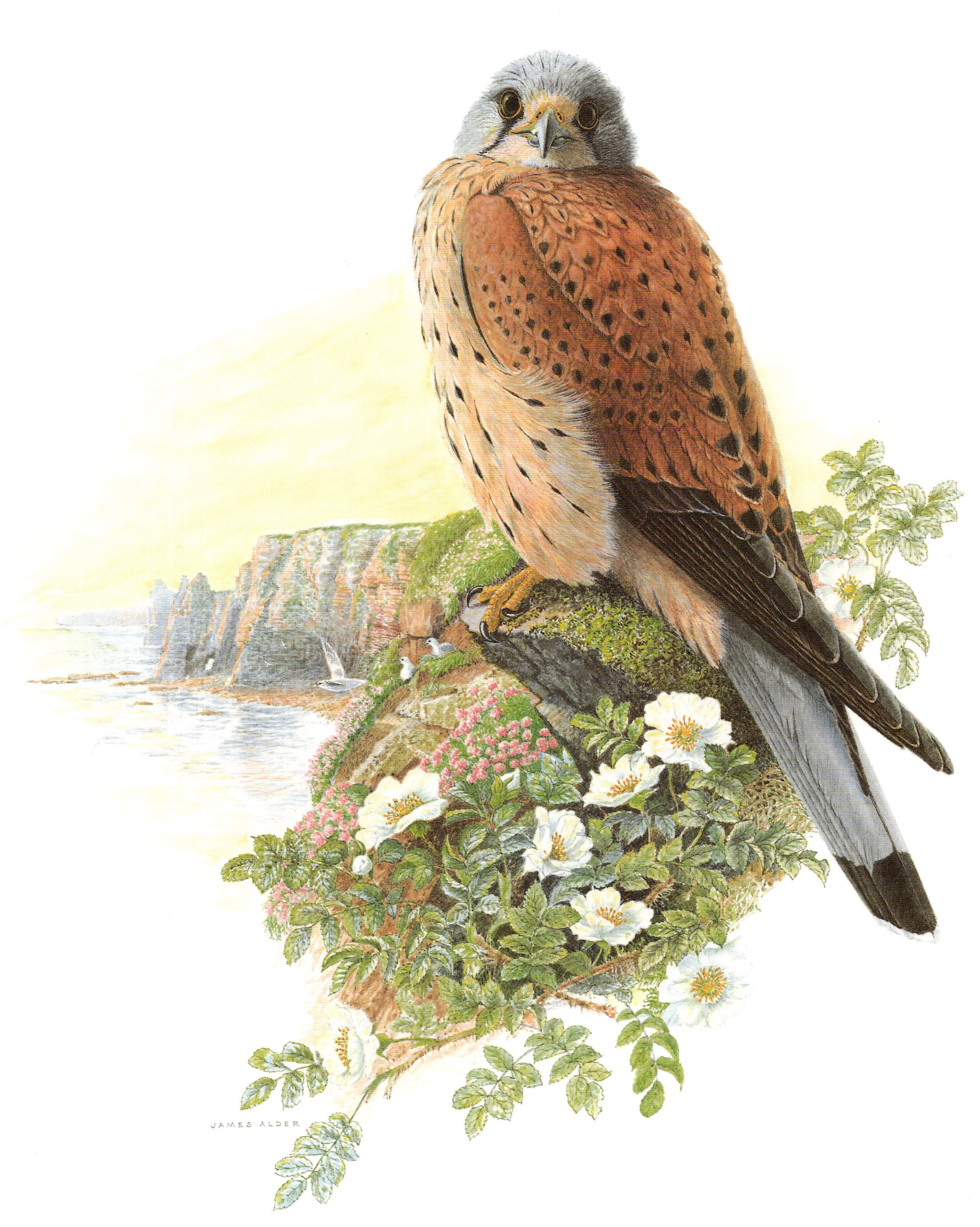
JAMES ALDER

KESTREL *(Falco tinnunculus)* PLATE 4

The beautiful flower festooned setting of Duncansby Head provides the inspiration for this drawing of the "Windhover," where he can soar and hang effortlessly, vying with the gliding fulmars in masterful use of the devious updraughts of air.

The ten worldwide species of kestrel are ubiquitous, occupying almost every ecological niche between the Polar Regions, from wilderness to polluted urban wastes. In their choice of nesting sites they are almost creative. Office blocks and warehouses become impregnable crags, cathedrals are sacred peaks, shipyards iron castles, from which the bold little falcons sally forth against their prey.

I once studied a pair for many weeks in a famous Tyneside shipyard, where they nested below the engine house at the top of a crane, overlooking the muddy, rat-infested river. They had evicted a pair of rooks who had originally built the nest, the ultimate in avian urbanity, of welding rods and packing case wires, with a fistful of straw for comfort. After great skirmishing the kestrels threw the rook's green eggs overboard, and replaced them with five brown ones. All hatched and fledged successfully, despite the crane's screeching protest as it built a ship!

One fledgling did come to grief; it fell into a bucket of bilge oil. I rescued and cleaned it and, after much training, rehabilitated it. His name was 'Kek,' and he became the emblem of the Young Ornithologists' Club of the Royal Society for the Protection of Birds (RSPB).

In the hierarchy of falcons and hawks, the kestrel was given the lowest status – anybody could keep one because their prey was of the humblest kind.

The now obsolete name 'coistrell' was given to it in mediaeval times, while, in Shakespeare's *Twelfth Night*, we find Sir Toby Belch vowing 'he's a coward and a coystrill' to describe a knave, a base fellow!

Over the years I have rehabilitated many of these beautiful falcons back to the wild and, to me, they stand high in intelligence and courage. One lovely female, who ranged freely in a territory around my house and roosted in my studio, came one day to the window ledge. Various stuffed specimens of hawks and skins littered my desk, and a camera was at hand. She bowed to me deeply, her banded tail widely fanned, head tilted sideways, and softly 'kee-kee-d.' She turned abruptly, and flew away fast in a straight line towards the distant coast. I never saw her again. In an illustrated talk on kestrels, I described this, a moving event to me, which I had photographed. The slide, showing her display, also revealed the stuffed hawk. A crushing Yorkshire voice came from the anonymous darkness and said 'Don't you think, Mr Alder, that the bird was saying if that's what he does to his birds, I'm bloody well off!'

BURNET ROSE *(Rosa pimpinellifolia)*

An attractive dwarf shrub of our coastal dunes, heaths and inland limestone areas is the burnet rose, *Rosa pimpinellifolia*. It is recognised by its often short stature and suckering stems usually densely covered in prickles and bristles, by its quite large white fragrant flowers and in autumn by the purplish black more or less globose fruit. The leaves are divided into five, seven, nine or eleven roundish leaflets with finely toothed margins.

PLATE 5 WILLOW WARBLER *(Phylloscopus trochilus)*

Willow warblers are delicate in form, colour and song, and are naturally among the Queen Mother's favourites. At the very limits of their northern breeding range in Britain, they nest in open glades in Her Majesty's woodland by the castle, and, who knows, may be the very last individuals of a great unrolling carpet of perhaps six million birds which began their long migration weeks before in South Africa.

After such a long journey, for a species whose weight may be no more than two sheets of writing paper, one might think that any suitable territory would be acceptable. Research has shown that both experienced adults and one year old birds seek out their natal territories, some adults re-nesting on the very plots of turf occupied by them in preceding years! Even their young, returning for the first time, may inherit the vacated territories of lost parents.

The nest is built on the ground by the female, among tufted grass and is domed, with a side entrance, and is warmly lined with feathers. The eggs, six or seven in number, are incubated by the female. Willow warblers are confiding birds, and, with patience and care, I have persuaded them to sit on my fingers, from which perch they have passed food to their young.

Although they are ground nesters, they specially like open glades in mixed deciduous woods, or young trees and growing conifer plantations, where they find their main food, caterpillars, moths, flies and spiders. They are urgent and acrobatic in their search, and constantly examine the undersides of leaves, earning their generic name, *phylloscopus*, which means 'leaf looking.'

On their southward autumn migrations, they are not averse to eating small soft fruits, which no doubt provide them with energising sugars for the long return flight to warmer climes.

ROSE "Iceberg"

'To many gardeners it remains the perfect rose with both a lovely form and an astonishing fragrance.' Add to that its long flowering season, its suitability for hedging, for cutting or as a climber and it is easy to see why 'Iceberg' is still one of the most popular of floribundas. Introduced by the German firm of Kordes in 1958, it has remained a firm favourite with rose growers ever since.

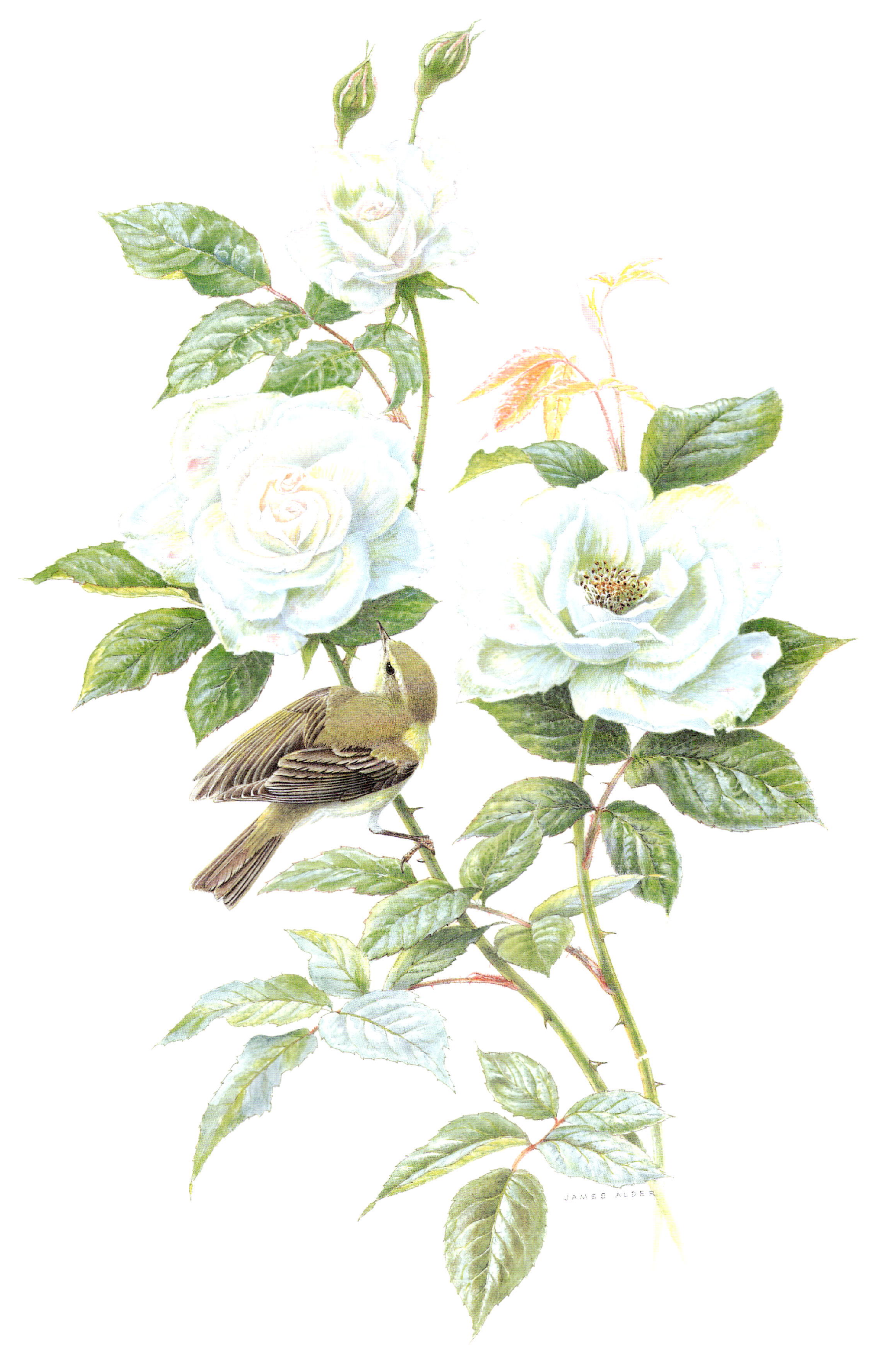
JAMES ALDER

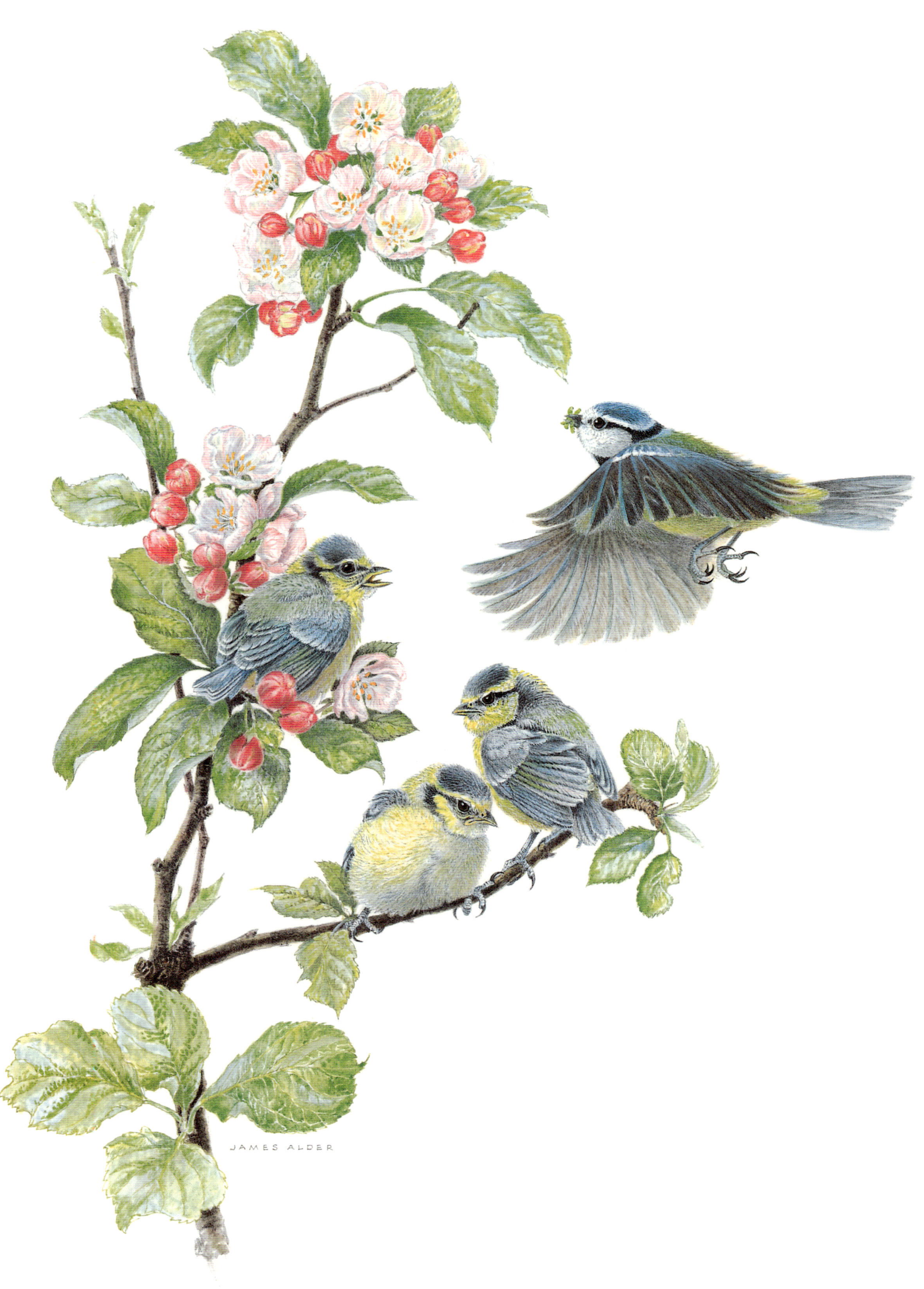
JAMES ALDER

BLUE TITS *(Parus caeruleus)*

PLATE 6

Blue tits, among the smallest and most successful of birds, are wide spread throughout Britain wherever there is sufficiency of trees and bushes, rarely thinning out in numbers until they reach the Scottish Central Highlands, Sutherland and Caithness.

Research has shown heavy concentrations around centres of human populations, where, collectively, small gardens become quite large nature reserves. Ornamental trees, hedges and various fruiting bushes can provide an almost inexhaustible food supply throughout the year, nest boxes in their thousands may exceed demand, tons of nuts and seeds are supplied throughout the winter and cats are given their comeuppance especially when young are fledging.

It has been shown that blue tits gear their breeding season to the peak supply of caterpillars, and unsprayed apple trees and bushes guarantee success. The eggs are seven to fourteen in number, and I have had ten fledglings pop out of one of my nest boxes. Poised with various expressions of expectancy along a floral spray, they are a happy sight, although regrettably they may soon become the favourite prey of the little male sparrow hawk, and their losses are high. However these losses are balanced by high fledging success.

Their ubiquity is equalled by their intelligence, and they gained notoriety some years ago because of their new habit of piercing milk bottle caps to sip the cream. Where they have difficulty in clinging to a string of peanuts, they will haul these up, 'hand over fist,' and quickly solve intricate puzzles to attain their prize of food. They can be little bullies, and will face up to and grapple with the much larger great tits at food tables, and are fiercely aggressive with them in defence of nest sites.

My own colour-ringed blue tits showed renewed activity that they were reasserting their authority in anticipation of spring. A pair that already owns a tried and tested breeding site is clearly advantaged. Bird ringing has shown that many blue tits are already paired in autumn, and I suggest that one of the pair at least had formerly bred at the selected site.

APPLE (blossom)

By the time Patrick Neill published his treatise 'On Scottish Gardens and Orchards' in 1813 a very large number of market gardens, nurseries and orchards had been established in Scotland including a seven acre 'public garden' at Thurso in Caithness. Apples had been grown in orchards and as espaliers or on walls for many years and a huge number of varieties were known including many raised in Scotland as their names revealed: Lady Wemyss, Luffness Pippin, Tower of Glamis. Some of the favourites are still grown today and Neill quotes of the Ribston Pippin 'A universal apple for these kingdoms. It will thrive and even ripen at John o'Groat's, while it deserves a place at Exeter or at Cork.'

PLATE 7 SWALLOWS *(Hirundo rustica)*

Swallows, originally cave dwellers, must have associated themselves with early man, continuing this relationship as he developed into herdsman, farmer and builder. This special symbiosis reaffirmed the cycle of life as the friendly birds mysteriously returned each spring, the livingest of creatures, from nowhere. For thousands of years mankind of all races has eagerly looked for their return. A Greek vase, showing a bearded man, two youths, and a flying swallow, celebrates the migrants return. The written dialogue, surely an early comic strip, translates as, First boy, 'look, there's a swallow.' Man. 'By Herakles, so it is.' Second boy 'It must be spring.'

The cupped nest, pellets of mud, saliva and broken straw, is traditionally made in byre or barn, and is long lasting. After 25 years, a disused nest in my garage is still intact, not a pellet displaced. Then, when the garage was a studio, the happy birds would sweep between my face and the drawing board, or flitted twittering, around the kitchen in the morning sun. Did primitive man feel my pleasure?

Adults normally return to the same barn, often to their original nests, but the first year birds must explore, many spreading to neighbouring farms to breed. The early birds have two broods, sometimes three, a replacement requirement to meet their heavy losses incurred during long hazardous migrations. As a rule, the birds breeding furthest north migrate furthest south. The Caithness swallows may twitter their way to South Africa! A quite different species of bird, the eskimo curlew, which breeds in Arctic Canada, flies southwards down the length of America to 'winter' in Tierra del Fuego!

My drawing of the swallows with apples was inspired by the Queen Mother's query, 'Why are there so many swallows in the garden – most seem to be just sitting around?' I replied that they were catching flying ants which had just emerged, they were crawling over the leaves and fruit, making sitting targets! The apples are 'old apples,' unnamed, and Her Majesty who had confided that she had not tasted them, was pleased to learn that they made a very good pie, after they had posed for their portrait!

APPLE (fruit)

Apples have long been cultivated in Britain and techniques for dwarfing and pruning probably were introduced around Roman times. John Reid in 'The Scots Gard'ner' published in 1683 has much to say on spacing, pruning and varieties: 'Apples may be from 8 to 10 ells distance... begin betimes to prune your fruit trees, spare them not while young: reduce them into a good shape, and order while such; so they will not only soon overgrow the wounds, their branches being but small, but also when they should come to bear fruit, you shall not need to cut so much, only purge them of superfluities; and this is the way to make trees fruitful as well as pleasant... the best apple for the table is the Golden Pepin, we have also Rennets, Russets, etc... and for the kitchen the Codling, Lidingtown and Rubies.'

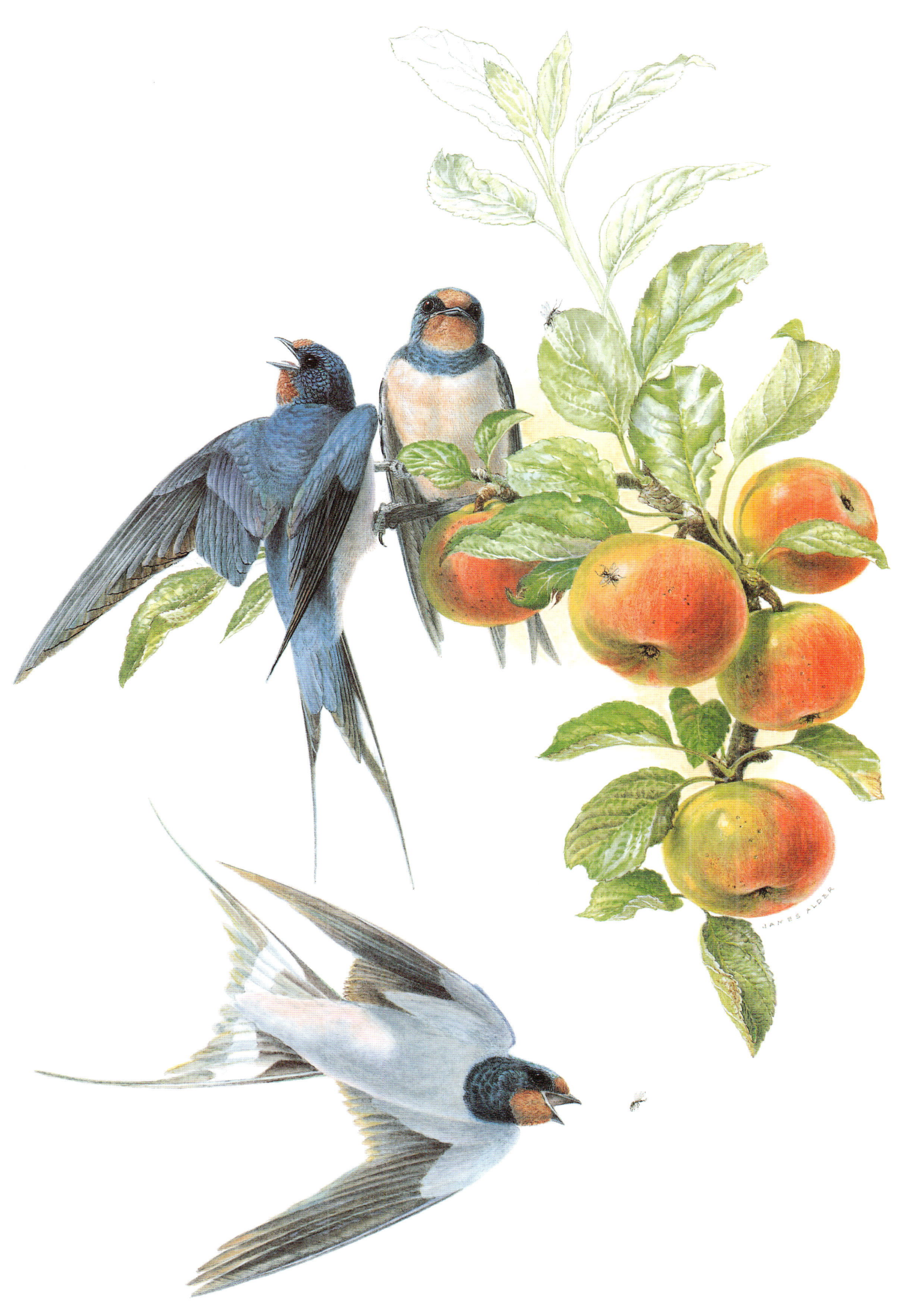
JAMES ALDER

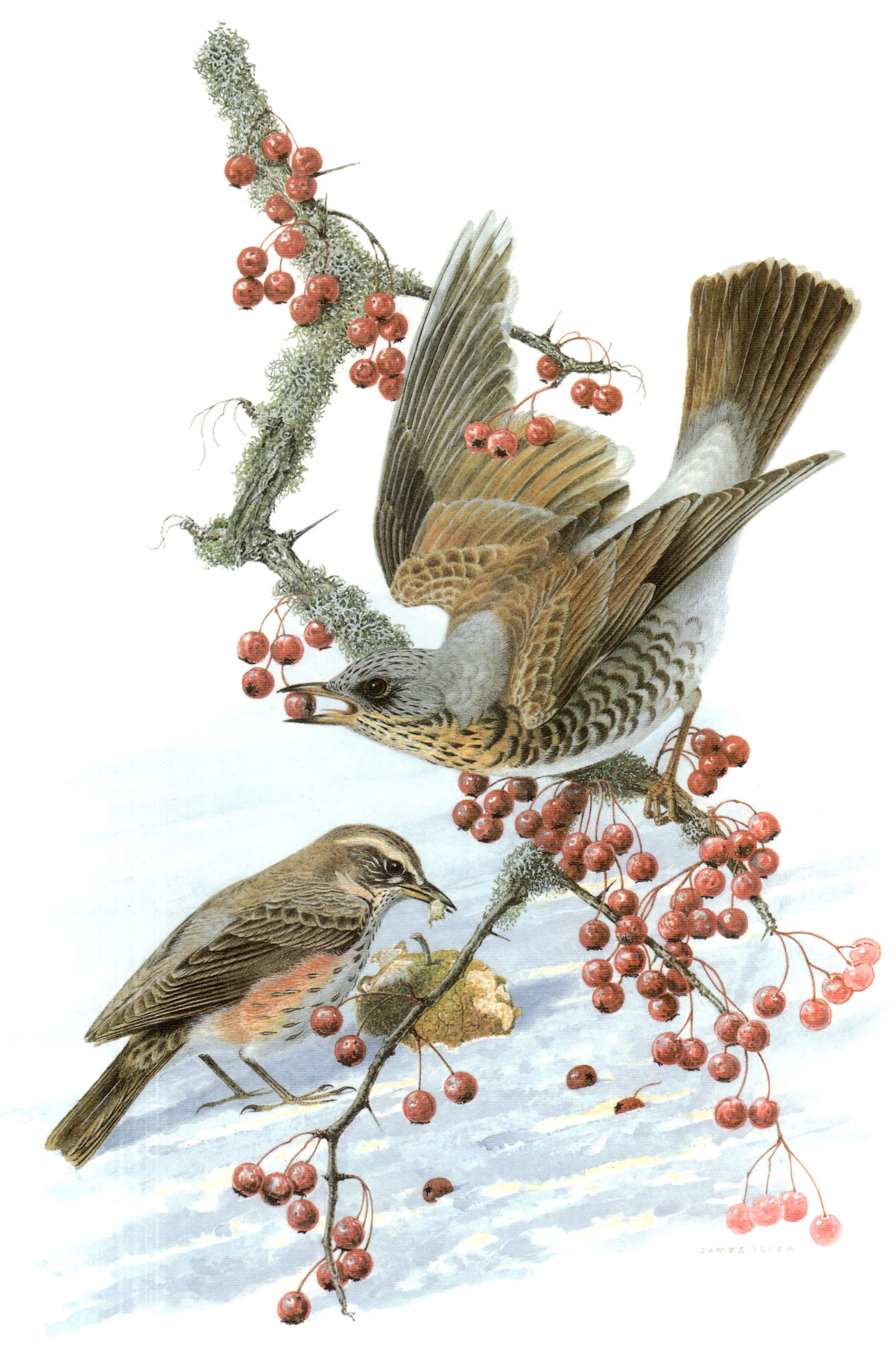
JAMES ALDER

Fieldfares and redwings are strongly nomadic birds, whose movements in autumn much depend on the availability of wild fruits; rowan, holly, hawthorn and fallen apples. The combination of cold weather and depletion of their food supply signals departure from their breeding grounds in Scandinavia and Finland, to Britain. First arrivals of the fieldfares occur in Scotland from September onwards, when their noisy 'chacking' readily identifies them as they flock to their crimson harvests.

In the summer towns and parks of Norway I have found them as tame as domestic pigeons, whereas in their winter quarters in Britain they are suspicious and unapproachable. This wildness prevents them from exploiting our gardens as our blackbirds so successfully do, and sudden hard weather will drive these handsome birds further south in huge numbers, when they may eventually find their way to Southern Europe.

During the last half of this century, fieldfares have established themselves as a British breeding species, although in small numbers. The first record of breeding was for Orkney in 1967, and they now nest in the north and Central Highlands, with a few records from Northern England.

Redwings arrive in northern Scotland at about the same time as the fieldfares. Many will have flown the dangerous route from Iceland where they breed, to link up with the great Scandinavian flocks. Their flight call, a thin, high 'seeip,' often heard as night-flying migrants pass overhead, is quite different from the fieldfares hard 'chack-chack.'

Bird watchers, or in this case bird listeners, get a lot of pleasure out of identifying night-flying birds from their calls, while some well tuned ears are able to identify 'dialects' within a species!

Although they are less sociable, redwings will mix with fieldfares and starlings on open stubbled fields. Individuals will feed happily in undergrowth, stirring leaves like blackbirds, or enjoy a frost-wrinkled apple, unlike the fieldfares that prefer open spaces.

Redwings, like the fieldfares, are now breeding in Britain. The first Scottish record was for a pair in Sutherland, 1925, since then they have built up small but stable populations from the Central Highlands, northwest to the coast.

HAWTHORN *(Crataegus monogyna)*/Lichen

The hawthorn or may, *Crataegus monogyna*, is one of the commonest shrubs used for hedging. Left to itself it will develop into a low tree, intricately branched and armed with thorns, which when thickly covered in scented white or pink flowers in spring is a common feature of all but the most northern landscapes. By late autumn the fruit, the haws, have matured into pea-sized dull red berries which remain on the tree until devoured by a host of winter feeding birds.

Lichens are formed by a close association between certain fungi and microscopic algae. They are found clothing rocks, tree trunks, walls, fences and gravestones but cannot tolerate anything other than a clean atmosphere. As a result their presence, or absence, is a useful indication of pollution levels. Many of the dyes used in former times were prepared from lichens.

PLATE 9 HERON *(Ardea cinerea)*

Looking back to the age of fifteen, I vividly remember lying face down in the shade of stunted alders by a peat-stained pool, watching the beautiful brown trout playing there. I moved slightly to get a better view, and there was a harsh yelp of alarm as a heron, about to land, almost stalled flat into the pool as it braked violently. Wrestling with gravity, huge grey and black wings thrashing gracelessly, it seemed to pause momentarily on giving rungs of air as it climbed, still reviling me for invasion of its private fishing ground.

Later, trying to convey to old Turnbull that spellbinding swirling of wings and sunlit spray, my own eager struggling for verbal flight stirred him to story-telling.

'Herons,' he said, 'are funny birds. Their legs are so long and ackward, when they're nesting they stuff them doon through holes either side o'the eggs.' I laughed, thinking that he was joking; he wasn't. Unfeelingly, I told him that I had watched herons folding their legs around their eggs and couldn't they stand on one leg with the other folded up and wouldn't it be difficult for them to remove their legs from the holes when danger threatened?

My tumbled words, without subtlety, arraigned me against a thousand-year-old myth, and I was defeated and 'sent to Coventry.' But he was a beautiful old man; he soon forgave me, told me how to catch wild rabbits and fish with my bare hands, and filled my eager being with his own inherited lore. His own daughter, more modern and bookish than he, nevertheless called the heron by its ancient Northumbrian name, pronounced 'haronshoof,' based on the old French *heronceau*, which even earlier meant, 'a young heron.'

The heron fishes in the Queen Mother's ponds near the castle, and breeds in a nearby sitka spruce wood, where I found moulted feathers and large blue eggshells.

SITKA SPRUCE *(Picea sitchensis)*

Sitka spruce will forever be associated with the two Scottish plant collectors in western North America. Archibald Menzies from Aberfeldy who found it and David Douglas of Scone who introduced it. Sitka has probably provoked more controversy and aroused more passion than any other forest crop, covering as it does acres of Scottish moorland in gloomy geometric stands which do, however, create a habitat of their own for various forms of wildlife. The tree is fast growing and when assured of adequate rainfall tolerant of a wide range of exposure and altitude doing best on peaty soils. The timber is pale, strong and fine-grained.

In gardens it can be a spectacular conifer, pyramidal in outline with a long spire, growing well over 100ft in height with lower branches that arch and droop gracefully. The leaves are blue-green, flattened and sharp pointed while the cones borne towards the top of the tree, are pendent, light brown and have crinkly edge scales.

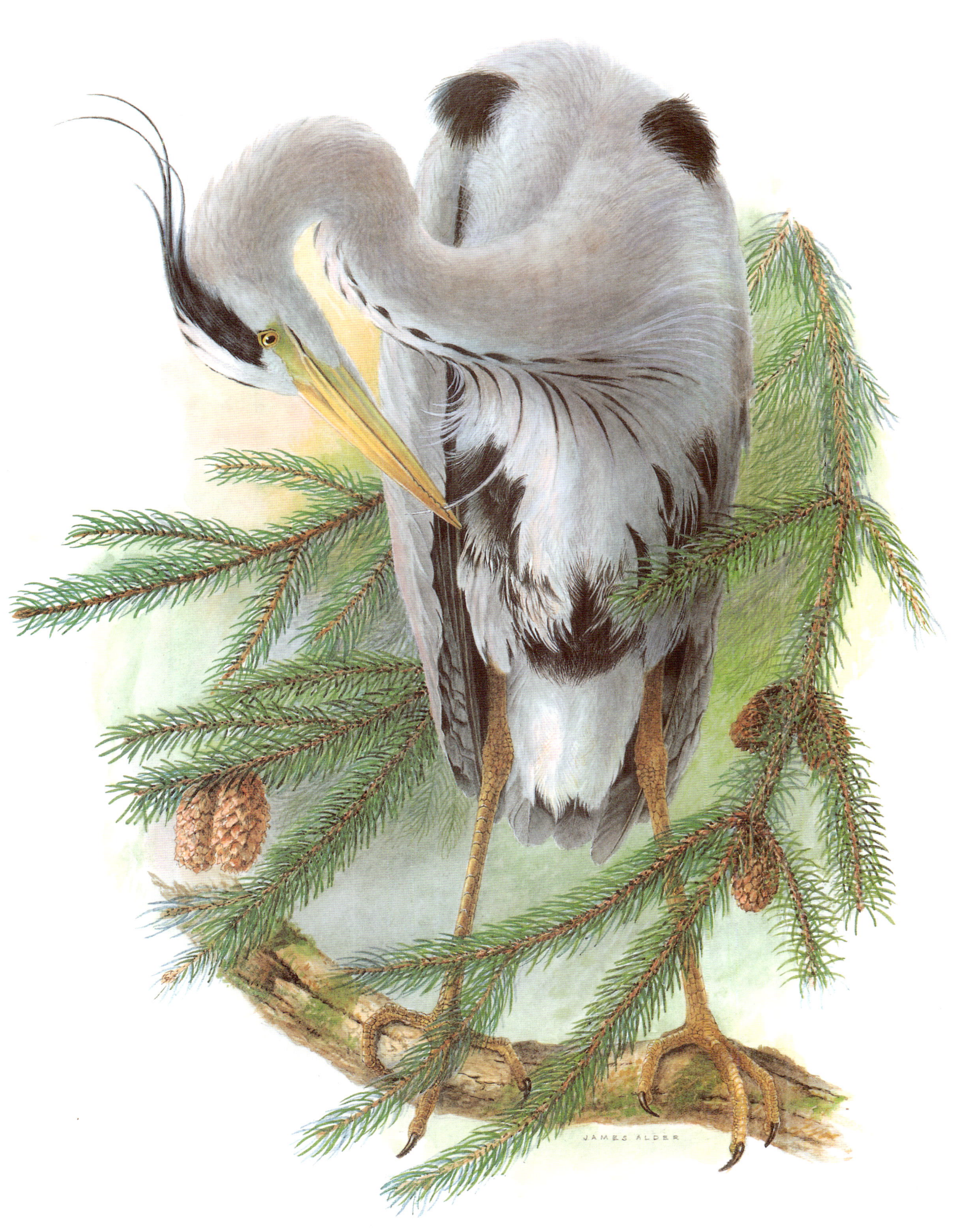
JAMES ALDER

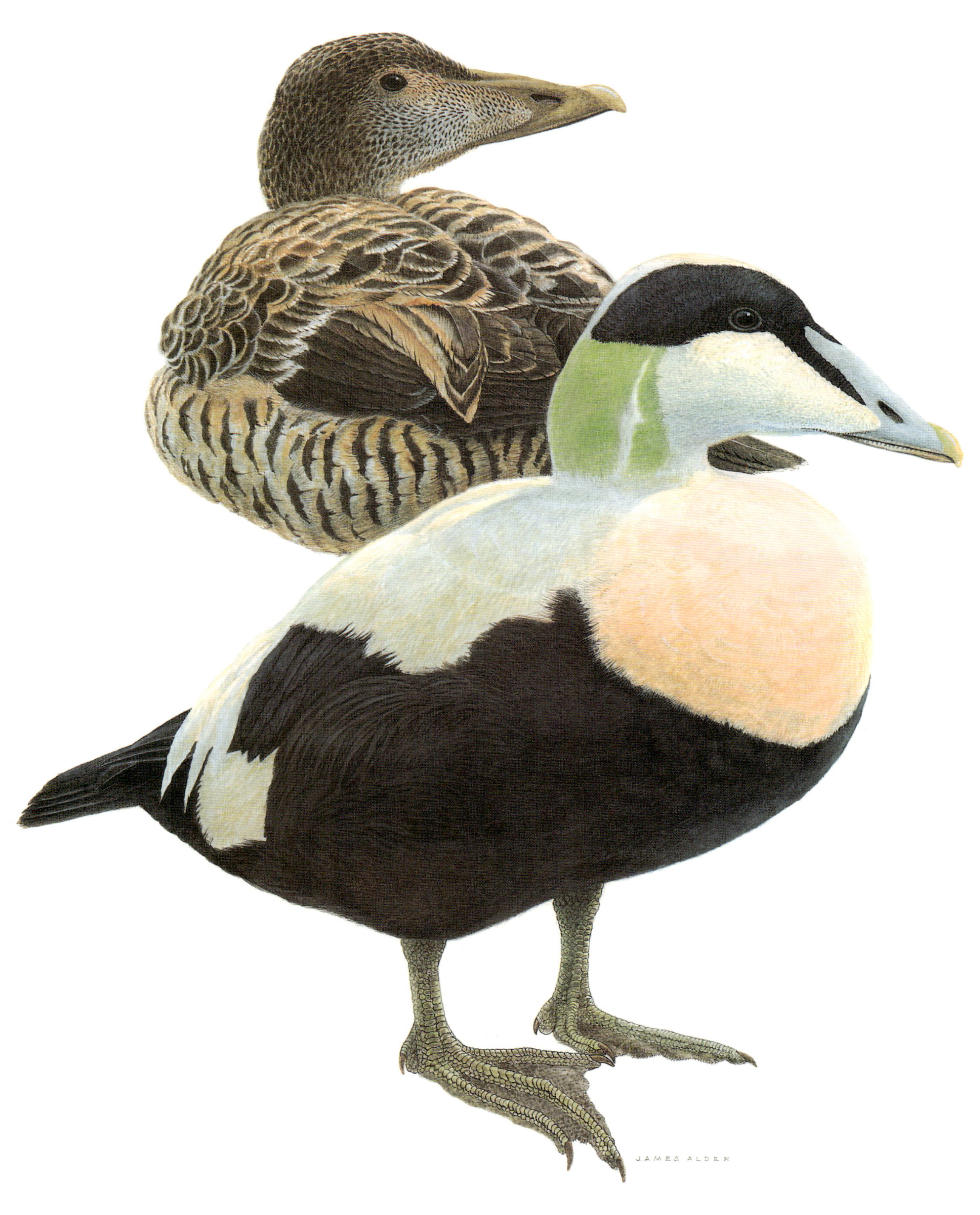

JAMES ALDEN

St Cuthbert, the illustrious Northumbrian monk (c.635–687) is traditionally supposed to have tamed the eiders during his hermitage years on the Farne Islands. To this day the locals refer affectionately to this beautiful bird as 'Cuddy's Duck.' When not breeding, though tamer than most wild ducks, eiders still keep a respectful distance from observers. During incubation however, the brown females are almost immovable, perhaps catatonic, and allow themselves to be stroked. It is the duck's nature to 'sit tight' – rarely will she leave the eggs until they hatch after 25–28 days or so. Soon after hatching, when dry and fluffy, the sturdy ducklings are bustled down to the sea by an anxious mother, the proud-stanced male often in attendance, when they will join a crèche, forming little floating rafts. They feed themselves, any mother will do for comfort, and they are well protected against hungry gulls.

If eiders are famous for anything, it is for the soft down which the ducks pluck from their breasts to make luxurious beds for their eggs. Down has been used for centuries to make quilts and pillows, the wise and careful collector taking only a handful from each nest. The eider's scientific name is coined from the Greek, *soma* for 'body,' *erion* for 'wool,' *mollissima* for 'softness.'

Eiders are almost completely maritime in all they do, and dive effortlessly for their favourite food, mussels and other shellfish. In Britain they are found all around the coasts of Scotland and Northern Ireland, and are common in the Queen Mother's little bay. Her Majesty can observe them easily on her daily walks when she is in residence, and takes great pleasure in their bold beauty as they ride the green waves or rest on the up-tilted, stratified rocky outcrops that guard the haven

PLATE 11 YELLOW BUNTINGS *(Emberiza citrinella)*

The yellow buntings nest in a dense, lichen-encrusted hawthorn hedge leading down from the castle to the sea. The Queen Mother is fond of these beautiful birds and sees them in small flocks, gleaning autumn's stubbled fields, sometimes accompanied by reed buntings.

I learnt most of my bird watching as a youth in Hexhamshire, a glorious corner of Northumberland, where they are called yellow hammers or yaller yowley. The earliest literary reference to this name appears to be J Withals Dictionary (1556) 'A yelambre, luteus, vel lutea' which describes the bunting's clay and yellow colours. Yarrell, Brit. Birds (1856) says 'I have ventured to restore to this bird what I believe to have been its first English name, yellow ammer. The word *ammer* is a well known German term for bunting.' They are also called 'yellow yowlring,' while 'yarling' is heard near the Castle of Mey, all names which may be derived from the old English geolca, meaning yelk or yolk.

There are about sixty or more names for this formerly common species, indicating its popularity. Among these we find 'scribbling lark' or 'schoolmaster,' referring to the elegant markings on the eggs, so often resembling fine penmanship. Many of the common names refer to this 'mysterious writing' and a Scottish name, 'devil's bird,' suggests the work of evil forces.

In the North, from Cumberland to the Humber, it is known as 'the blakeling,' blake meaning pale, thus without colour, therefore shining white, or yellow, with the further complication that blake is confused with the Old English 'blaec,' meaning black. With this information in mind, the reader will be able to fathom the old saying 'as blake as a cowslip!'

'Cry baby bunting' (Somerset) refers to the repeated song which all children once knew 'a little-bit-of-bread-but-no-o-cheese,' while blacksmith, Salop, and 'tinker,' Sussex, surely have in mind the ringing of hammers on an anvil.

RED CLOVER *(Trifolium pratense)*

TUFTED VETCH *(Vicia cracca)*

HEDGE WOUNDWORT *(Stachys sylvatica)*

Three of our commonest field and hedgerow plants are the tufted vetch, the red clover and the hedge woundwort. *Vicia cracca* the tufted vetch seems ineptly named for, far from being a tufted plant, it uses tendrils on the ends of its leaves to climb and scramble through surrounding vegetation for as much as six feet. It thrusts up short flower stalks holding clusters of bluish-violet 'pea' flowers which mature into pods containing two to eight seeds. Unlike the vetch which has no smell, the red clover, *Trifolium pratense*, has a sweet honey scent which attracts bees to its purple-red flowers which are held in dense more or less globose heads. The leaves are trifoliate and each leaflet often has a whitish crescent-shaped patch in the middle. It is frequently cultivated and used for hay. The vetch and the clover both belong to the pea family but the hedge woundwort, *Stachys sylvatica*, is a relative of the mints, the sages and the dead-nettles. Its stately spires of dull red flowers can grow to over three feet high. The leaves are heart-shaped and stalked and the whole plant has an unpleasant smell when bruised.

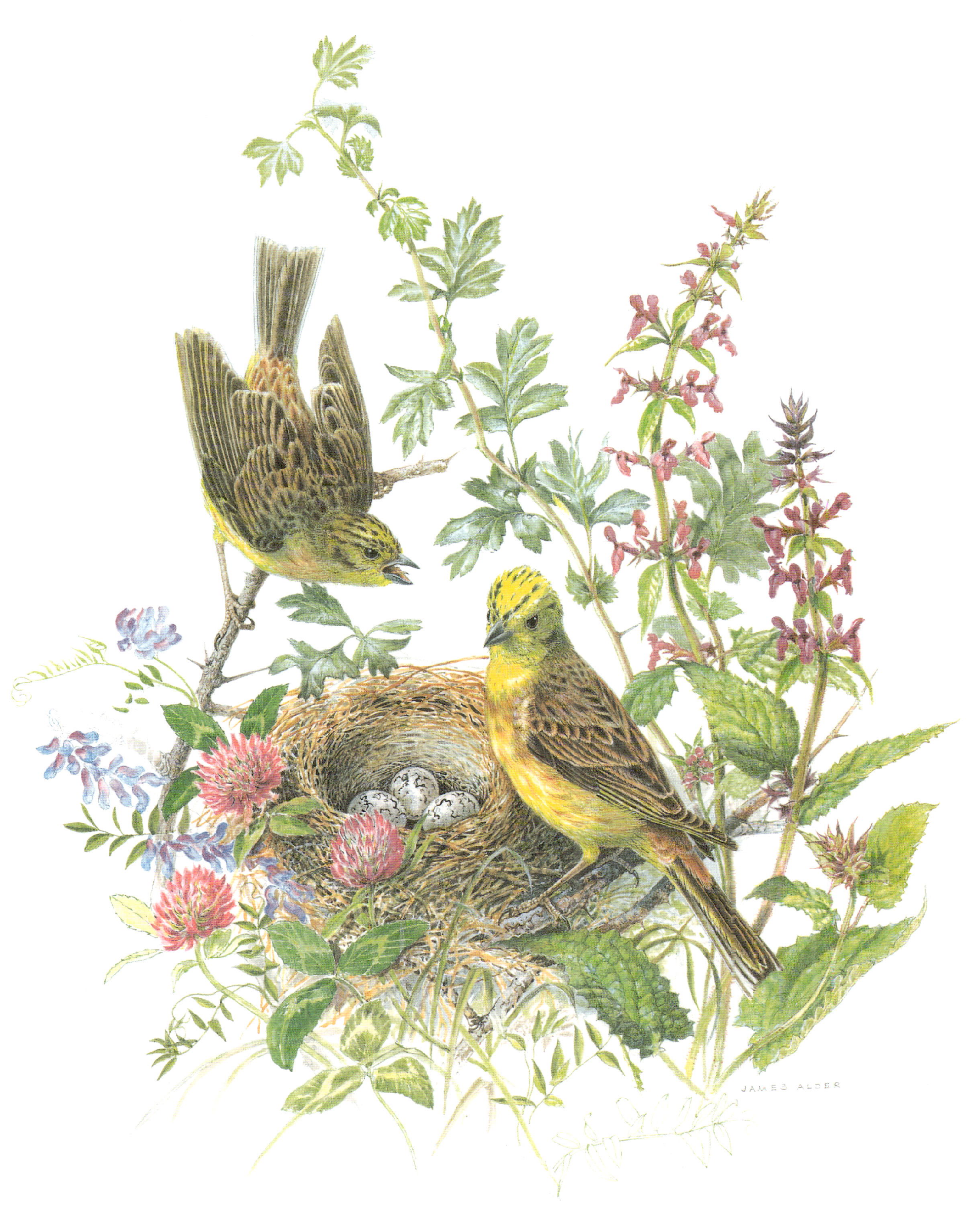
JAMES ALDER

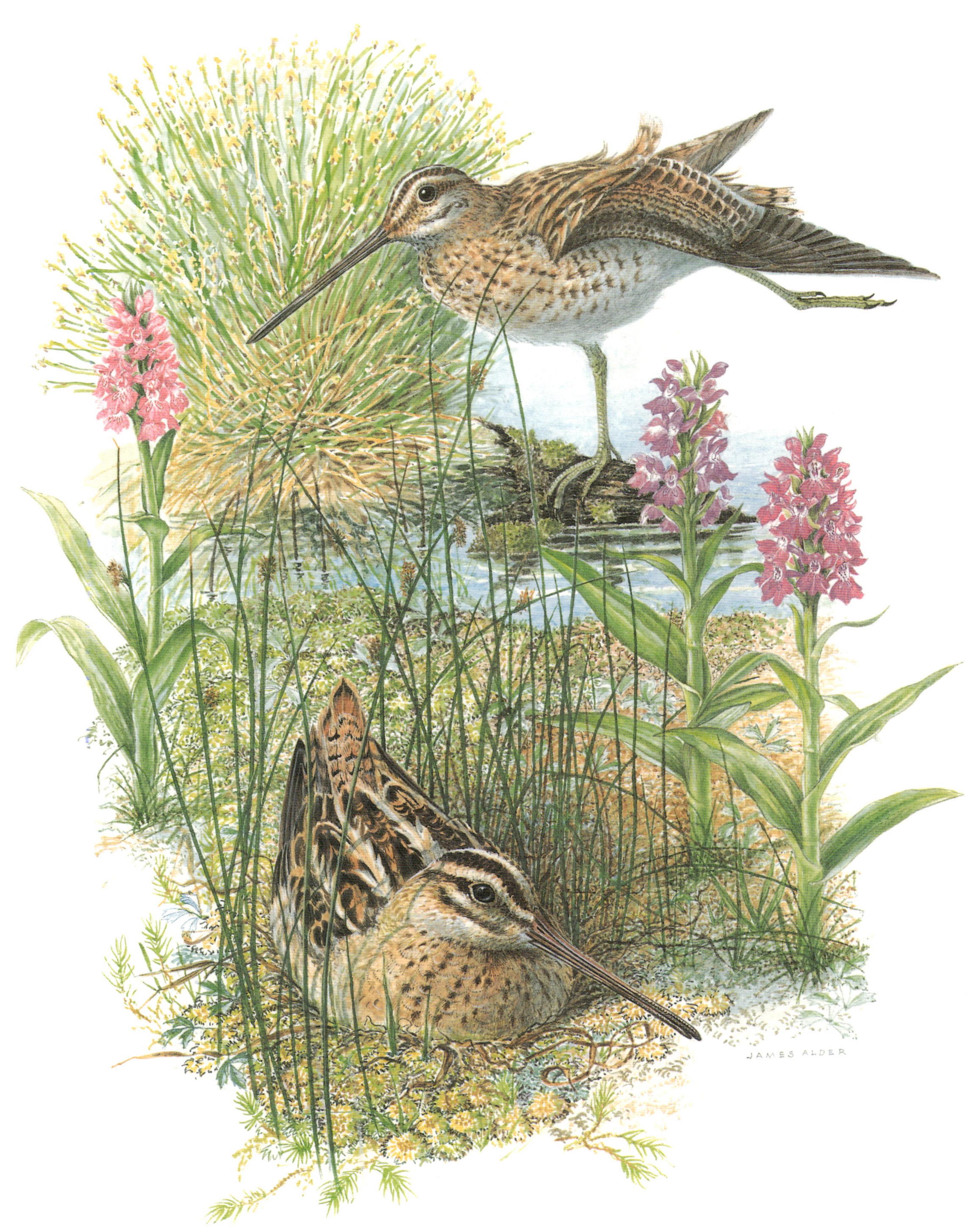
JAMES ALDER

It will not have been overlooked that the common thread running through these observations is the relationship between wilderness, big skies and the aerial displays and songs of the birds. The snipe, not a large bird, is able to compete with the best in the delivery of his spring message. Climbing rapidly to hundreds of feet, he then tips over and dives, wings beating rapidly, each outer tail feather widely spread and tail fanned, producing a 'drumming' or 'bleating' sound as the rushing air vibrates his stiffened tail feathers. His true vocal call is a brittle 'chip-a, chip-a,' uttered from moorland post or wall, and during his other switch back flight, when he rolls alternately from side-to-side.

Snipe belong to the great Order of Charadriiformes, which also contains other ground nesters such as the ringed plover, lapwing and woodcock. Typically they lay four eggs, roughly pear shaped, often large for the females' size. They are arranged pointed ends inwards, occupying the smallest possible incubation space for a clutch of big eggs, permitting the bright eyed chicks to emerge precocial and ready to go. When the chicks are threatened the parents will feign mortal injury to distract intruders, and share their nidifugous brood between them, parting for good!

They are crepuscular in habit – beautiful is the memory of a snipe feeding or preening by silvery moonlight at the edge of a hoar-frosted pool. They probe deeply in mud with their long beaks, which are sensor-tipped and can part slightly below ground, allowing the swallowing of small prey without withdrawal.

Snipe are related to woodcock, and both species are reported to carry their young for short distances. I once saw a woodcock pick up her most active chick between her legs and carry it away, her flight laboured. I was elated to have joined the favoured few in this observation, but, after euphoria, I became cautious. I counted the remaining young, huddled together: they were three! The fourth was still there, a metre away, crouched on broken bracken. I had been well and truly deceived by avian sleight of hand!

NORTHERN MARSH ORCHID
(Dactylorhiza purpurella)

The northern marsh orchid, *Dactylorhiza purpurella* is one of the more common of the 28 orchid species native in Scotland It is also one of a group of species which are rather similar in appearance and also quite variable and which often grow intermixed in the same habitat where to confuse things further they may hybridise. This all means that they are sometimes not easy to identify.

They occur often in large numbers in damp permanent pastures or rich coastal dune slacks and meadows or even derelict wasteland sites and new roadway embankments. Whatever the ease or difficulty in identifying them, large drifts of the purple, pink or magenta flowers when seen in early summer are of great beauty.

The natural history of orchids is a study in itself. Throughout their almost worldwide distribution these highly specialised plants have evolved in a close relationship with the insects which pollinate them.

PLATE 13 PEREGRINE FALCON *(Falco peregrinus)*

The Castle of Mey is situated near the shore between the great cliffs of Dunnet and Duncansby, where peregrines nest. These falcons can be observed patrolling the shoreline and, in the spring and summer, paired birds are seen gambolling in the air, touching wings, or feeding and training their fledged young in spectacular aerial food passes. Few of us fail to be stirred and not a little envious of such exhibitions of grace, power and almost total freedom.

The British assume themselves to be a nation of bird lovers, although the literature tells us that bird watching (and with it affection for our feathered friends) did not really begin until the eighteenth century with the joyous writings of Gilbert White of Selbourne, and later, the brilliant wood engravings of Thomas Bewick of Cherryburn, Northumberland. Bewick tells us that yellow and ortolan buntings were fattened for eating in Italy, but with us 'accustomed to grosser kinds of food, it is too insignificant to form any part of our repast.' A hint, perhaps of British Beef is Best!

Increasingly, we have become intolerant (correctly I think) of the slaughter of vast numbers of small birds, often in the name of sport, as they migrate through Europe to and from Britain. Shakespeare's Hamlet tells the Players 'we'll e'en to't like French falc'ners, fly at anything we see.' Now substitute shotgun for falcon, and we recognise a familiar and ancient resentment!

I find no evidence that Shakespeare was a falconer although he must have mixed with the gentry and have known the rules. London at that time was full of wealthy falconers and craftsmen/tradesmen who supplied the appurtenances of hawking-hoods, jesses, leashes, cadges, gloves, lures, varvels, blocks, bells, bewits, imported birds and imping needles!

In those days, the large and edible heron was a formidable and favourite prey of the falconer. In *Hamlet* we find him saying to his anxious friends, 'I am but mad north-north-west; when the wind is blowing southerly, I know a hawk from a handsaw.' This was the first published reference of the phrase. Since he knew his birds, Shakespeare should have written 'heron' or *'heronceau,'* French for a young heron. But then, an audience may not know one flying bird from another, unlike though they may be, and, I suggest, his deliberate use of the very different 'handsaw' with its comically similar sound, lends emphasis to his knowing more than his doubters.

SEA PINK *(Armeria maritima)*

One of the most attractive of our seaside plants is the sea pink or thrift, *Armeria maritima*. Forming tight cushions of narrow leaves it is covered in summer with stalked rounded heads of rosy pink flowers which are fragrant. It grows between rocks at sea level, on sandy or muddy shores, on cliffs or cliff tops, sometimes producing a comfortable springy sward over considerable areas. It is, however, not restricted to the coasts but occurs on mountain cliffs and rocks well inland. An alternative name, the Sea Gilliflower, was the one used by the nineteenth century Thurso naturalist, Robert Dick. From 1937 until 1952, the duration of the reign of King George VI, husband of Queen Elizabeth the Queen Mother, a plant of thrift was depicted on the 12-sided 'threepenny bit.'

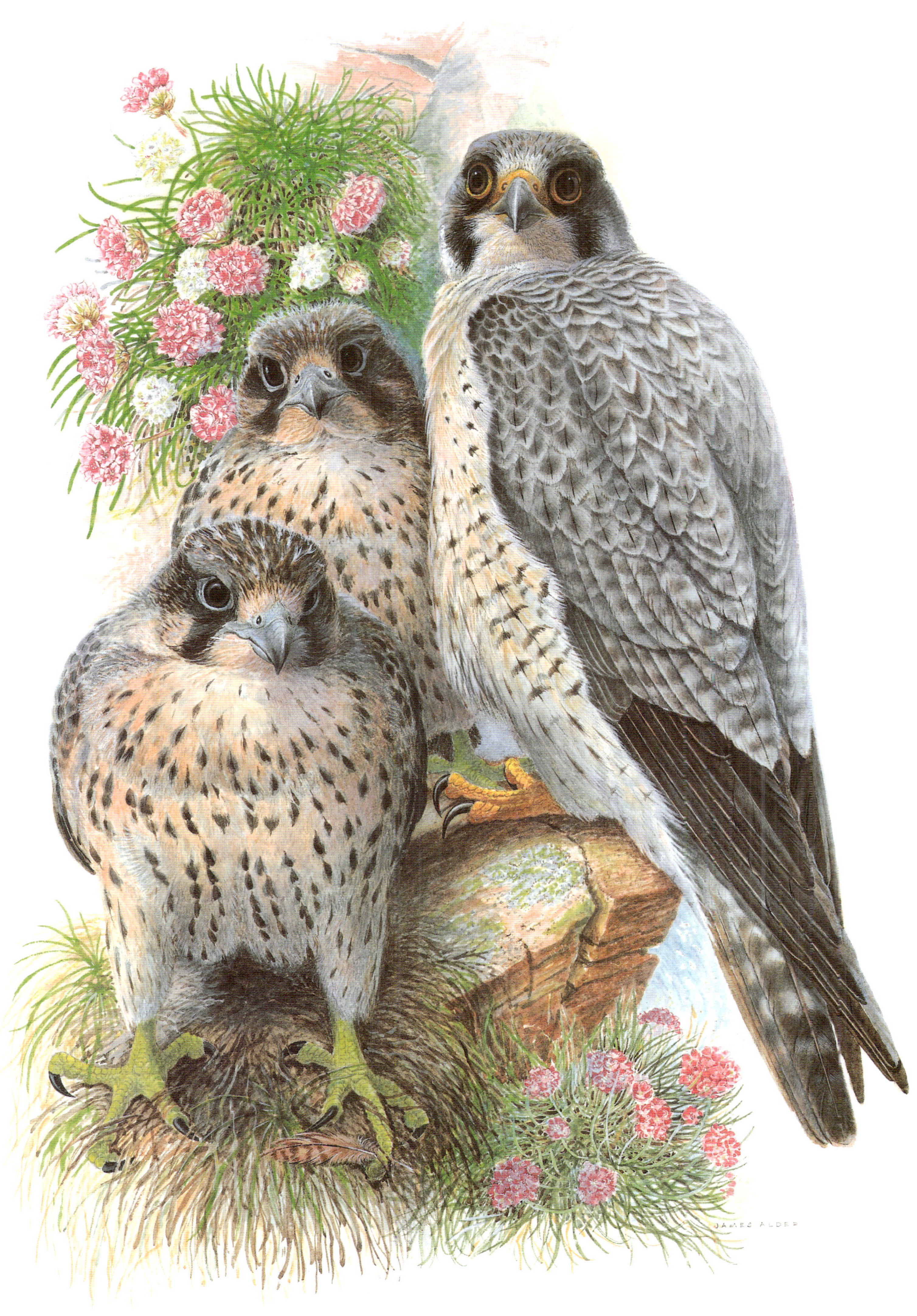
JAMES ALDER

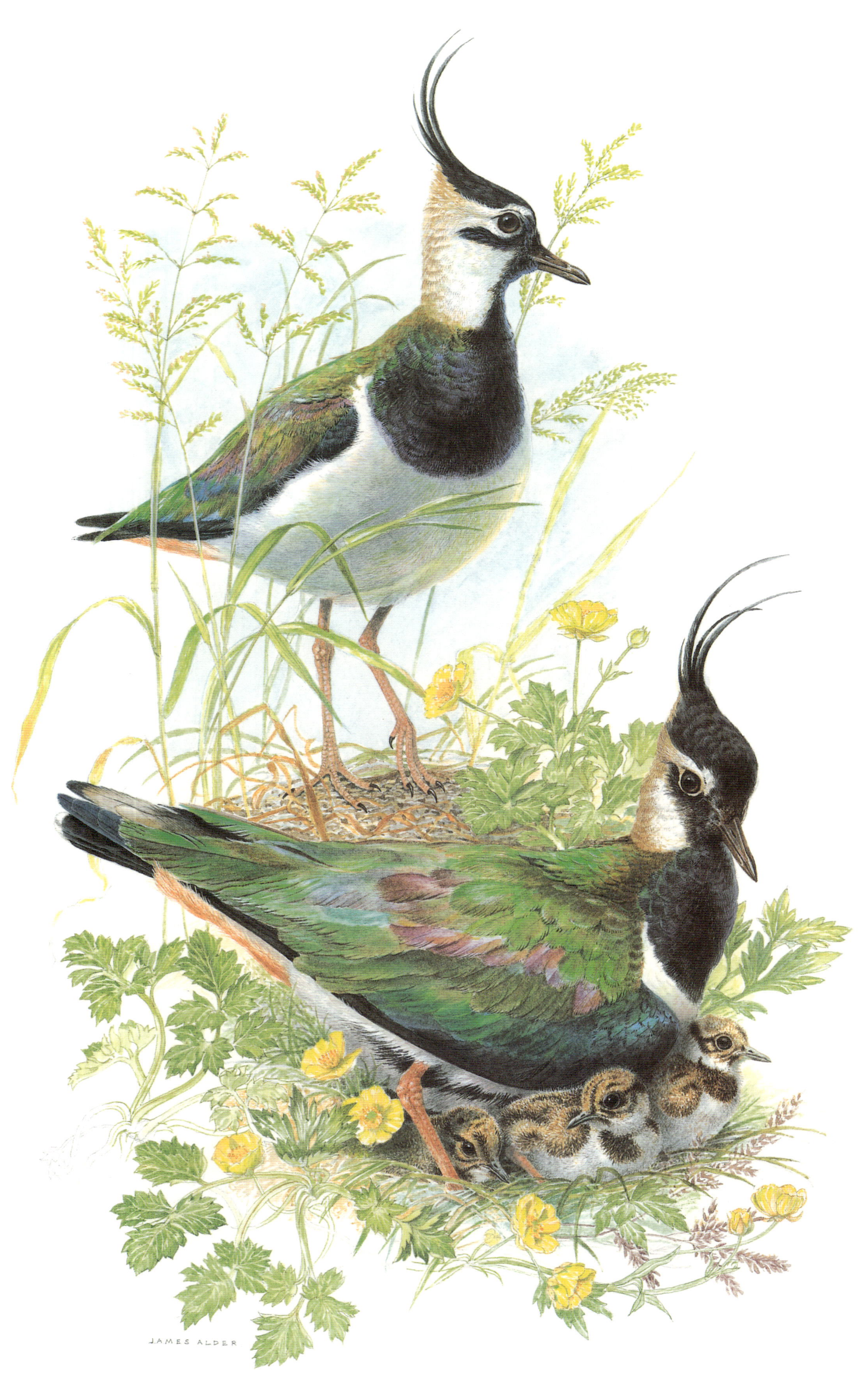
JAMES ALDER

Nearly forty years ago, I was studying and photographing a curlew on a Northumbrian hill farm. I had finally positioned the hide about 10 feet from the nest after a series of closer moves, ensuring after each that the birds suffered no distress. Getting into the hide became a problem – the wary birds refused to return to the nest until I departed. My friend the farmer accompanied me, then left. Still the curlews were uneasy, two had come, two must go! Then I asked my friend to remove his jacket and carry this at arm's length as he departed, talking to himself. The birds were satisfied and the female returned!

My next task required the conditioning of the sitting curlew to the sound of my noisy plate camera's shutter. This I achieved by tapping the tripod gently, progressively increasing the volume until the sitter became accustomed to any sound from the hide, including my request to lift her head a little!

Later, using the same tricks, I successfully moved the hide towards a peewit's nest on the brow of a hill. After an hour of tapping, the female being thoroughly relaxed, I stopped abruptly. The peewit raised her crest, gave an alarmed 'pee-eep' and flew off the nest to a higher knoll, where, on tiptoe she pirouetted anxiously. Seeing no danger, she confidently flew back to her nest and quickly settled on the four eggs. To keep her there I now had to blend the shutter noise with continued tapping. Silence it seemed, now meant danger!

Later, recounting this tale to my friend, he told me that he had been "driving" fencing posts the day before, just out of sight below the hill. 'Tap-tap' for minutes on end, then seeking new posts, he would appear in view to the peewit, causing her departure.

Apart from peewit (sound of its voice) 'lapwing' (sound of its wings) and 'green plover' (colour of plumage) and many others, its Caithness name is 'shochad' or 'shcoket.' After much research through the Oxford Dictionary, I conclude that this comes from an old Germanic name '*schoker*,' to shake, agitate, vibrate, with reference to this and other plover species habit of vibrating one foot on muddy surface or in shallow water, to disturb small prey and make it visible. Then, they adopt an elegant posture portrayed in my watercolour drawing.

CREEPING BUTTERCUP
(Ranunculus repens)

A 'buttercup meadow' conjures up a picture of carefree sunny childhood days. The farmer, however, would not be so delighted if the meadow was made up of the creeping buttercup, *Ranunculus repens*. Although it is a lovely plant when looked at dispassionately with five golden yellow glossy petals and trifoliate leaves, its habit of sending out creeping runners which root, produce more plants and send out more runners soon encroaches on surrounding vegetation, smothering it and preventing further growth. In this way it can colonise very quickly and A E Holden in his 'Plant Life in the Scottish Highlands' describes it as a 'mischievous weed' while William Hooker in 'Flora Scotica' of 1821 protests simply 'too common!'

PLATE 15 OYSTERCATCHER *(Haematopus ostralegus)* REDSHANK *(Tringa totanus)* TURNSTONE *(Arenaria interpres)*

In Britain and Ireland, oystercatchers are mainly coastal birds, although they are to be found breeding in suitable environs mainly from Lakeland northwards, through Scotland to Shetland. A trend to breed inland by shingly rivers and lakes, and in stony fields has occurred during this last century.

An old Orkney name 'scolder,' from 'skeldro,' tells us that they are bold and noisy birds, especially on their breeding grounds, where in display they may be seen tripping, shoulder to shoulder, red beaks angled down, piping loudly. On shingle they nest typically in shallow scrapes, but some nests may be in odd places, such as the tops of rot-hollowed gate posts, stone walls, even roof tops. Oystercatcher chicks hatch ready for action, but are fed by the parents at first. Remarkably, the young serve an apprenticeship – those fed mainly on worms become independent early, while those receiving bivalve food (cockles, mussels, limpets) will remain much longer with the parents until they have acquired the greater skills needed to open the shells!

Redshanks are distributed widely as breeding birds and winter residents through Britain and Ireland, increasing in numbers northwards to Scotland and Shetland.

In the breeding season they are found in damp places, marshes and rushy fields, where their nests are concealed in strong tufts of grass. They usually lay four eggs and the pretty chicks are nidifugous, leaving the nest soon after hatching. Appropriately called 'tattler' by the Shetlanders, the redshank is a noisy bird, warning all around the approach of danger. Their food is small crustaceans and shellfish, small fish and worms.

The coastal, Arctic breeding range of turnstones almost encircles the North Pole. They do not breed in Britain, although they are near enough on Scandinavian coasts, but they are passage migrants and many winter here. Those migrants through Britain, after refuelling, go on to west African coasts, while birds breeding in Alaska will fly down to Chile, and others from far eastern ranges make epic flights to New Zealand. They have a wide range of adaptations to survive long journeys, such as the ability to swim and take off from water, and they have a wide choice of food. Few of us would ever see them in their lovely spring attire, if it were not for the fact that they moult at stopover stations on migration, when in August they may still retain much of their variegated plumage of tortoise-shell, white and green-shot black.

(BLADDER-WRACK) KNOTTED-WRACK *(Ascophyllum nodosum)*

There are two brown seaweeds in Britain whose branches are buoyed up in a swell by gas-filled bladders. The long fronds of *Ascophyllum nodosum* are confined to sheltered waters and are haven to a multitude of varied sea creatures. They drape the rocks in thick curtains at low tide and are among the species collected for use as manure.

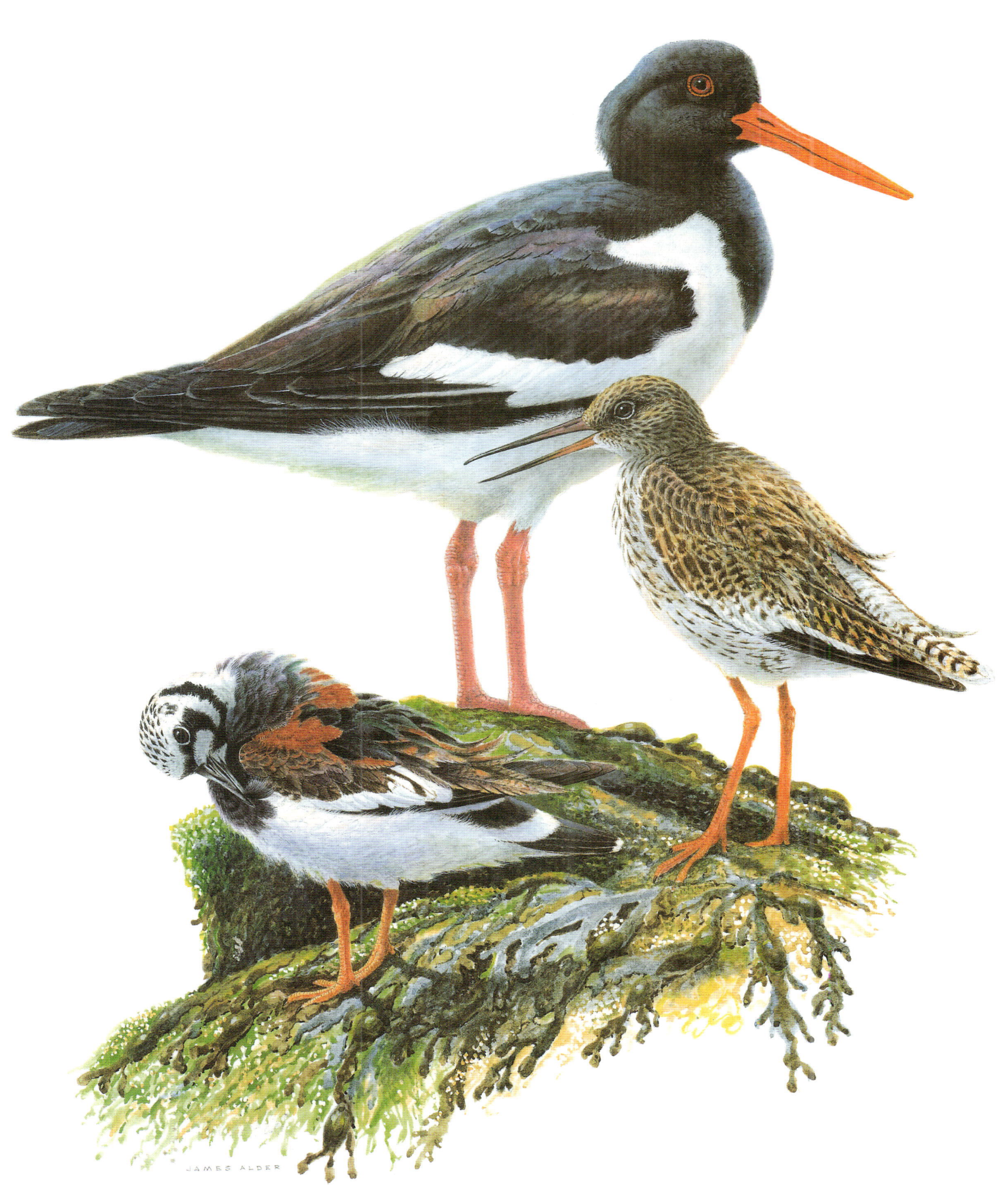
JAMES ALDER

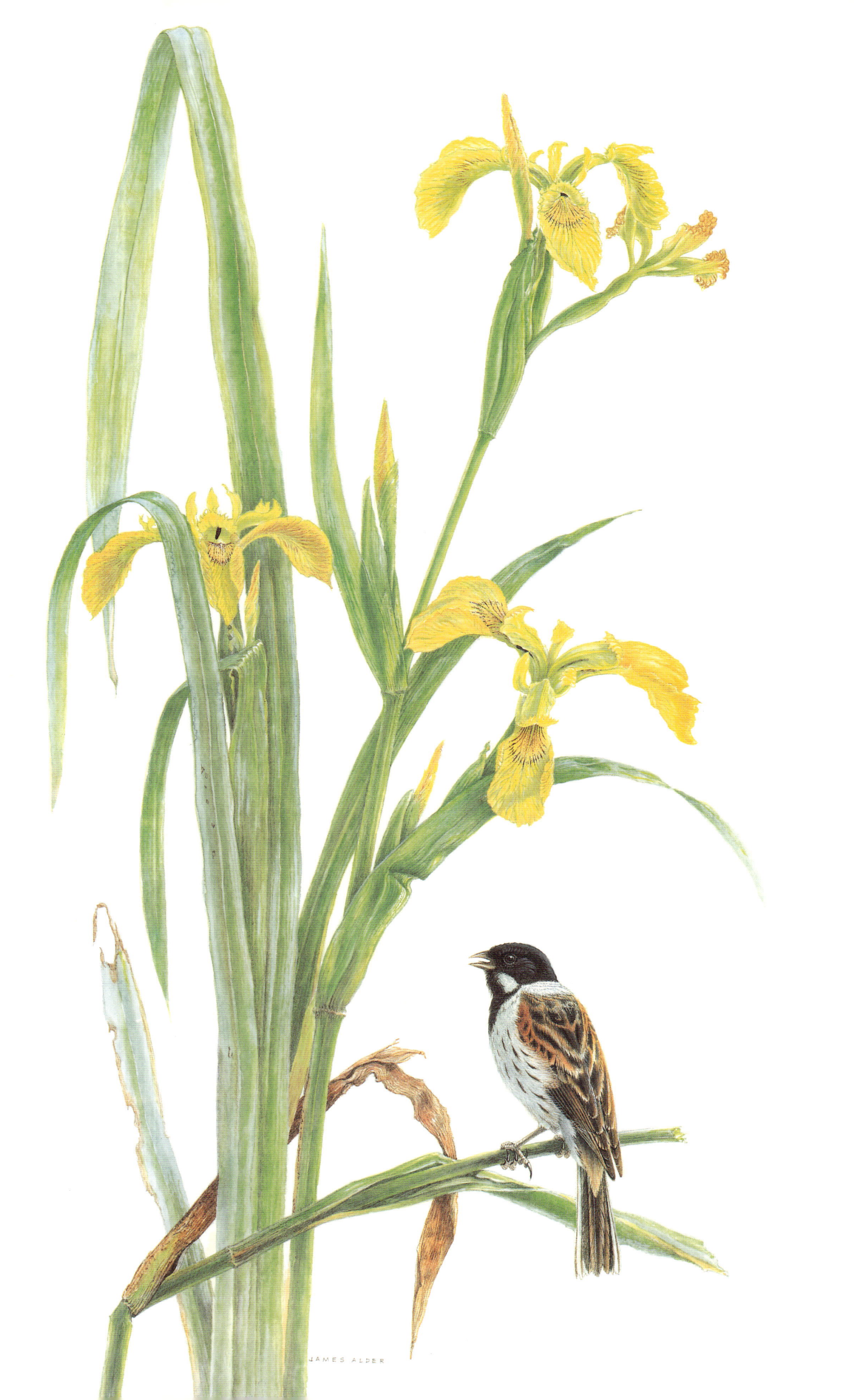
JAMES ALDER

REED BUNTING *(Emberiza schoeniclus)*

Earlier this century, reed buntings would normally be found close to reedy ponds, damp and rushy places and wet ditches. Since then the species has widened its choice of habitat, and may be found in the drier environs of scrub and farmland much favoured by yellow buntings. Reed buntings are sturdy little birds with a wide distribution throughout Britain and Ireland, including the islands, and may be observed the year round in northern Caithness and Orkney.

The male is smartly clerical with his black cap and broad white collar, the female resembling more a hen sparrow with blackish face and moustachial stripe. In courtship the male raises his black head feathers and plumps out his white collar, ruff-like, to form a frame for the head, a display which may be followed by a swirling chase of the female and a fluttering struggle among the herbage.

Nest building is by the hen only, the cup being made of strong grasses and moss, lined with thinner grass, often finished smartly with black horsehair. The brown streaked eggs take 14 days to hatch and the young fledge at about 12 days.

During autumn and winter both sexes have drabber plumage, and their jerky, undulating flight is characteristic. Their diet in winter is the seeds of marsh plants, grain and grasses, while in summer they add to this a variety of insects and their larvae. The buntings in general have beaks specialised to eat grain and grass seeds. The beak is conical and pointed, the cutting edges of both upper and lower mandibles being slightly inward curved. Most have a bony 'knob' or 'boss' situated in the palate, both yellow and reed bunting having this feature. By mandibulating the seed or grain against the boss, with rapid sideways movement of the beak's sharp edges the buntings are able to sift the husk from the edible content.

The name bunting came into the literature about 1300. Since then, bunt and bunting can mean, short and plump, a blow, mottled, buff-coloured, a swelling, parti-coloured, brown puffball, infected wheat – one take's one's pick as to the origins of the bunting's name! However, the one I like best is bunt or bunting, an ancient machine for sifting meal or separating husk from seed!

YELLOW FLAG-IRIS *(Iris pseudacorus)*

The name *Iris* comes from the Greek for rainbow reflecting the wide range of glorious colours exhibited by the genus as a whole. The stately yellow flag-iris, *Iris pseudacorus*, is found throughout the British Isles where there are suitable damp habitats ranging from inland mires, canals and streamsides to coastal strands. It avoids chalk lands and is absent from upland areas. The thick rhizome which creeps over soggy ground sometimes even immersed in water was formerly used as a black dye or as an ink. The leaves which come to a fine point are about the same length as the somewhat flattened stem and have been used for thatching as well as being woven for chairs. From 4–12 flowers are borne in the inflorescence, each a clear golden yellow, beloved by bumblebees. Fruiting capsules consist of three compartments containing closely packed brown seeds reportedly of use as a substitute for coffee.

PLATE 17 HEN HARRIERS *(Circus cyaneus)*

Hen Harriers were once found throughout Britain, perhaps nesting in close proximity to towns and villages, where they may have been welcome as rodent catchers. The nineteenth century, with its growing interest in game-keeping, taxidermy and egg collecting, soon brought them close to extinction. Their last havens were then Orkney, Shetland and Northern Ireland, where they just managed to survive, until recent protectionist and conservationist attitudes permitted their spread and restablishment elsewhere.

Opposite Orkney, where they still breed regularly, the northern coasts of Caithness have always been a good place to watch these harriers, and they are firm favourites of the Queen Mother. In conversation she has expressed her pleasure at the gold and green light of evening. My drawing, showing the blue-grey male in flight and the female with her downy chicks, tries to capture this atmosphere.

The breeding season begins about May, when the 4–5 eggs are laid on alternate days, the female only incubating. The smaller male is at first responsible for feeding his mate and, later, the growing chicks. As they develop in size and strength, the female now joins in the hunt for larger prey. All nicely timed for the male, who may be polygamous and required to feed another little brood of harriers in an adjacent territory!

Water voles and field voles, rats and young rabbits are among the mammalian prey, while the male, despite his leisurely hunting technique close to the ground, is nimble enough to catch pipits and larks. The heavier female may take duck and partridges, when available.

Both sexes are spectacular aerobats and their exhibitions are now aptly known as 'skydances.' The male's repertoire includes a series of deep undulations containing, in rapid succession, standing on the tail, barrel rolls, loops, somersaults and tumbles. When the female joins him in ecstatic flight, the dance becomes art, pure and natural, displaying with consummate grace the crafts shared by them as potential begetters of their race.

HARE'S TAIL COTTONGRASS *(Eriophorum vaginatum)*

The blanket bogs of Caithness are studded in the summer with the snowy-white fluffy fruiting heads of the hare's tail cottongrass or bog cotton, *Eriophorum vaginatum*. This, the only single-headed British cotton grass, forms tussocks which can reach 1ft in diameter and live to a great age and indeed the species itself appears to be a survivor of the ice age. The leaves are narrow, only about 1mm wide, and the stems, growing to 1–2 feet are round below but 3-angled at the top. The name *Eriophorum* means wool bearing. It is not a true grass but a member of the sedge family.

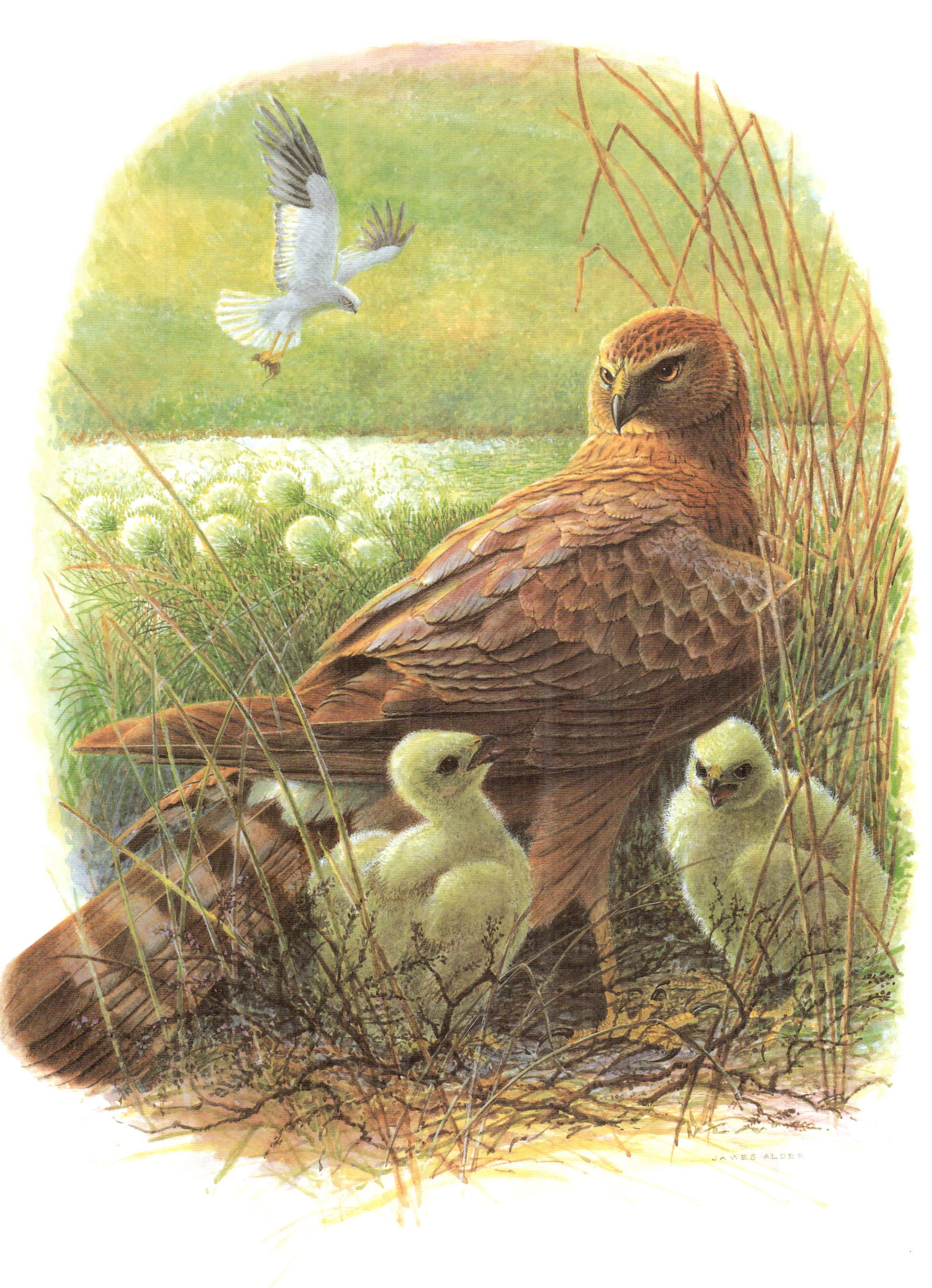
JAMES ALDER

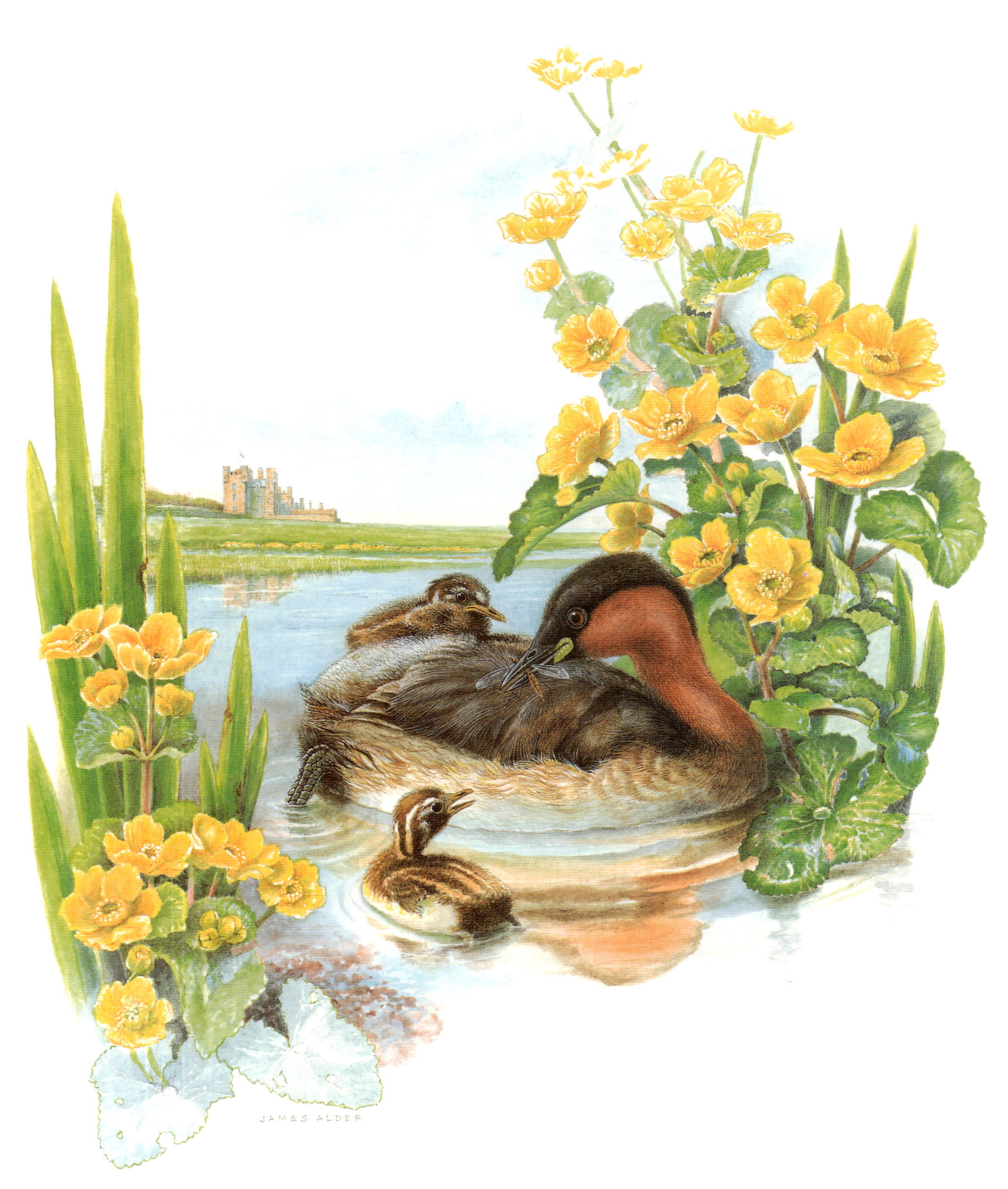
JAMES ALDER

LITTLE GREBE *(Tachybaptus ruficollis)*

At first sight duck-like when swimming, the little grebe is more buoyant, short of body and plain dumpy, its rear end high wide and blunt, with a comical tuft of feathers that is but an excuse for a tail. The whole family of the *Podicipedidae* seem cut out for comedy in voice, plumage and eccentric courtship displays. This is recognised in the little grebe's fifty or so common names found throughout Britain. 'Dabchick' and its variants are mainly heard in the south, while up north more vulgar and imaginative names are given – 'Tom Pudding,' 'Rolling Pin,' and in Scotland 'Mither o'the Mawkins,' translated I think as 'Mother of the Mop.' Well, look at it! I have often likened it to a bird Haggis. Having shown the 'cleaning lady' a live, slightly injured one, she took the thought seriously and her reaction was that 'they' ought to be ashamed of themselves, treating a gentle little thing so. I excuse myself as a Frazer, a Bruce and a Scot!

The dabchick's nest is a floating platform of rotting weeds, securely attached to growing vegetation, and is built by both sexes. The eggs 4–6 in number, hatch after about 3 weeks and the chicks are immediately active. The striped young are charmingly carried on the parents' backs, and will peck at the adult's white tipped beak or the pale green base patch, probably as a signal to be fed.

Their food is mainly aquatic insects, larvae, and small fish, found on the surface or by diving. To this end, the grebe's legs and lobed feet are fitted, propeller-like, at the very rear of the sturdy boat- shaped body.

Little grebes have a variety of calls... wild whinnying and trilling which easily identify them hidden among the reeds. If thoroughly scared they may submerge, head and beak just above the water. Waterhens snorkel like this with only their beaks showing.

MARSH MARIGOLD *(Caltha palustris)*

The marsh marigold or kingcup, *Caltha palustris* is a common and attractive wetland plant flowering from early spring till late summer throughout the British Isles where it is found in stagnant pools, ponds and lochs, slow running rivers or swift mountain torrents. It is a widespread species known from North America and the temperate regions of Europe and Asia. Its growth form is variable probably dependent on habitat and altitude but the shining golden flowers and bright green heart-shaped to kidney-shaped leaves although varying in size make it easily recognisable.

PLATE 19 MERLIN *(Falco columbarius)*

A 'Jack' merlin was once brought to me with a breakage in its carpal joint. This is a sinew-bound group of small bones, akin to our wrist, which permits great flexibility of the wing, enabling the bird to 'row' through the air.

The wing hung heavily, yet the little falcon permitted handling without protest. After feeding it, I designed a double-sided wing pocket made of soft but strong leather, fitted to keep the wing naturally folded, the bony carpel joint protruding slightly at the front. The merlin made no attempt to remove it, as happens so often with bandages taped on, and the joint healed rapidly.

Meanwhile he was taught to walk to me for food and to step willingly onto my extended, ungloved hand. Within three weeks he made little flights of a few feet, and learnt to return to his perch or 'block' on command. The great day came when I took him into a nearby field and set him free on the stump of a tree.

At my call he flew straight to me, was rewarded with food and scratching of his feet, which he liked, then returned at commend to the same stump! After this he quickly learnt to fly to any perch, rock, or fence post, to which I pointed. The old falconers knew all about the intelligence of these bright little birds – one can't bully a falcon into submission – and learnt to love their hawks and were very unwilling to 'hack them back' to the wild.

Shakespeare finds great poetic inspiration in the lores of falconry – most of his plays make reference to birds of prey. To his contemporaries, to whom the jargon of hawking was still part of their living language, he could say through Northumberland, in *Richard II*, 'Imp out our drooping country's broken wing,' with very powerful effect. A falcon with damaged wing and tail feathers is not at its best!

Imping, from the Saxon and earlier, means 'to graft' and was the delicate skill of replacing old with matching feathers in good condition. I remember refitting the tail of a female kestrel, which had lost the original while in 'illegal possession.' However, all I had was a set taken from a dead jackdaw. On release, the kestrel swooped and soared with ease, and I swear that it finally power-dived at me to demonstrate that the rudder really worked; but I do wonder what bird watchers thought when later they spotted a 'black-tailed kestrel!'

Because of its intelligence and gentleness, the merlin was of course the 'ladies hawk' of mediaeval times, and it was not unusual for the gentry to take their pets to church, hooded, jessed and belled!

SEA CAMPION *(Silene uniflora)*

Like the sea pink, and often growing with it, the sea campion, *Silene maritima* or more correctly *Silene uniflora* is also to be found on inland mountains. However, as its name suggests, it is more common around our coasts, where its grey-green somewhat fleshy leaves clothe prostrate stems forming loose mats or cushions. The flowers, held on short stalks are white with bilobed petals while the surrounding calyx, often pink tinged, inflates with age emphasising the beautifully reticulated pattern of its veins and creating a bladder-like structure around the developing capsule. The trailing stems are often used by sea birds for nesting material.

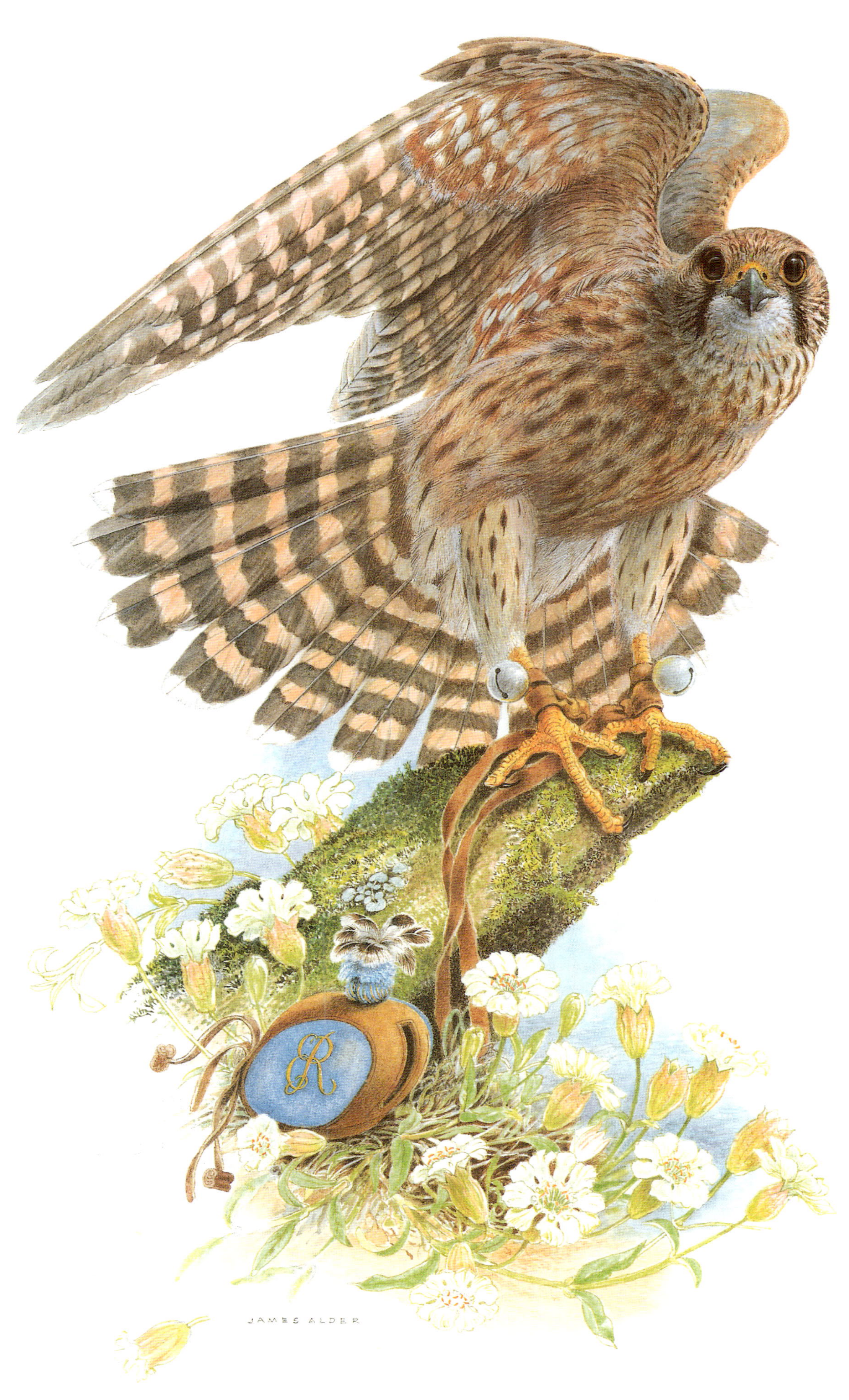
JAMES ALDER

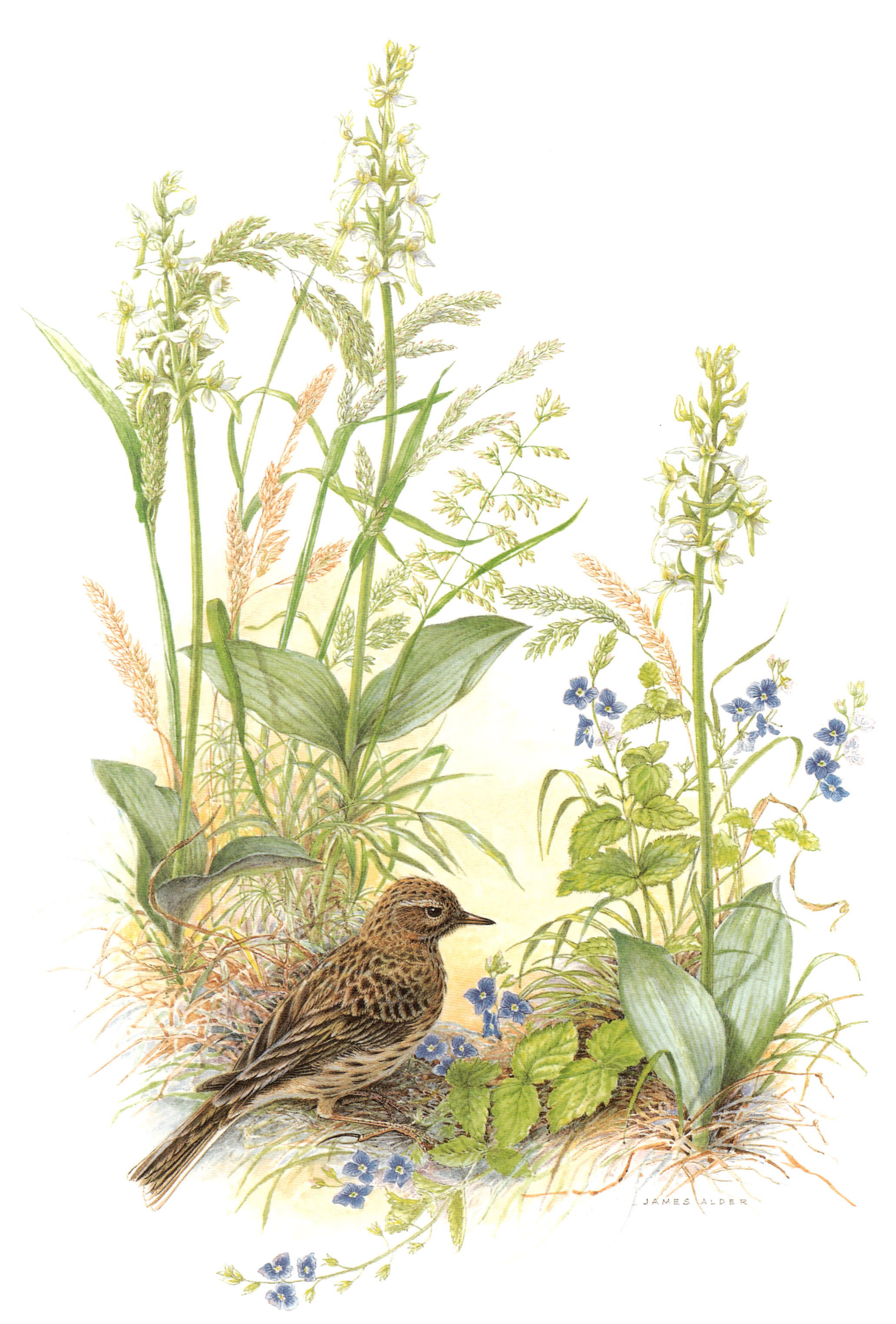
JAMES ALDER

MEADOW PIPIT *(Anthus pratensis)*

It is a human failing that the neophyte bird watcher will claim his common birds as rarities. It is diplomatic to reply that all birds seen for the first time are, in their newness, rare, and that rarely are rare birds seen until one knows ones common birds first!

The common little meadow pipit is a 'little brown bird,' excelling in modesty. Little in song, unspectacular in flight, by its very unobtrusiveness singling itself out for ready identification in a land that seems far too expansive for its survival.

How does one describe it? When flushed out from the heather, it rises, small, brown and speckled, and utters a mouse-like 'tsiip,' followed perhaps by a call note that becomes more confident, a high-pitched 'tissip-tissip.' In song flight, the gentle bird rises almost lark-like, fluttering up to a hundred feet or so, all the while uttering its feeble, tinkling song, which gathers momentum until, aspiring no more to greater heights it hesitates, then safely parachutes down to mother earth.

To another male pipit, in a land where no other species does this kind of thing, it is a firm territorial claim, and to the watchful female a spirited statement of his intentions, both great achievements attained with minimum expenditure of energy!

Watching the pipit being pursued in aerobatic flight by its greatest predator the merlin, twisting and side-stepping its fate, one can only cheer when the little bird escapes, as it so often does.

Among its other enemies are the hen harrier and the short-eared owl, while the parasitic cuckoo causes heavy egg losses. The meadow pipit has evolved a simple trick to equalise the species great losses from year-to-year – it rears two broods, sometimes three, and they populate Britain and Ireland in their millions.

LESSER BUTTERFLY-ORCHID *(Platanthera bifolia)*

GERMANDER SPEEDWELL *(Veronica chamaedrys)*

Two species of butterfly-orchid are native to Britain and each has a similar and somewhat western distribution, particularly in Scotland where the lesser butterfly-orchid, *Platanthera bifolia*, has a slightly wider, though local incidence, occurring usually in open undisturbed grassland or moorland. The white, scented, flowers attract visits from night-flying moths which feed from the long nectar-containing spurs. This usually results in the pollen masses becoming attached to the moth's long tongue eventually to be carried to another flower which may then be pollinated.

The germander speedwell, *Veronica chamaedrys*, with its bright blue, white-eyed flowers has a trailing stem which has two distinctive opposite lines of hairs. The word germander, derived from the Greek, refers to the oak-like shape of the leaves and the prostrate habit.

PLATE 21 GOLDEN ORIOLE *(Oriolus oriolus)* HOOPOE *(Upupa epops)*

On presenting this drawing to Her Majesty for her approval, she expressed surprise that these exotic birds could be seen so far north, although she was aware that as rare migrants and occasional breeders here, both were accepted as British birds. I explained to the Queen Mother that both species reached Britain, the extreme north west of their range, during warm anti-cyclonic conditions in spring. I had consulted the local bird recorder, and he had assured me that they were listed as very rare visitors to Caithness. Her Majesty's private wood may have provided occasional sanctuary for hoopoe and oriole during the last 40 years and we agreed that they should be included among the illustrations. Although the possibility of seeing one is very remote and the chance of both being together surely impossible, artist's license has solved that problem! The first breeding record for the golden oriole in Scotland is 1973.

In their southern environments, golden orioles inhabit woodlands of oak, birch and alder, feeding on insects in summer and fruit in winter. The nest is a rough hammock of straw, grass, bark and wool, slung firmly between strong thick twigs, and is built by the female. The only occasion that I have encountered this species was on an island in the Baltic, at the northern edge of its range. I heard it first, a pleasing fluty whistle, ventriloquial in the dense canopy and then, despite its brilliant colouring in the open, I had difficulty in seeing it among the waving, sun-dappled foliage.

The sighting of a rare species is always a very special affair, and my first hoopoe, seen on a cold Spring day, on a Northumbrian farm, remains forever imprinted. It fed among grazing cattle, often raised its fine crest in excitement, and permitted close approach before taking flight, when it dramatically resembled a huge, buff-pink, stripe-winged butterfly.

On the sunny hillsides of its continental habitat among open woodland and scrub, the hoopoe nests in holes in rotten trees and old walls. Its main food, lizards, grasshoppers and insects, abounds there.

Here in Britain such a diet preference will be found mainly in the South of England, where the hoopoe occasionally breeds. Luckier people who have studied its nesting habits say that the unfledged young are very foul smelling, no doubt to disenchant the over curious and to discourage the predator!

SYCAMORE *(Acer pseudoplatanus)*

Few trees can withstand the rigours of the Caithness climate and those that can are bent and contorted by the wind into untypical silhouettes. The sycamores at the Castle of Mey seem to prop each other up in a great archway within the gates or gather like a protecting shawl about its southern side bent tight where the wind has relentlessly hammered over the surrounding wall. The sycamore, *Acer pseudoplatanus* is not a British native and was not extensively planted in this country until the late eighteenth century although it had been known in cultivation long before that, introduced from continental Europe. However, it has become naturalised and is as much a feature now of the countryside throughout Britain as is many an indigenous species. It can form a large tree, the branches spreading and, the greyish bark flaking with age. The five lobed leaves, often infected by autumn with the black spots of Tar spot fungus (Maple blotch), and the double winged fruits are unmistakable. Hooker states that 'the wood is used for bowls and trenchers and other turnery work; and the Highlanders are said to make a wine of the sap.'

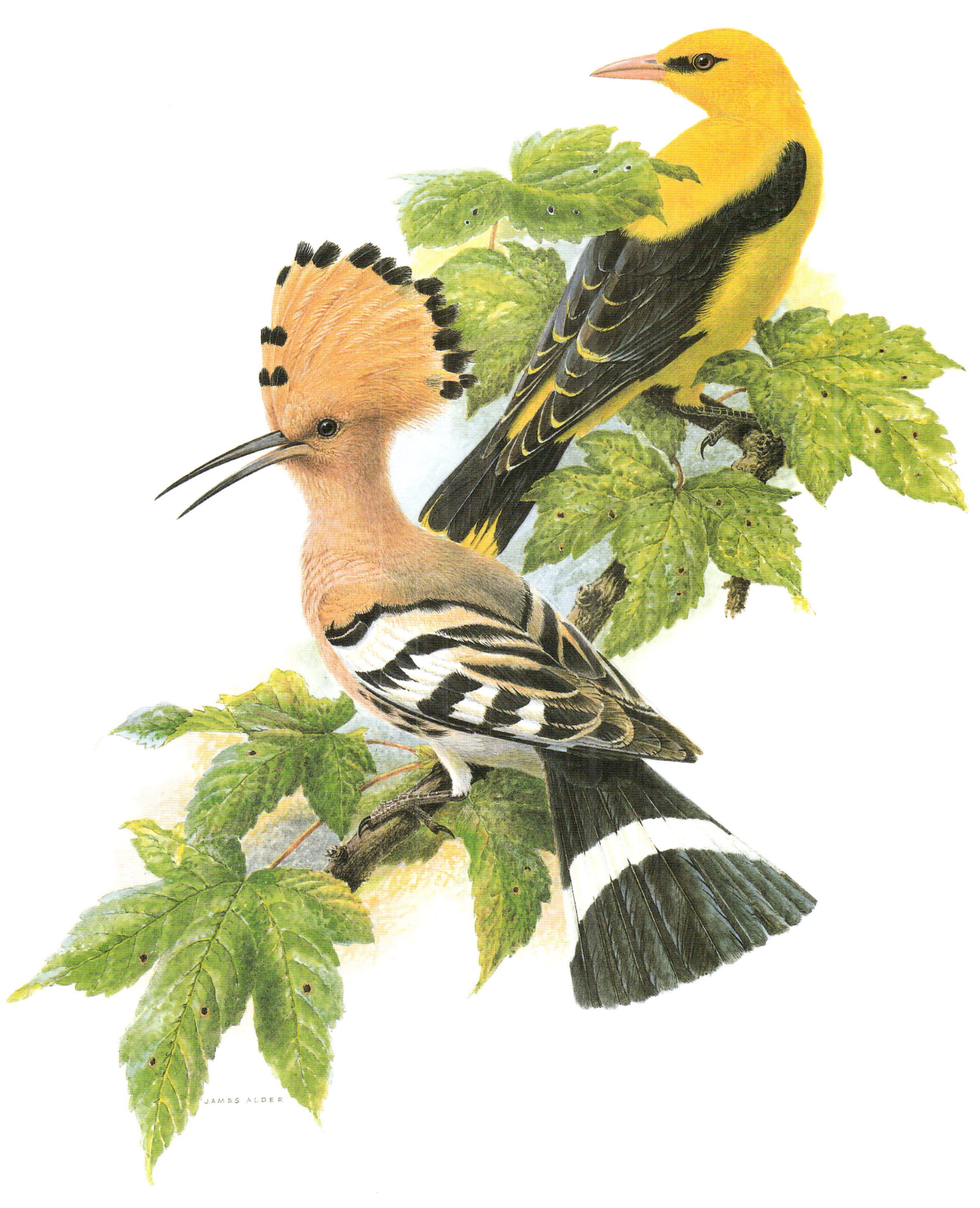
JAMES ALDER

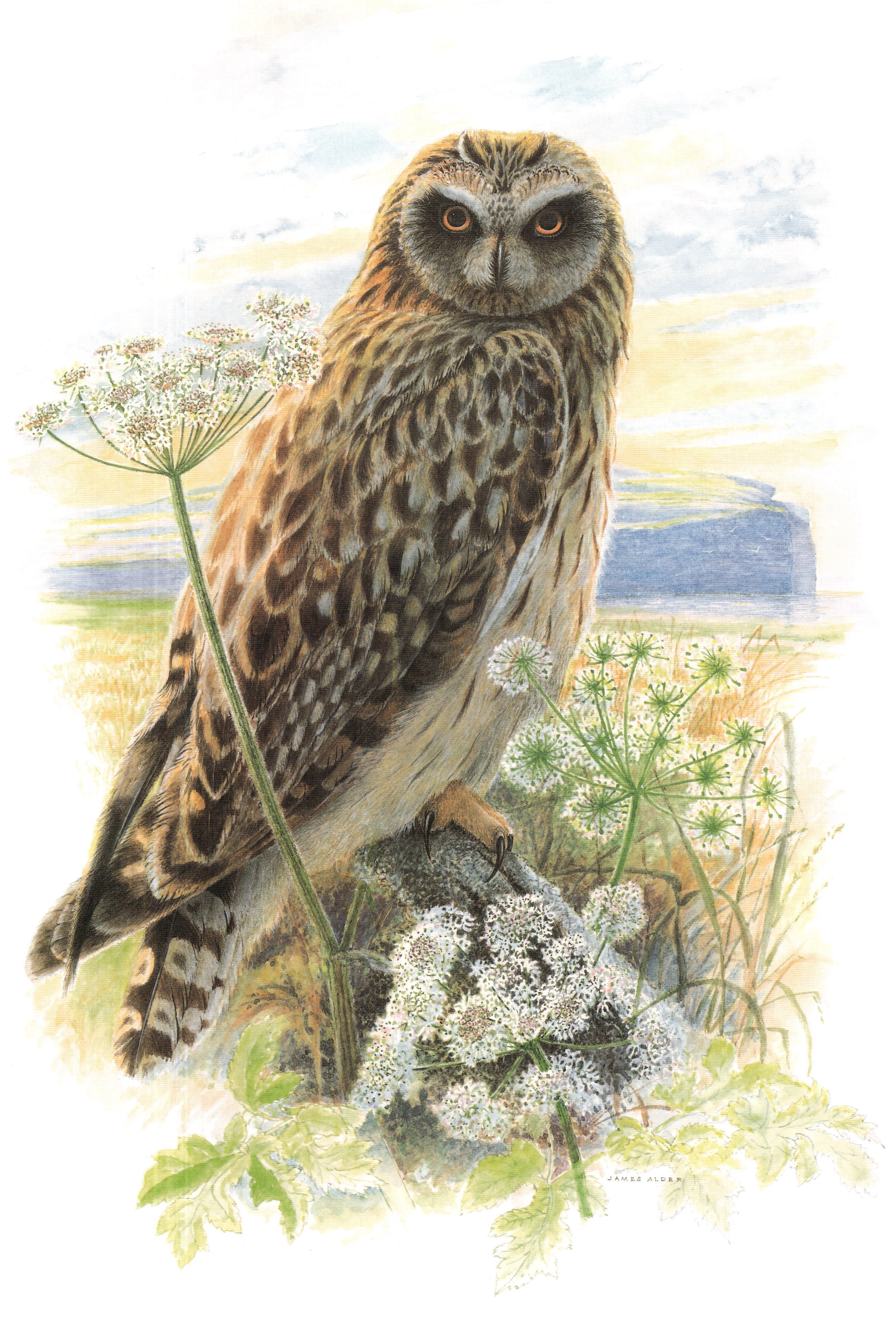
JAMES ALDER

Short-eared owls regularly quarter the foreshore and the rough grazing near the castle, their slow rolling and wheeling flight, interrupted by sudden pounces on their prey, being characteristic. A wide variety of suitable breeding habits are available along the flat coastal lands, deep heather, boglands, dune and dense gorse, where the male on his territory advertises himself in song, a deep 'boo-boo-boo' and displays his prowess with exaggerated rolling flight, wing clapping and diving.

He mobs intruders enthusiastically, while the incubating female remains incognito, only leaving the nest at the last moment if disturbed. The 4–8 white eggs are laid in a shallow scrape at 2-day intervals, incubation commencing at the first egg. When hatched, the comical grey-white chicks, yellow eyes frowning from blackened face, are therefore staggered in size and look like a family of resentful gnomes.

The successful breeding of this species seems to be linked to the prevalence of its main prey, the field vole. Where 'vole plagues' occur, these owls gather in numbers to breed. In Ireland, where voles are not on the faunal list, 'shorties' are rarely seen. Among my own observations I noted that, when prey was plentiful, surplus items of voles and mice were deposited in little runnels near the nest, a kind of larder. During food shortage (and empty larders), the small owlets often disappeared, leaving perhaps two out of five. Davison, the gamekeeper, had noted this over many years, and expressed surprise that if this were ordinary predation, why hadn't all disappeared?

A possible solution to the mystery was presented on a cold, wet afternoon in June 1953, when I sat in a hide on a Northumbrian fell, trying to photograph these owls.

The owlets were huddled together waiting patiently. The female suddenly flew to the nest, dropped a vole beside the chicks and was away before I could blink! The largest owlet swallowed the vole, his siblings beak-snapping and hissing protest. After a few minutes, he affectionately nibbled the ear of the smallest chick, picked her up, and, to my horror, swallowed her! 'Unnatural' this appears to be, but the behaviour is now known to occur in many species, and has a name, Kronism, after the ancient god who sacrificed his son to ward off calamity.

The watercolour portrait shows the short-eared owl against a backdrop of Dunnet Head.

HOGWEED, COW PARSNIP *(Heracleum sphondylium)*

In the same family as the carrots, parsnips and parsley of our kitchen gardens or the poison hemlock that killed Socrates or indeed the ornamental eryngiums and astrantias of our herbaceous borders hogweed *(Heracleum sphyondylium)* is one of the commonest and most obvious of hedgerow plants. It is widespread in the British Isles and whether flowering or fruiting its stately umbel-topped stems never fail to enhance the roadside verges in summer and autumn. The flowers are usually white though occasionally pink to purple or greenish, with the outermost petals radiating and deeply bilobed giving a lace-like appearance to the often flat-topped umbels. Large leaves are shaggily divided and have inflated petioles sheathing the stem while the flat dry disc-like fruit are dispersed by autumn winds. In the past the stems and young shoots have been used as a vegetable: pigs are fond of it and it has been used as a fodder for domestic animals hence the common names of hogweed or cow parsnip.

PLATE 23 SEDGE WARBLERS *(Acrocephalus schoenobaenus)*

Most of our British warblers are secretive. To my mind, only two of these, the sedge warbler and the whitethroat, have distinctive advertising flights and these are not dissimilar. The songs of the warblers are, to a good ear, clearly identifiable and the sedge warbler's is one of these. It is a patchworked song, vigorous and hurried, containing many repeated phrases and single notes, interspersed with harsh chattering; to me resembling some modern music where once a tune emerges, almost accidentally, it is instantly dropped to be replaced by cacophony! Yet it is far-carrying, especially on still summer nights when I have listened to it, completely charmed, as I waited for barn owls to return to their nest. The song is imitative as is the song of that greatest of nocturnal singers, the nightingale, which also is not averse to dropping a musical clanger or two! Perhaps the best songs do need occasional stridency.

Because of its occasional nocturnal singing, the sedge warbler has been mistaken for the nightingale, especially in the North, where the latter is not found. I have frequently assured (if that is the right word) excited callers that they have heard sedge warblers, not nightingales. One went to the trouble of tape recording the song. I visited the marshy ditch where it sang – still it was a sedge warbler! I left feeling that the recording would be kept safely until a more compliant ornithologist gave him the prize he so desired!

The 'Caithness triangle' as I like to think of it, has many suitable wet habitats for the warbler, where reeds, rushes and rank vegetation are available for nesting. My study of the sedge warblers recalls a devoted pair which I watched for many hours. After feeding their chicks they often sat side-by-side, as if admiringly discussing them. Probably, the banal truth is that they were waiting for faecal sacs to be voided, instantly to be removed and dropped well away from the nest!

HOARY WILLOW HERB *(Epilobium parviflorum)*

Epilobium parviflorum the hoary willow herb, is not so common in the north as in the south but can still be found quite frequently growing in marshy places, river banks or loch sides. It seldom grows more than 2ft in height, and like its relatives, has four-petalled pink flowers set on top of a long ovary borne in a lax raceme. In the autumn the four valves of the long capsule split and recurve releasing quantities of seeds each bearing fluffy plumes of hairs which are caught by the wind and drift through the air for long distances. In addition the stem produces basal leaf rosettes which over-winter thus providing an alternative method of propagation.

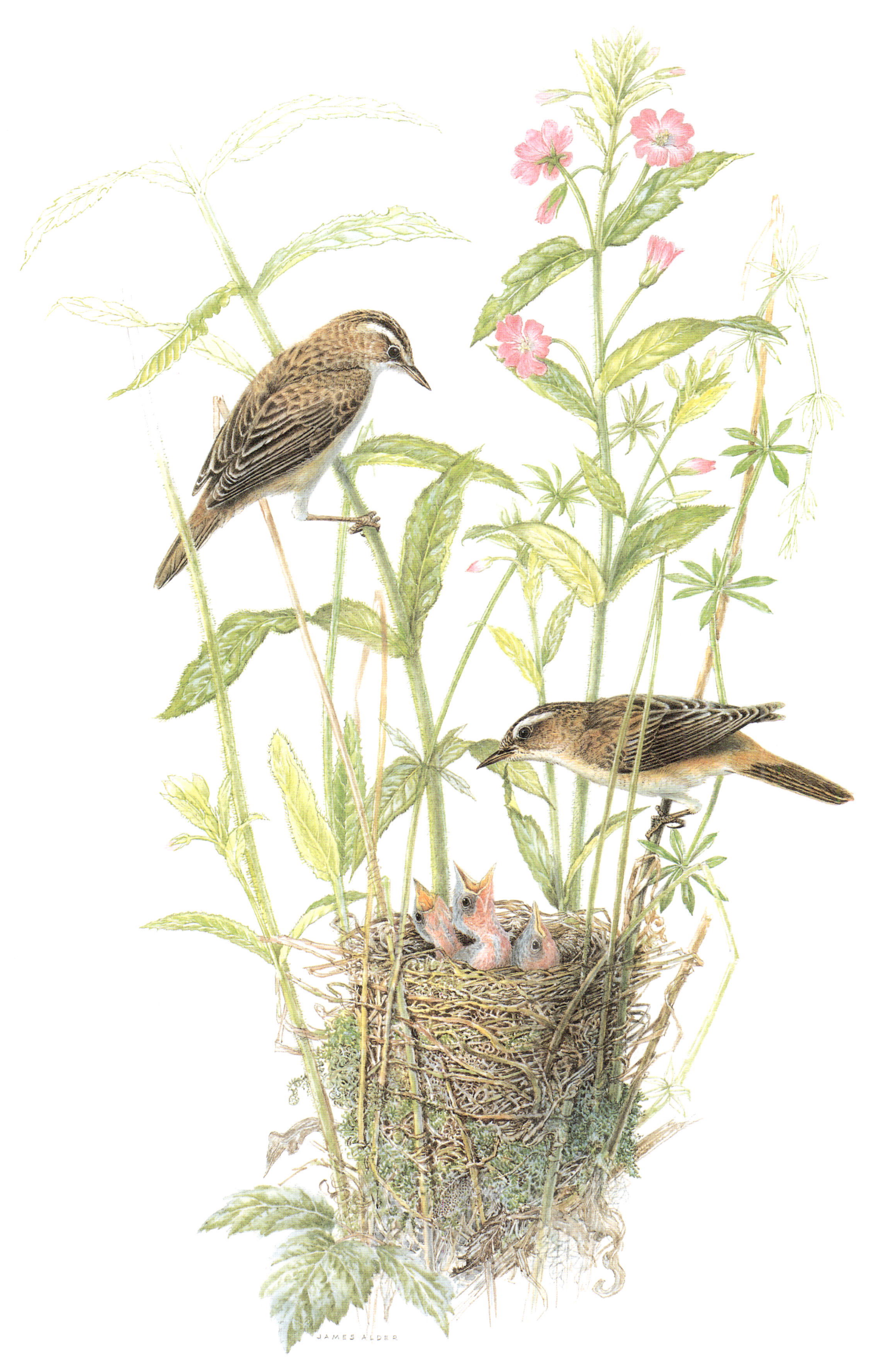
JAMES ALDER

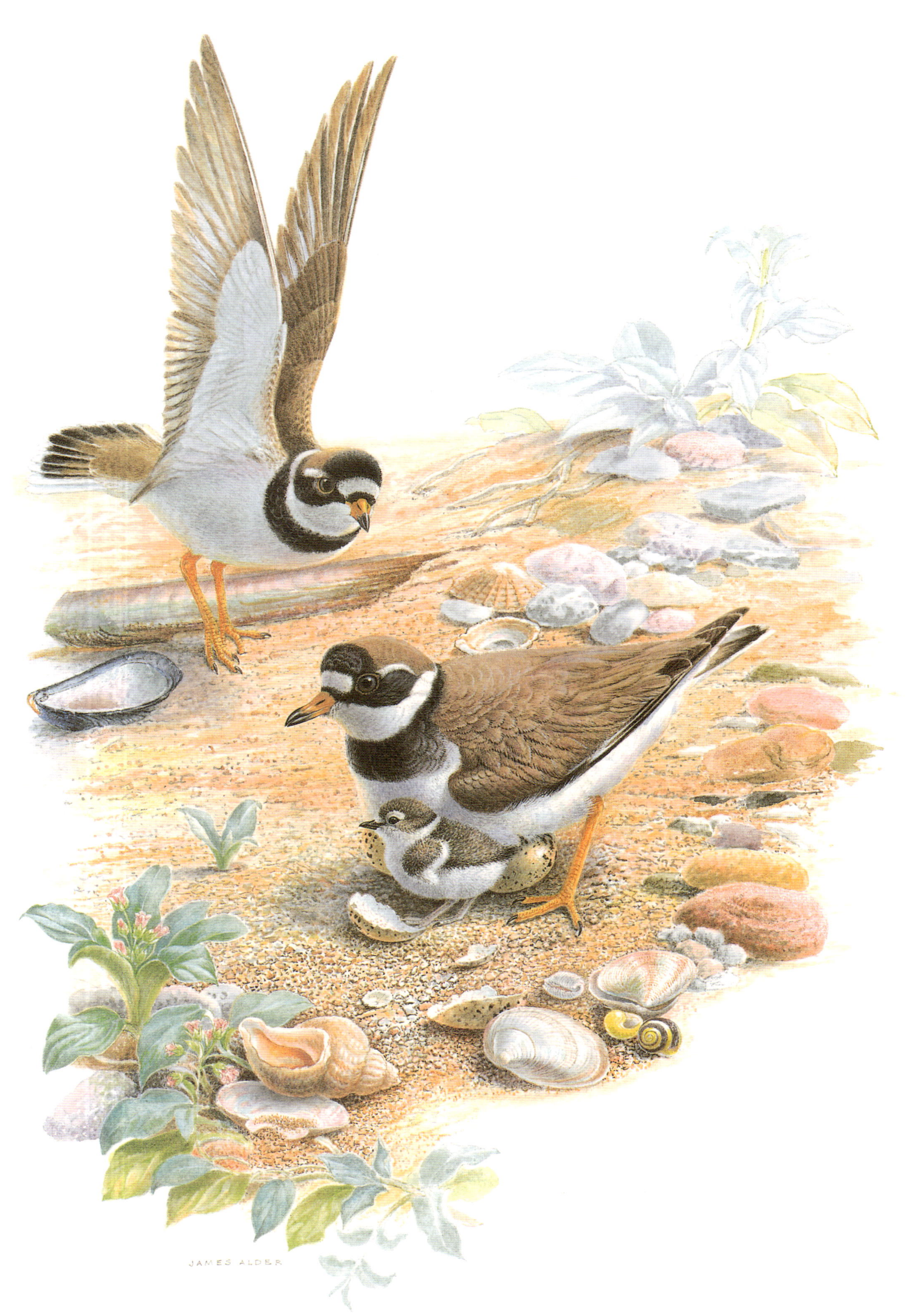
JAMES ALDER

RINGED PLOVERS *(Charadrius hiaticula)*

The great open spaces are the shapers of the plover tribes, of which the ringed plover is a typical example. Despite their bold plumages, often black contrasting with brown and white, their protean behaviour both on the ground and in flight presents bewildering, changing shapes to the over-eager predator, while closely knit patterns of a wheeling flock make choice of a victim difficult.

The cryptic arrangement of their colours also make ground nesting birds difficult to detect, the eggs are but pebbles, while at the cries of ever watchful parents, the nidifugous young instantly squat, motionless.

I have observed several species of ground nesting birds from hides, among them redshank, sandpiper, curlew, golden plover, peewit, woodcock and short-eared owl, and all have impressed me by their apparent unconcern while incubating and brooding. They are relaxed, preening, adjusting nest material, dozing. Let their watchful 'off duty' mate shout a cry of warning and they become alert. Perhaps they squat, warily raise their heads or, crouching, quietly leave the nest although unable to hear or see the dangers. Surprisingly, a curlew raised her head to sing a glorious greeting, 'curlee-curlee' to her mate flying low over the nest, a give away, if it were not for the fact that his confident contact calls had informed her that all was well!

They 'talk' to their young before hatching, reinforcing the comfort of the warmth of incubation with sounds that can only be described as 'crooning', so that the chicks on hatching may react to a simple range of communications, necessary for early survival.

Their simple vocal exchanges, though genetically coded, may have more immediate survival value than our complex grammars are to us. I have for many years, believed that flocks of birds 'gossip' a murmuration of genetically inherited sounds that keep a community informed. They quickly sort out the false alarms and seem to recognise a general alarm call that has interspecific value.

OYSTERPLANT *(Mertensia maritima)*

'Whole plant very glaucous; and, if the bloom is rubbed off rough callous points appear which become white and almost stony in drying when the rest of the plant turns nearly black. The flavour of the leaves resembles that of oysters' so wrote William Hooker and George Walker-Arnott in 1860 of the oysterplant *Mertensia maritima*. Growing from a very deep twisted and much divided tap-root this distinctive plant is confined to the seashores of circumboreal regions. In Britain it is a rare and decreasing species though locally abundant and not uncommon on the Caithness coast. With its prostrate, mat forming growth, greyish blue-green fleshy leaves and pink to blue funnel shaped flowers it is often found in the seaweed and wrack of the tide line. It withstands fierce winter storms and the shifting of the shingle thanks to the huge complicated root system.

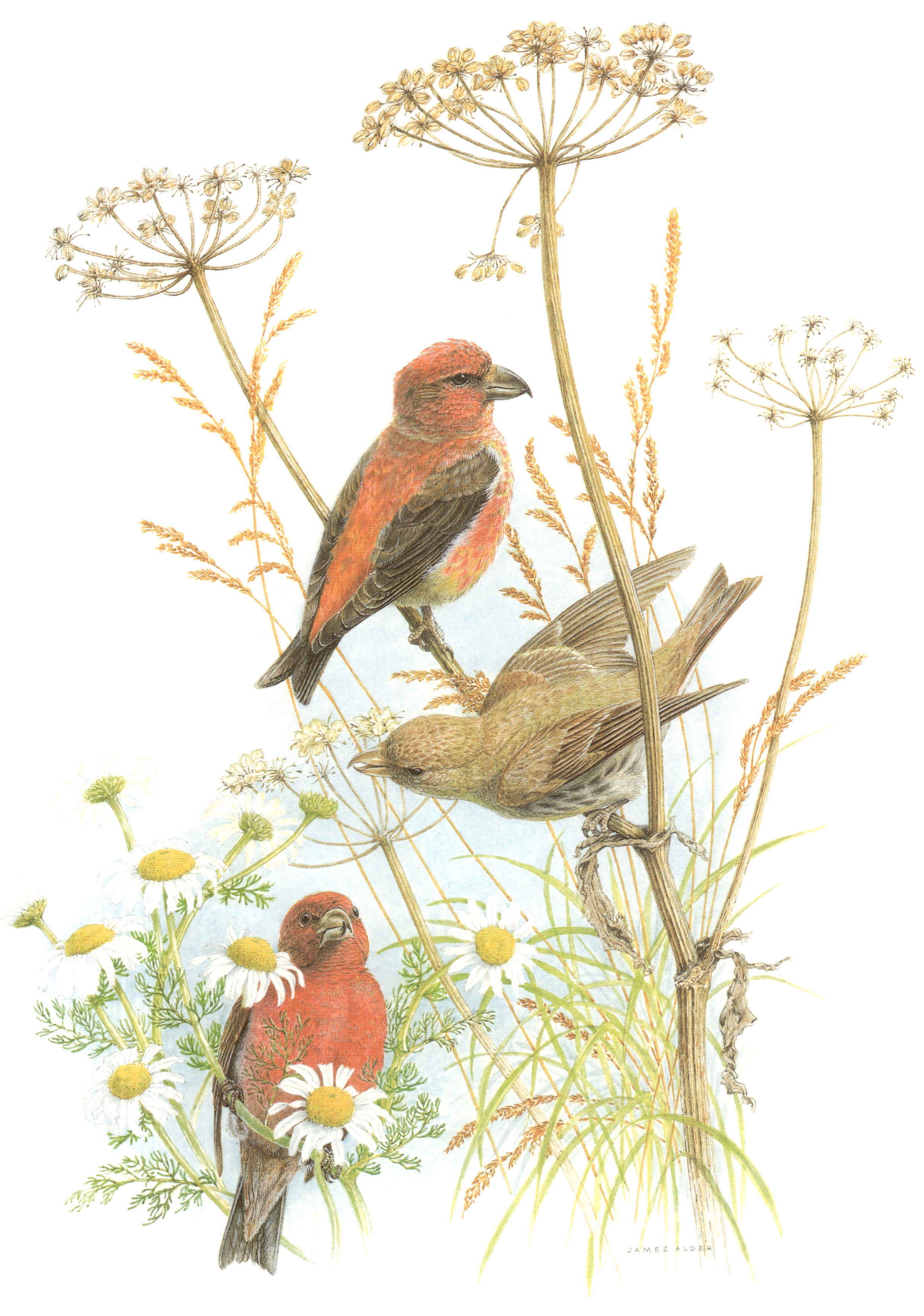
JAMES ALDER

The crossbill was not on the short list of the favourite birds which the Queen Mother had produced, although I half expected to find it, having collected sitka spruce cones in a small wood near the castle. Their scales had been snipped, clearly by a crossbill. Later, near John o'Groat's, I almost stood on a juvenile, which fed on crushed weeds on the ground!

This bird joined two others, feeding on hogweed and scentless mayweed, so tame that they permitted approach to within four feet. Obviously they were tired and hungry, having flown from Scandinavia. Two hours later, fed and rested, they flew southward down the coast.

I had never before observed this species at such close range, and was able to study the sturdy frame, the head thickened to support the heavy beak, and the crossed mandibles which may cross either way. It is now known that their parrot-like and acrobatic feeding postures are adapted to suit the way the beak is crossed! The birds that I saw were all juveniles, greenish grey in colour, although I have portrayed two in the fine red plumage of the adult male. (females are greenish).

The behaviour and morphology of the crossbill is almost entirely adapted to exploitation of their staple diet, the seeds of pine, spruce, or larch cones. The crossbill is therefore an 'irruptive' species, moving in flocks from cone-exhausted forests to new harvests, where they may breed. Large flocks may find their way to Britain, where breeding may continue from August through winter to the following spring. Given a good supply of fresh cones, they are adapted to survive in freezing conditions, and I have seen in Kielder Forest, a brood of naked chicks in February, their nest rimmed with frost and snow.

The eggs are three to four in number, laid one each day, although incubation begins at the first egg. The young may vary in size, and the smallest will die where there is food shortage, at least giving the sturdier chicks a chance of survival.

SCENTLESS MAYWEED *(Tripleurospermum inodorum)*

The white and yellow daisy-like flowers and much divided leaves of the mayweeds are a common sight both along the coasts and on wasteground and arable land throughout lowland Britain. The scentless mayweed, *Tripleurospermum inodorum*, is a more or less erect growing annual plant with pointed leaf segments which are not succulent in contrast to the sea mayweed, *Tripleurospermum maritimum*, which is often perennial, has rather fleshy leaves and is restricted to coastal areas. Unlike some of their relatives neither species has much scent. Both are occasionally used in dyeing, resulting in various shades of yellow.

ACKNOWLEDGEMENTS

To Sir Martin Gilliat, Sir Alistair Aird, the Staff of Clarence House and the Castle of Mey, I owe my grateful thanks for guidance and hospitality.

I am especially indebted to Sir James Steel for his patient involvement at every stage in the development of this book; and I extend my lasting gratitude to Sir Yehudi Menuhin, who as a boy, inspired me with his beautiful music.

Alder, Stella, Secretary
Arnold, Lawrence, MA, MB, B.Chir. DOMS
Arnott, Joan, Secretary
Attewell, Arthur R., Artist
Backhouse, William, Forester
Barnes, Herbert Abner, Solicitor, Ex RAF Officer Pilot
Bertram, Robert, (J.S.), Master of Design
Capes, Douglas, Craftsman
Caris, Athol K., BSc, Headmaster
Davison, James, Gamekeeper
Denyer, James H, OBE, MA, Ex RAF Officer Pilot
Evans, William, Company Director
Hickling, Grace, MBE, MBOU
Hindmarsh, Myrtle
Lumsden, Pauline, Secretary
Morris, George, Master mouldmaker
Scott, Stanley, Artist
Stobbs, Edward, Farmer
Turnbull, Robert, Farmer
Tynan, Antony, MBE, BSc, Museum Curator
Woods, Paddy & Jennifer, Botanists
Young, Matthew, Curator, Shipley Art Gallery
To my wife Lilian who has patiently helped
'ab ovo usque ad mala'.

By Gracious Permission of
Her Majesty Queen Elizabeth II

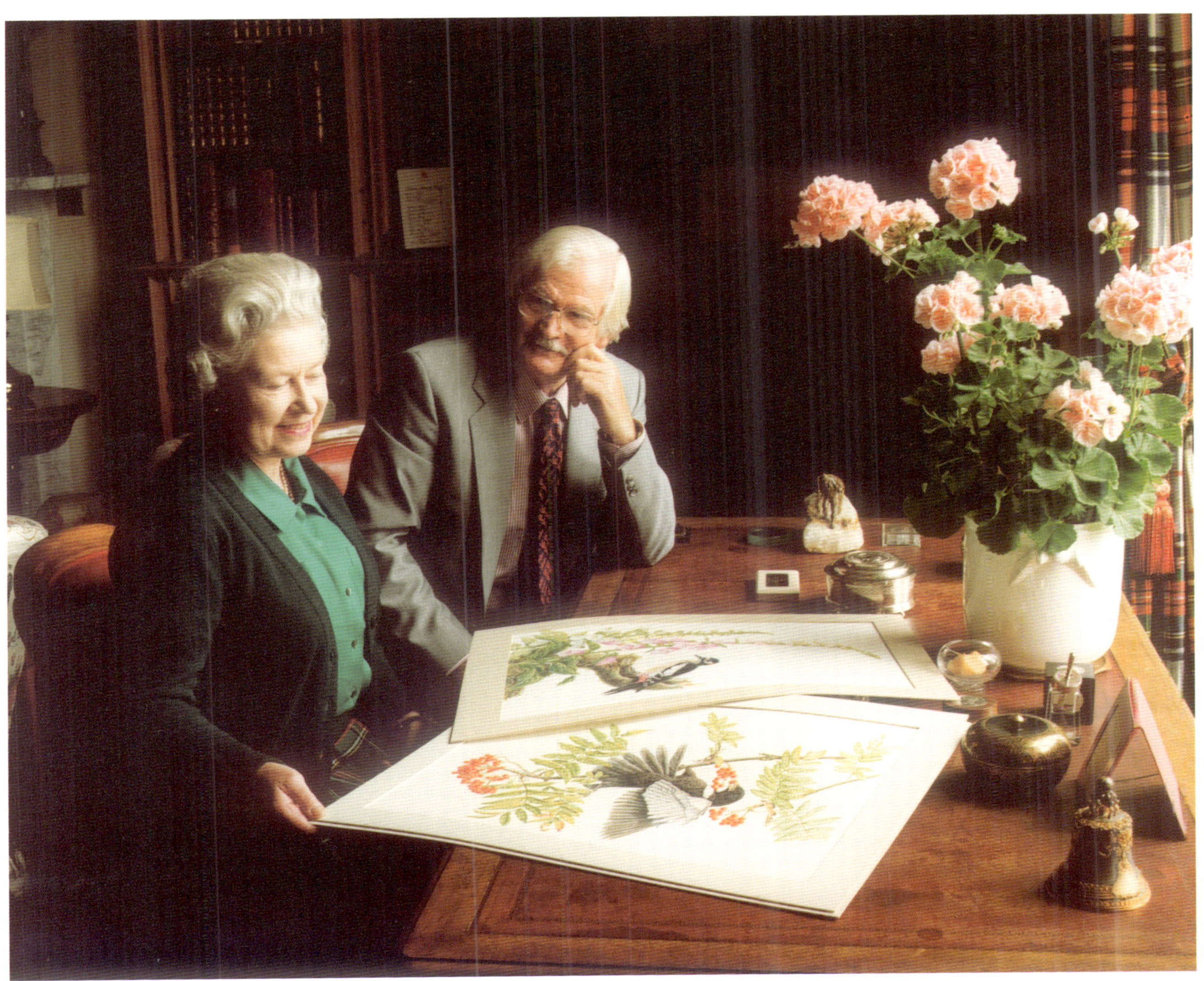

Her Majesty Queen Elizabeth and James Alder in the Library, Balmoral.
Photo: Malcolm Crowthers

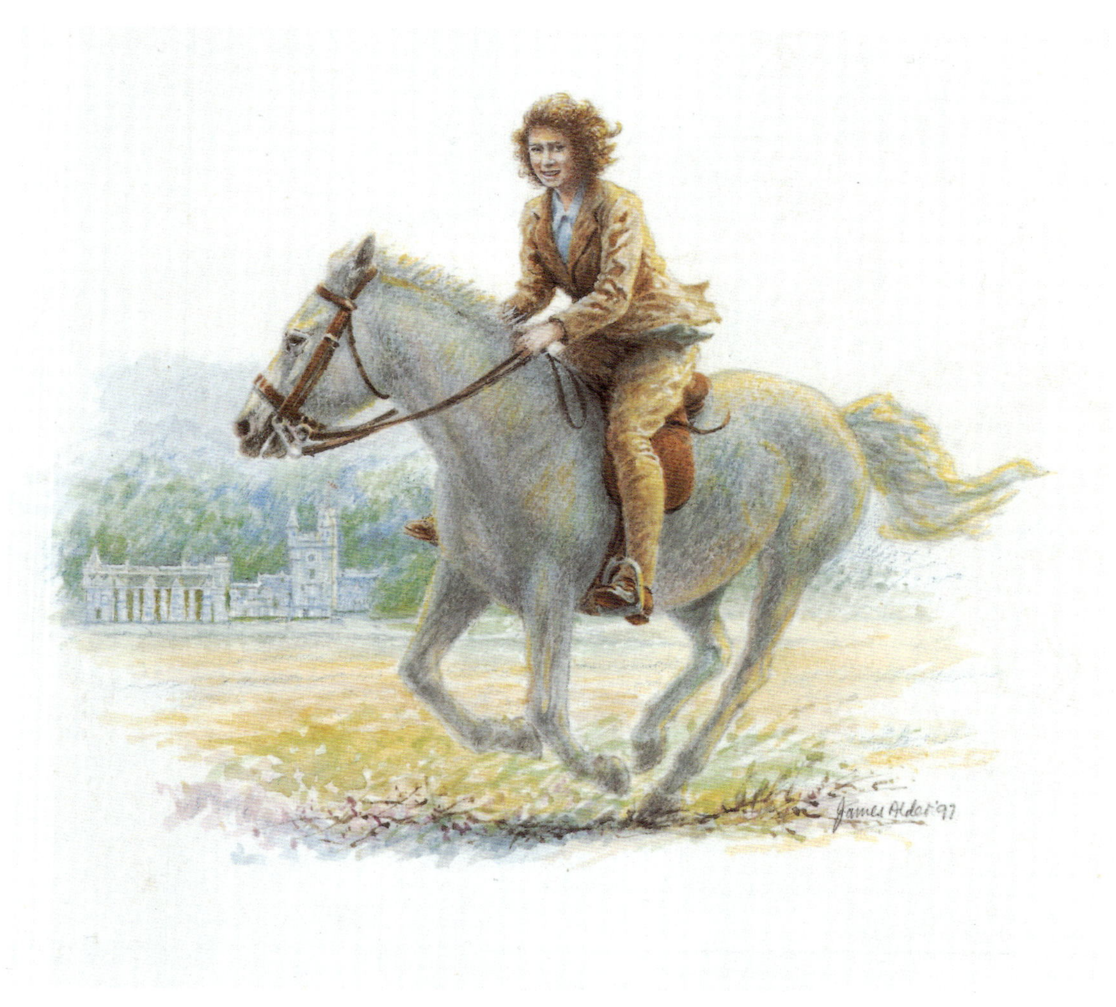

Her Majesty, as a girl, riding at Balmoral.

BIRDS and FLOWERS *of* BALMORAL

by

James Alder

Preface by Viscount Ridley

Botanical Text by Jennifer and Paddy Woods

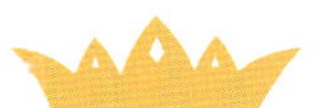

1947–1997

Published in the Golden Wedding Year of
Her Majesty Queen Elizabeth II and His Royal Highness Prince Phillip

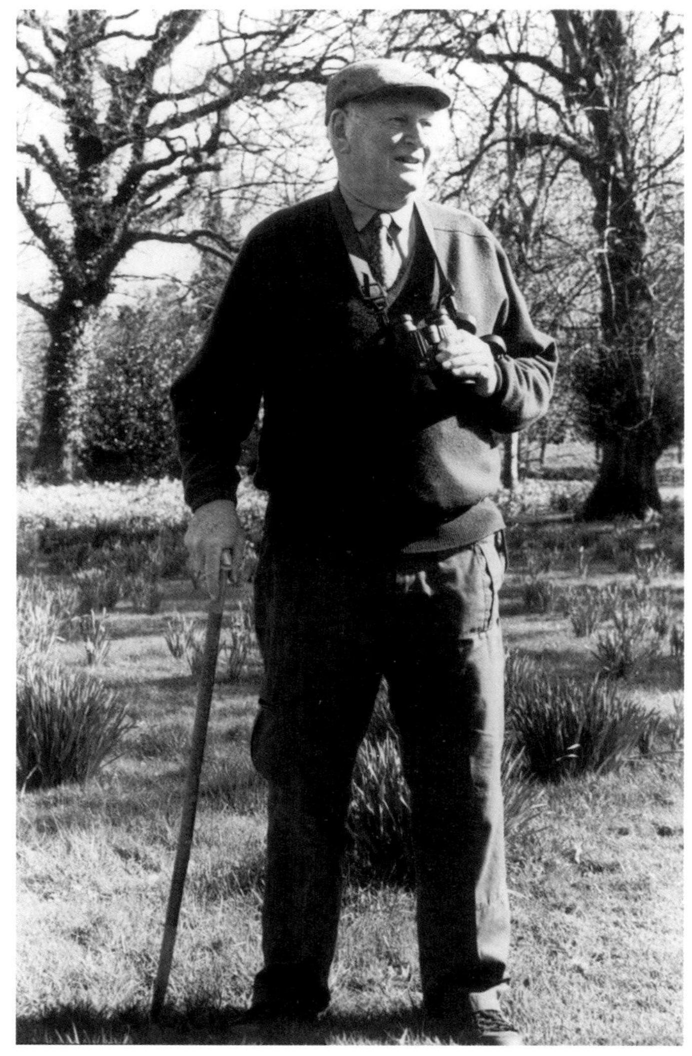

Viscount Ridley at Blagdon.

PREFACE

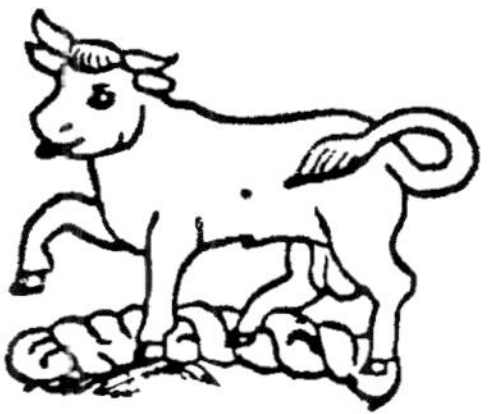

I am honoured and delighted to write a preface to James Alder's second book 'Birds and Flowers of Balmoral' which complements his magnificent first volume, Birds and Flowers of the Castle of Mey'.

James Alder follows in the tradition of the famous Northumbrian naturalists of the last century, John Hancock and Abel Chapman, while his paintings clearly draw inspiration from our great Tyneside artist and engraver Thomas Bewick.

He has devoted many years to the study of the Dipper, the world's only amphibious song-bird and has entranced many audiences with his remarkable experiences. While fishing, I have long shared his pleasure, listening to the Dipper's winter song.

My own observations, sadly, show the disappearance or fall in numbers of species once common in Northumberland. Skylarks are fewer and it is a long time since we heard the Cuckoo. The Blackcock, illustrated herein, which before 1939 used to breed near where we both live, not far from what is now Newcastle Airport, is now but a memory. Ornithologists throughout Britain have observed similar losses and changes.

Interesting to note that the rarer species such as the Capercaillie, Snow Bunting and Dotterel thrive on Deeside and long may this be so. We only wish we could see these birds in Northern England.

This book does not dwell on the subject of conservation: perhaps more subtly, the paintings, invoking both the power of the Golden Eagle and the colours of the Woodpecker's plumage, encourage us to share our world with beautiful creatures.

I hope that all who have the good fortune to see this book will realise that it is a great tribute to the enlightened conservation policies of Her Majesty Queen Elizabeth II on her Balmoral Estate where these magnificent birds have been preserved to be chronicled and illustrated.

Viscount Ridley

INTRODUCTION by James Alder

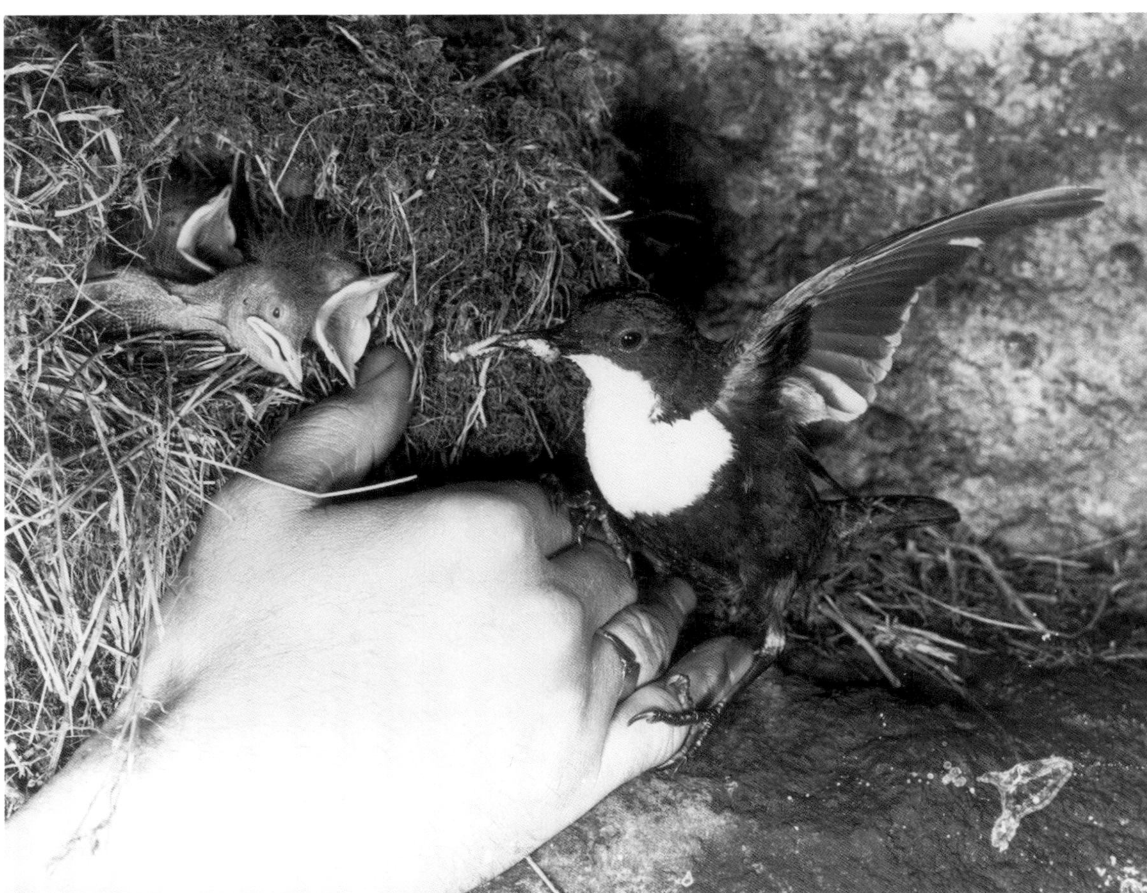

I remember an evening, at the age of thirteen trying to write an essay, with illustrations, on a 'sparrow wedding.' This is the noisy pursuit of one female by many males, which, according to modern wisdom co-ordinates the breeding season of local sparrow populations, something then that I could hardly have guessed at!

My mother and her elder brother were gossiping nearby. 'What have you written?' I was asked. On reading the details I detected uneasy glances between them and felt that I trespassed into a taboo area. I never finished the essay. How I yearned then for bosky and book-shelved environs, where beautiful birds could pop up from pages and branches. How could I know that the lovely triangular stamp in my notebook, showing a 'savage' with magnificent Bird of Paradise head-dress, should presage the reality, sixty years later, of sitting alone in the mist-silvered forests of Highland New Guinea, with Birds of Paradise dancing above?

Already however, the Fates were at work. I had at that age, won a scholarship for art. Immediately my headmaster, Athol K. Caris fitted me with satchel, real watercolour paints, sable brushes and heavy textured paper. Despite my teacher's protests that I was a near idiot, Caris sent me out to draw, *every day* for the rest of my life at school! Would that happen now?

But... I was born on the banks of the River Tyne, in the heart of the old city. Pollution was reaching its heights. There were sparrows and starlings, various gull species; and feral pigeons (which abounded) who often made their nest from wire! I recall no blackbirds in song. 'Dirty British Coasters' steamed out with coal and iron: timber from

Scandinavia, fruit from the Middle East and South Africa, live stock from Scotland and Europe sailed in with their pungencies. This was my horizon and a boyhood playground. I watched the engineering miracle of the New Tyne Bridge arching from either bank, and King George V opening it. And not much later the child Princess Elizabeth arriving in a barge.

Somewhere, in that rather stony ground, were scattered the seeds of curiosity about words. Trying to understand their origins fixed my pursuit of the new science of ornithology. A hard-earned bicycle gave me new freedom and my ambitions now extended to the hills thirty miles away. The humble gamekeeper, the poacher, the peasant farmer were sought out instinctively. Thomas Bewick's beautiful woodcuts and his autobiography were a driving force and I could still find 'glens' where my instincts *knew* that he had bird-nested here or climbed that crag. His inspiration gave me an instant rapport with my subject, birds and men.

Among my kind nobody knew the curlew's song! Twenty miles away they were 'warps', green woodpeckers were 'yaffles' because they laughed, and chaffinches were 'apple-shielies' because they shelled the flower buds. The scientific names of birds too were intriguing and I discovered that they were verbal collages of Latin, Greek and the Latinized names of ornithologists. The nutcracker's, *Nucifraga caryocatactes*, is quite onomatopoeic and the beautiful wall creeper of the high Alps, *Tichodroma muraria*, informs us first in Greek, that it runs up walls and again in Latin that it is found on walls.

As a boy, keen on bird art, a 'mural' was not a wall but a painting on a wall. From this I learnt that names could be lost through modification. The telescope through which I watched my dippers was so-called from the Greek 'teleos', afar, and 'scopein', to see, a lovely inventive idea. However, its brass tubes, so handily recessing one into another, invited in later centuries the verb 'to telescope', an equally vivid description for a report of a train crash, although hardly relevant to seeing from afar!

Now I can say, I think with some certainty, that any shortcomings of this work are mainly attributable to the fact that I was, more or less, self-educated: but with absolute conviction that its joys are the inspiration of the many friends past and present, who 'saw afar' and pointed 'that way'.

'*Birds and Flowers of Balmoral*' is a natural extension of '*Birds and Flowers of the Castle of Mey*', although each environment presented its own challenges. Mey is a small estate, set in a few private acres, open and sloping to a wild sea and shore. The thick castle walls encroach almost crushingly on the small rooms, which are modestly furnished, with well-used books, memorabilia and paintings. A narrow flight of stone stairs leads up from a kitchen to the Queen Mother's dining room where visitors are made to feel at home, and, at tea, whistling kettles steam ceaselessly.

On one occasion there, after she had shown pleasure at my work, I said shufflingly that I knew of better bird artists. 'Ah well', she said comfortably, 'that may be, but you're here, aren't you'.

On reflection that seems to have been a splendid apprenticeship towards the production of the second book, '*Birds and Flowers of Balmoral*'!

Four years later, I remembered the endlessly long red-carpeted corridors of Windsor and Buckingham Palace, and the tartan of Balmoral. Sandwiched between Rembrandt and Rubens and the almost overpowering wildlife of Landseer, when painted human and luminous animal eyes questioned my right to be there. I confessed in audience to Her Majesty the Queen that these were a little un-nerving.

'I have always loved Landseer's work. He gets into the spirit of things' she said, neatly dismissing my discomfort, while giving useful advice.

'The Queen Mother was interested in every aspect of the development of her book' I said, 'and showed extensive knowledge and remarkable memory'. 'Oh, mother is a clever woman... always reading books and keeping up with things' she replied.

'Did you, ma'am pick up this knowledge naturally, like a mother tongue?'

'Well yes... I was born to it', she said, which seemed to sum up everything. 'I remember as a small child running happily down long corridors, a sort of freedom'. (I had a quick vision of red carpets and Rembrandts strobing past). 'I was encouraged to learn about history and all kinds of things by visiting the libraries of Windsor. And then it was strange growing up during the war. All the grand treasures and paintings disappeared... buried in some cavern I suppose. Even the lovely cabinets faced the walls... only their drab backs to look at. I don't recollect much of Balmoral as a small child. I remember the garden... I was only four. When I was about eleven my parents lived at nearby Birkhall and I remember my first pony rides through the forest. The huge pines were pink in the evening... and I did encounter a young golden eagle.'

'The Queen Mother was uneasy about the larger species but clearly loved the small hedgerow birds. Your Majesty has hinted at a similar wariness?'

'I also have been attacked by Skuas – not much fun that. And on the Farnes off Northumberland the terns draw blood from one's scalp... pickterns, they call them, don't they? But they all have their place in the scheme of things.'

'During my privileged access to Balmoral, I have come to see it as a special nature reserve. I have seen more unusual species and predators in a day than anywhere else.

Do you see Queen Victoria's hand in this?'

'Yes, certainly. Those were times when some things were discouraged. But, Balmoral is a Victorian creation – she did much to preserve wildlife, and it was she who wisely bought the first of the remaining pine forests to add to the estate. We have continued this work... there is a duty involved. Prince Phillip is doing his best to achieve a balance between the pressures of increasing public access and the need for a policy of successful conservation. It is a continuing problem. I am glad by the way that you were able to paint the beautiful ring ouzel... the smaller birds seem to be fewer in number. Your woodcock painting reminded me of an occasion when I saw the mother carrying its chick. A rare event I am told, I scared it in the woods, when it stopped, gripped the chick between its legs, and flew away.'

The Queen's evident pleasure at seeing this persuaded me to recount a similar experience.

'I had', I told her, 'conditioned a Woodcock to accept me near her nest. She was brooding her newly-hatched young when suddenly she stood up and grunted softly to invite a chick to follow. In a flash she stooped, grasped the chick between her legs and flew away, her flight obviously laboured. Wonderful, I thought: this is something I believed was fable...'

'Caution persuaded me to check the spot. The chick was still there, crouched motionless and almost invisible among the leaf litter. I had been deceived, for the remaining three were still in the nest! The "chick" between her legs was her swollen undertail coverts and her laboured flight, drooped wings and dangling legs were the catatonic effect of fear for the safety of her brood.'

At this the Queen's eyebrows rose. 'No Ma'am, I hastened, I am not denying your observation, I am reporting mine as is was experienced. Greater ornithologists than I agree with your observation… the latest bird books record the return of the mother to take away the rest of the brood.'

'Then we are agreed', Queen Elizabeth said, 'that this clever bird can deceive us into believing that she has carried her chick away to safety, and that at other times she truly does so.'

This, I think, was as fair a diplomatic exchange as one could hope for!

Between 7000 and 8000 years ago scots pine flourished throughout Britain and Ireland but then declined when the climate became warmer and wetter. The forests retreated northwards and, although displaced to some extent by oaks and other broad-leafed trees, the pine forests were still fairly extensive in Scotland. From about 2500 years ago, however, the decline was accelerated by man's influence, and by the middle of the eighteenth century the changes became devastating due to increased farming and demands for more timber. Now only scattered relics of the ancient Caledonian pine forests survive in parts of the Highlands and western Scotland.

In the nineteenth century, timber from the Deeside forests, of which Ballochbuie is one of the largest, and significant in the context of these essays and paintings, used to be floated from the Linn of Dee to Aberdeen. As this was only possible when the rivers were in spate, the construction of a 12-mile tramway from the railhead at Ballater was planned so that the Ballochbuie forest could be exploited. Fortunately, in order to save the forest, Queen Victoria intervened and took first a lease then subsequently purchased the forest in 1878. A year later, on the 28th December, the storm which caused the Tay Bridge disaster, also caused extensive damage to Ballochbuie.

These relict pinewoods of the Central Highlands of Scotland, contribute something very special to the Balmoral landscape, and are the habitats for rare and unusual plants, fungi, birds and animals. They have been the subject of a number of studies and conferences, the most recent of which in 1994 was jointly organised by the Forestry Commission, the Royal Society for the Protection of Birds, and Scottish Natural Heritage – an involvement which bodes well for the future of the native forests, and I hope, beautiful Balmoral.

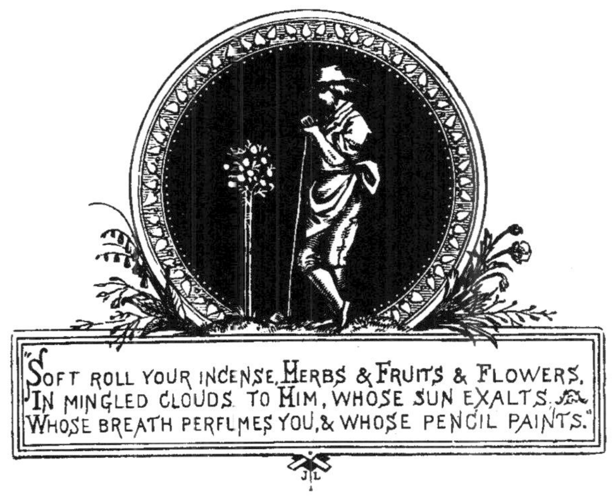

A PROOF OF THE ORIGINAL WOOD ENGRAVING FROM THOMAS BEWICK'S WORKSHOP. THE POEM IS BY JAMES THOMPSON, AUTHOR OF 'THE SEASONS'.

The Plates 26–50

PLATE 26 GREEN WOODPECKER *(Picus viridis)*

During the early 1900's the 'Yaffle' spread from the Southern Counties northwards, although they were present in Northumberland, though rare, at the turn of the century. Severe winters suppress their numbers easily: that and their sedentary nature prevents rapid dispersal. First breeding was recorded for Selkirkshire 1951, and by 1973 they had reached Aberdeen. Their presence in the lowland woods of Balmoral represents the most northerly part of the range. Her Majesty told me that she had seen one of them feeding on the lawn at Balmoral.

Unexpectedly, they spend much time feeding on the ground, their preferred diet being ants... and more ants. Their extendable sticky tongues, which are tucked away at the back of their skulls, elongate to about 10 cm. Because of this food preference, their beak, though large, has not evolved the strength nor shock-absorbing qualities of other woodpeckers. Nevertheless they are woodpeckers and hop up, or down tail first, and along branches with the best! The preference for tree-enclosed areas of old pasture with rotten stumps and logs assured me that I would see one of these beautiful birds on most visits to a favourite spot.

Their flight in the open is unmistakable for they bound through the air in long undulations. Besides ants and pupae, they devour huge quantities of beetles, larvae, wasps and worms. One was seen to follow the plough in the company of rooks and gulls. Seeds of corn, pine, acorns, rowan, apple and buds are taken.

The nest-hole is excavated to be about 6 cm, diameter and is unlined, the smaller woodchips acting as a bed. Smooth, glossy, white eggs average six in number, and both sexes incubate for about 18 days. The parents feed their family with huge quantities of ants and pupae. In one experiment seven nestlings consumed an estimated 1.5 million ants and grubs!

At fledgling the young are dull versions of their parents, heavily spotted on chest and belly, but this is very quickly replaced with new adult-type livery in autumn, implying an early competitive regime for survival.

Ninety common names demonstrate their popularity! 'Yaffle' describes their mad spring-time laugh, most describe their colour, and the remainder an association with mythology, probably Celtic. They are 'Rain Birds' in Sussex, 'Storm Cocks' in Salop, 'Rain Fowl' in Northumberland, as portenders of bad weather!

BIRCH *(Betula pendula & pubescens)*

'What tree is more graceful than the slender birch?' So questioned William MacGillivray in his 'Natural History of Deeside' published in 1855. Birch, with aspen and willows, would have been an early recoloniser after the last ice age about 10,000 years ago and still is an aggressive invader of ungrazed land. In most parts of natural or undisturbed landscape it is often the dominant tree where the delicate, sometimes weeping habit and white bark, particularly of young trees, give it a grace unmatched by other tree species. This is especially the case with the aptly named *Betula pendula*. The balmy air of a warm, still spring day is often strongly balsam scented from the sticky, unfurling buds and young developing leaves. Besoms are still made from tightly tied bundles of birch branches.

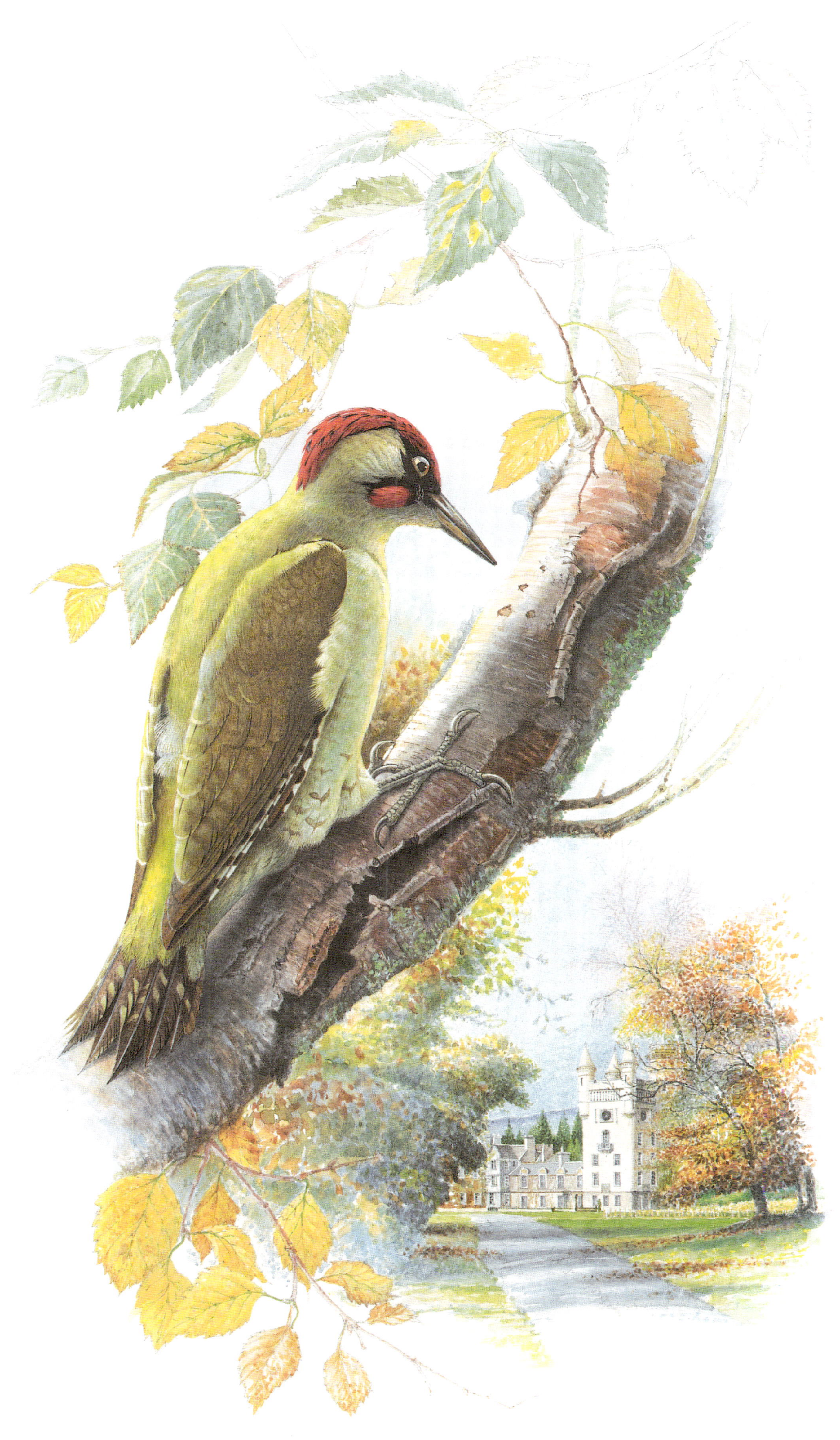

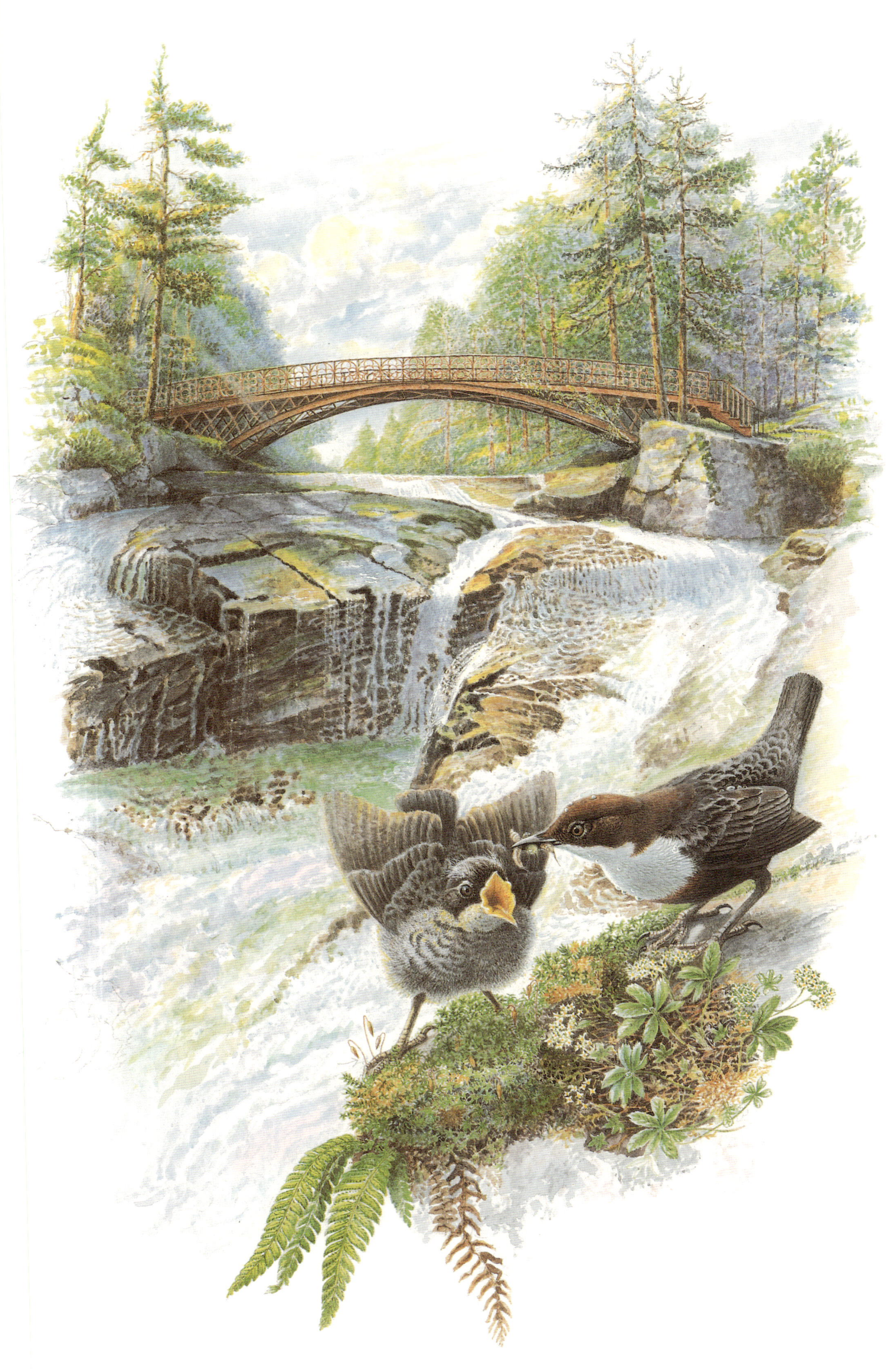

Having spent many damp cold mornings, beginning in the mists of crepuscular dawn, believing that I could tame the dippers, at last there came that magic moment. I reached out my hand and placed it on the nest ledge. The female dipper fluttered to me, unperturbed, and stood on my fist to reach her young in the nest, and fed them.

In that precious moment I was hooked, with unknown years of struggle ahead. I tramped those waters, was soaked, exhausted, injured, and almost drowned: I stood waist-deep in icy waters to catch and ring the dippers yet felt no cold until the adrenaline deserted me. My farming friends warned me 'you'll suffer later'... and I did... and how I wish I could do it all over again.

The precious notebooks with their scribbled data and smudged sketches grew in number, and a pattern of their life-style emerged, reinforcing a lust for more knowledge. Hundreds of thousands of words, some now indecipherable from immersion, were sandwiched between dog-eared and sagging covers.

I began to know that local population as parents, uncles and aunts, cousins and great-grandmothers, and felt a genuine sadness that 'blue-and-yellow' a date recorded 10-year-old, was no longer with us! Their average age, my graphs showed me, was about 3 years, older than those shown in other studies, so a 3-year-old was indeed aged.

'Triple-ring,' a mature female of cautious and strong hierarchal disposition, disappeared. Years later after my study was finished, I saw a female dipper wearing three ancient rings. Was this she? If so, she was 22, the oldest known wild passerine in the world!

Knowing my flock as individuals enabled me to anticipate their movements and relationships. As with all living things they were hierarchical. Those with the best nest sites and territories survived best, their young were heavier and inherited the best genes for survival. Determined young females lived next door in poorer territories until they inherited their dominant neighbour's possessions!

Powerful males could be polygamous, with mates spaced along three miles of stream, and, like wrens, built spare nests hanging over the torrents to entice their females. Raging spring floods washed out nests built by the immature, but experience taught them to re-build above the high water mark.

Yet the dangerous waters test their courage and invention. The compact nests of damp, air-saturated moss are igloo-shaped. If engulfed by rising waters they may become diving bells, enabling the young to survive in a bubble of air, while their entirely amphibious song-bird parents approach them with food by diving underwater!

One day I might write about it all...

ALPINE LADIES MANTLE *(Alchemilla alpine)*

One of the first plants to lift an observant townsman's heart as he escapes to the hills is the tiny Alpine Ladies Mantle. It is found, often abundantly, on moorland and rocky cliffs from over 1000 ft. and sometimes lower if washed down by mountain burns. It is a true indicator that the highlands are at hand. The dainty greenish flowers spring from rosettes of long-stalked leaves, each with five or six silver-edged, deep lobes.

PLATE 28 WOODCOCK *(Scolopax rusticola)*

The mysterious woodcock counts among my favourite birds. As a boy my first experience was to observe their 'roding' courtship flights, slow and owl-like along dusty glades. Almost unbelievably, the 'song' is a soft ventriloquial 'twizzick' and a grunt, proving that being different is what matters!

Perhaps only the nightjar exceeds the woodcock in exquisite camouflage of feather and egg. They are among the earliest species to nest. Encircled by morning frost, I have sat near an incubating female whose long brown beak and gold-streaked plumage might have been the stems of rotten bracken and leaves.

The enchanting downy young, quaint caricatures of their parent, are cared for by the female only, and are enticed to leave the nest immediately after drying out. There are many reports of both woodcock and snipe carrying their young away from danger, to which the introduction to this book refers in more detail.

Incubation of the eggs lasts about 3 weeks and they hatch together: soon the young are self-feeding and are able to fly long before they are fully grown.

Large numbers of migrant woodcock arrive from Scandinavian countries in October to swell our British population, and calculations from shooting records indicate that as many as 200,000 birds are bagged annually.

Gleaning George Bolam's 'Birds of Northumberland' I read that a Chillingham keeper, 1886, aware that they bred here says ... 'we always shoot them ... any that are bred here always leave before shooting in the autumn, so what's the use of sparing them..., Another reported 'far more would have stayed to nest, if we could only have refrained from shooting them...' Abel Chapman, a famous game-hunter, tells us with blunt honesty, that no sooner was a woodcock seen or reported than 'a gun was sent for and the "foreigner" shot, although probably nesting at the time.'

The Duke of Northumberland originated the marking of trapped migrant and breeding woodcock at the end of the nineteenth century. These careful recordings of East Coast autumn arrivals identified their later migration westwards. Marked near Alnwick, sample recoveries show their passage to Co. Wexford, Cork, Limerick, Antrim and to Pembroke in Wales, Somerset, Cornwall, Argyll and Brittany, France.

WOOD ANEMONE
(Anemone nemorosa)

LESSER CELANDINE
(Ranunculus ficaria)

Although at first sight dissimilar, two of our most attractive spring flowering woodland plants belong to the same family. The Wood Anemone has white or pinkish flowers, deeply divided leaves and a creeping rhizome. The flowers of the Lesser Celandine are golden yellow, the leaves glossy green and heart-shaped, and the roots tuberous. Both close their flowers at night and have similar fruiting heads. They spread quickly and carpet the floor of deciduous woods, but also flourish at the edge of pinewoods. They can be found growing near each other.

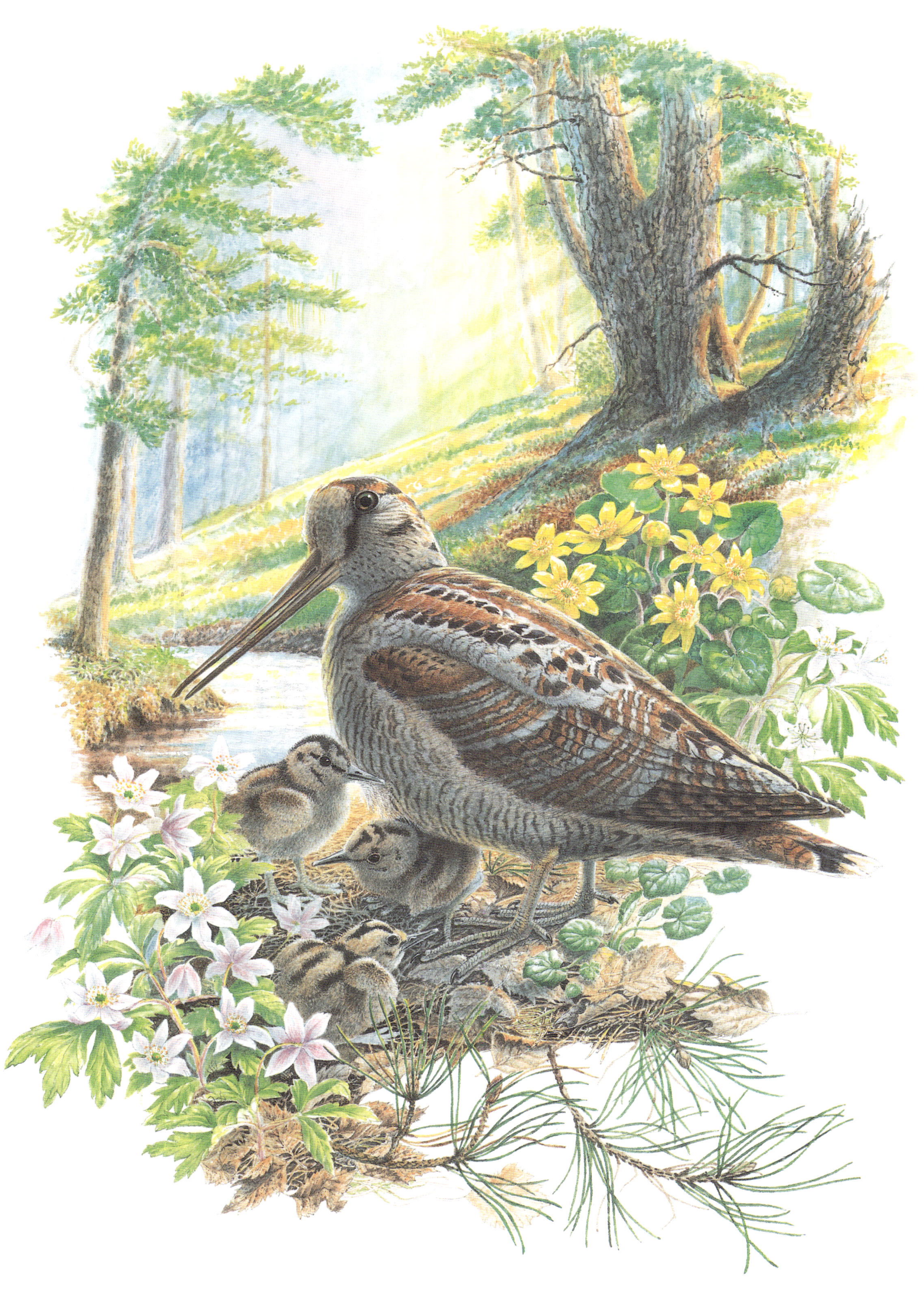
JAMES ALDER '96

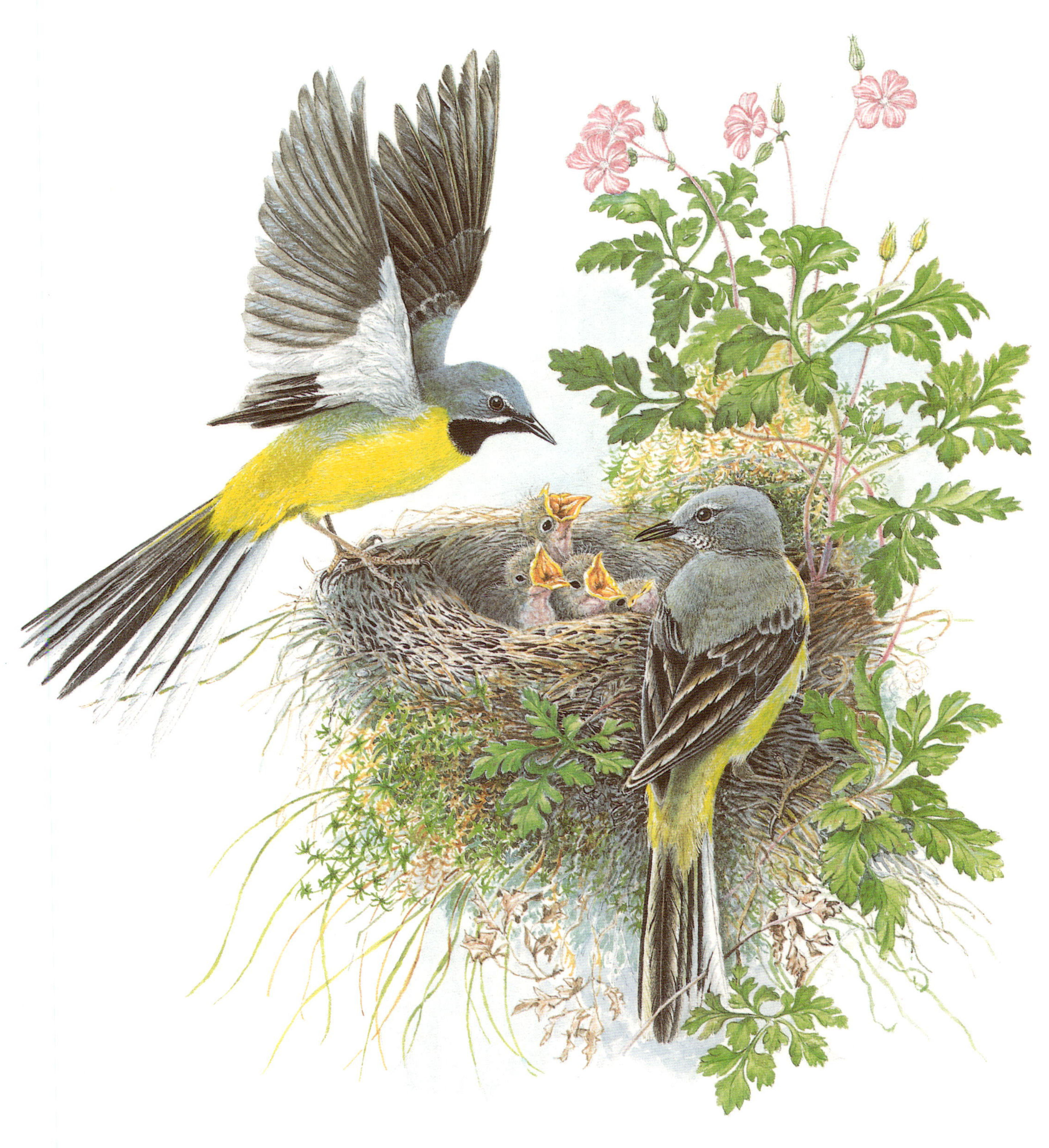
JAMES ALDER '96

GREY WAGTAIL *(Motacilla cinerea)*

Graceful in all its actions, the grey wagtail is a bird design of *haute couture*. French grey, citrine yellow, black and white are straight from the artist's palette for this creation. Complemented with a slim tail as long as a wedding train that beats to the birds every whim, the wagtail flirts and darts among the streamside boulders that it loves. In flight it even bounds through the air in a series of curvaceous arcs.

It is so elegant it seems to have defied imagination in its several common names; 'dishwasher' in Sussex, 'oatseed bird' in Yorks, and the most common 'barley bird,' a name also given to the common gull, the greenfinch, nightingale, siskin, wheatear wryneck and yellow wagtail! That's because all were supposed to appear during the spring-sowing of barley, some, no doubt like the gull and greenfinch to eat it, and others such as the nightingale and wagtail celebrating the arrival of spring. There is no evidence that wagtails eat barley!

In Britain they are fairly sedentary in habit. Although they may breed in Central Europe as high as 1600m; they are delicate birds and their numbers fluctuate due to hard winters. They begin laying in April to May, nesting in holes or crevices, walls and banks, usually near running water and waterfalls.

Their frequently beautiful herbaceous settings inspired my drawing and this one is based on a nest on the Devil's Water, Northumberland, where the pair were so confiding, the female allowed me to sketch her as she incubated her eggs. I regularly find these nests occupying old dipper's nests, indicating these species common territorial needs.

The elliptical eggs are glossy, creamy white, marked faintly grey and buff, and are usually five in number. Incubation takes 11–14 days, the pair taking turns. Both care for the growing and fledged young, feeding them on a diet of mayflies, stoneflies, lacewings and damsel flies, caught by low level fluttering aerial sorties along stream margins.

Grey Wagtails are found across the Palaearctic Region from Europe to Japan, except for a large yet unexplained gap from Poland to the Ural Mountains in Russia.

HERB-ROBERT
(Geranium robertianum)

The origins of the common name of this plant are obscure. The ancients used it medicinally, and in mediaeval latin called it *Herba Roberti*, possibly in reference to a Saint Robert or Ruprecht who, it is said, taught its use in medicine. The name may also be a corruption of *Herba Rubra* which refers to the plant's distinctive red stems. The common name for the genus is Cranesbill: it is derived from the beak-like shape of the seed capsules.

Botanically correct, if confusing, *Geranium* is the scientific name for the Cranesbills, but it is also the common name for the related, most southern African genus, *Pelargonium*.

Herb-Robert is an annual or biennial herb of dampish, usually shady places where the scarlet stems grow rank and brittle. The leaves when bruised have a strong fox-like smell.

PLATE 30 LONG-TAILED TIT *(Aegithalos caudatus)*

Long-tailed tits are birds of open woodlands, mainly deciduous, preferring oak, birch, sycamore, where family groups search in winter, in almost perpetual motion for insects, bugs and their eggs.

It is charming to see them trooping along a way-side hedge, always confiding and approachable, overtaking each other acrobatically, their delicate contact calls a constant 'chit-chat' of gossip. Only fourteen cm. long, of which the tail is nine cm., they are vulnerable. A hard winter may wipe out most of the population; yet they can recover rapidly, and this is achieved by a system of family unity and co-operation. I was privileged to observe this system at work in the early 50's.

The beginning was a few deposits of moss clinging to twigs in a budding hawthorn hedge. I suspected nest-building and set up a 'hide' to watch. The pair busied themselves fetching moss, spider's webs, lichen and wisps of dry grass. Each bird in turn sat in the centre of the yet unshaped nest and using their body as a former, reached out to place their material.

As it developed, spiders 'silk' was wrapped over the edge where it clung. Reaching over, the tit took hold of the edge of the silk and stretched it over and inside, where it again clung. The nest cup formed rapidly, and they probed it internally to 'felt' the wall.

When the rim was higher than themselves, they seemed to decide on the entrance position, and avoided that point when placing material, until the dome was finished. Always, they worked from the inside. Vast numbers of feathers were brought, and many eggs, perhaps 12, were laid.

The female only incubated, while the male fed her for about 15 days until the eggs hatched. Both adults then fed the large clamouring family, while the elastically structured nest expanded to accommodate them, yet remained intact! Calamity, however seemed certain.

'Tic-tac' came a call from nearby treetops and the pair flew up to greet two visitors. After an apparent 'conversation,' all flew down to the nest and fed the young in almost non-stop activity. The young fledged, leaving a sagging yet whole nest, and formed a family group including the new foster parents, whose own nest may have failed by predation.

Long-tails troop together, feed and roost together and defend their part of the woodland against other flocks. To ensure that in-breeding is minimised, some females leave their groups to join others. The affection with which they are held throughout Britain is shown by fifty or more common names, usually referring to the nest. 'Fuffit,' a Scottish name, refers to a soft ball of feathers.

COMMON HAWTHORN
(Crataegus monogyna)

Few hedgerows are not enhanced in late spring by the white, heavily scented blossoms of the Hawthorn or May, a small tree with intricate spiny branches. The flowers, borne in umbellate clusters, are followed later in the year by smallish dull red fruits, the 'haws,' which can make a fine jelly. The wood is dense and hard, useful for carving and has been used for furniture, bowls and tool handles.

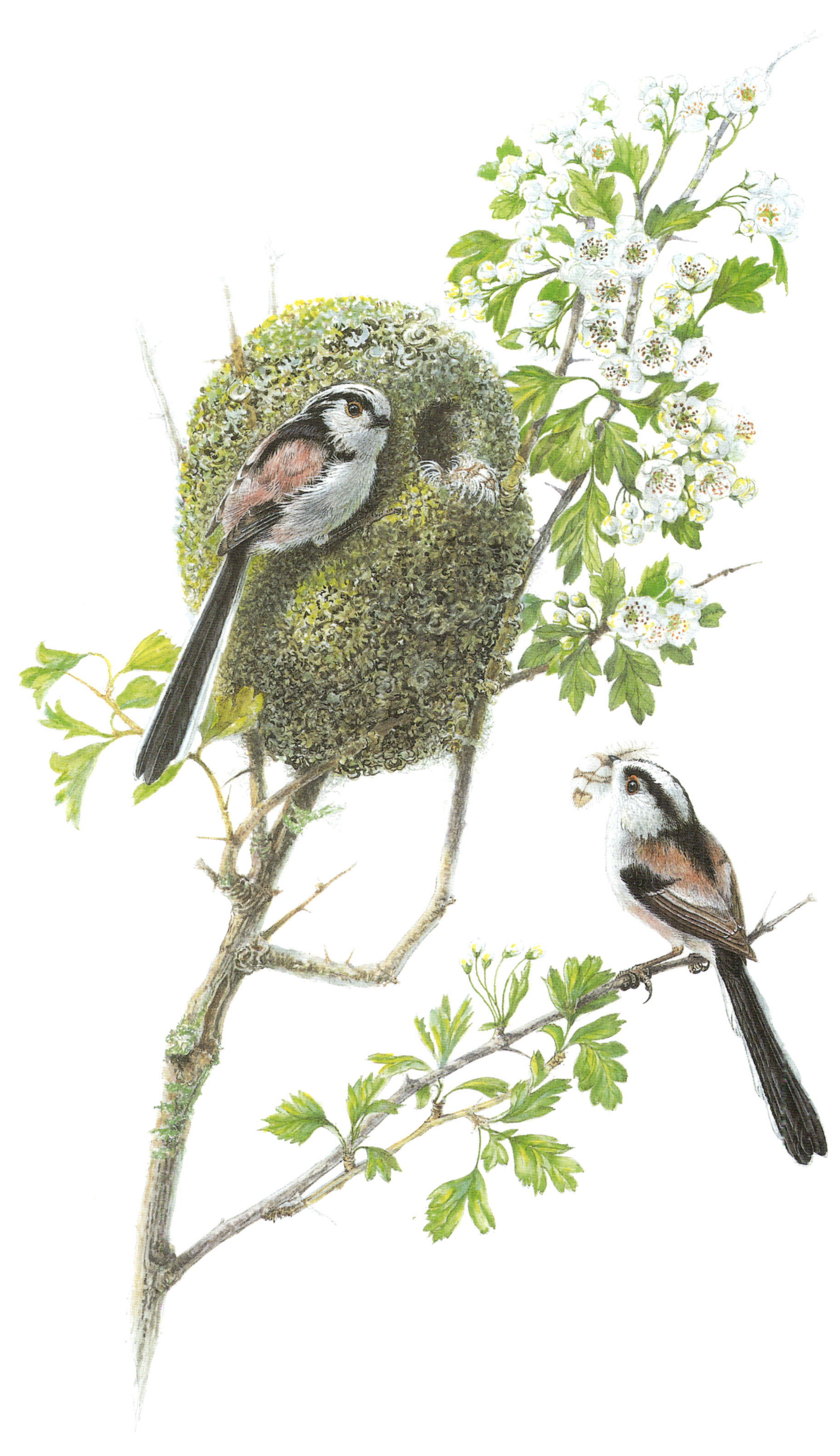
JAMES ALDER '96

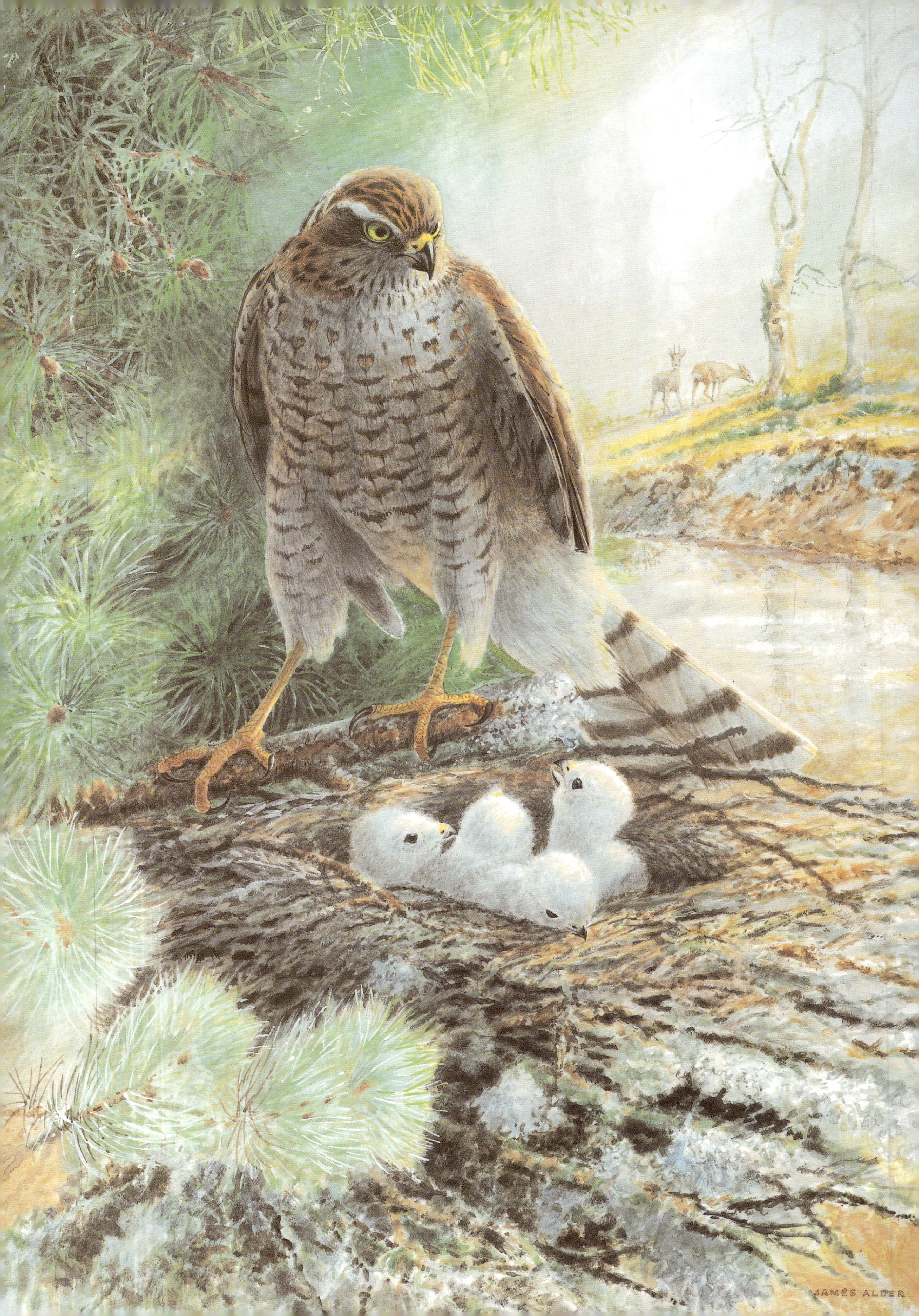
JAMES ALDER

In Scotland the sparrow hawk is a 'gleg,' the clever hawk. I know why. Across the estate not far away a pair nest in a private wood. As I work near my window overlooking the garden, which is planned to attract birds, I may count up to ten or more species. The hawks know my garden well and plan their attacks meticulously.

Soaring high over the estate the female defines her territory and gathers information. She descends slowly to the long hedge, gliding and occasionally beating her wings; down the neighbour's drive, turning left through the gate at road level where gaining momentum she rises up the 30 foot cupressus hedge and over... and she is among her prey. The earlier cry of the sentinel mistle thrush may have alerted the feeding birds. There is a confused blurring of pink and black, and the yellow of extended talons as the hawk misses her intended victim, a bullfinch. All scatter, but she pursues only her route; she has a plan and must succeed.

Where I have watched them nesting, I have always thrilled to that moment when the powerful female returned, still impassioned from the hunt. There is a click of talons, she glares down at her reaching young, and becomes the fond mother, delicately using beak and talon to feed them.

From recent scarcity, sparrow hawks have dramatically increased in numbers in Britain. 'Gleg' they are because they continue to colonize town centres and well-gardened estates.

Their food is almost entirely small birds, although species sometimes as large as wood piegeons and grouse are taken. The latter I doubted until a gamekeeper proved this to me. A female killed a grouse almost daily, but could not carry it, and returned to eat it. I have seen a pair co-operating to drag a wood-pigeon into a wood. The pair show prey selection. The 'jack,' the much smaller male, specialises in small bird catching. While she is incubating her eggs, he can feed her and himself, but when the chicks are growing much more food is required and the large powerful female joins in the hunt for larger prey.

When they are not persecuted sparrow hawks may survive for 12 years or more.

GOLDEN PLOVER *(Pluvialis apricaria)*

Modern bird watchers are supplied with a wealth of information, the work of thousands of zealous field workers. Distribution maps of species show us at a glance that British golden plovers breed mainly in Northern Uplands, and migrate to South East Lowlands and coastal areas for the winter, where they are joined by immigrants from Iceland and Scandinavia.

Winter is the easiest time to watch them. Although they have lost the rich black underparts of the breeding adult, they still have a gold, black and spangled beauty. The plumage is cryptic however, and a whole flock can be overlooked! Look for black and white peewits mixing with black headed gulls in damp, open pastures, and there you may see the plovers in scattered groups. The gulls may steal the worms from the plovers, but then, with enough to go round, the noisy gulls may provide an early warning system for the flock at large.

The golden plover's eggs and chicks show the same gold, black buff and brown colour scheme exhibited by the adult, exploiting so successfully the textures and tints of their environment, mainly dry, burnt, flat or gently sloping moorlands where far-seeing is important for ground-nesting species.

My drawing of the chicks is based on diary sketches some fifty years old. I returned to old haunts where these were made, where clear evening skies once echoed to the haunting far carrying 'too-roo' calls, rising and falling, of the displaying male. A dot in the sky, his slow buoyant flight, so unlike his normal sharp-winged dash, displayed him more certainly not as a passing traveller, but as a territory owner.

On this occasion I saw one where I expected many. I knew that numbers had fallen in many areas, perhaps due to overdrainage of the habitat, and was disappointed. However I returned a week later and counted 110 in an aerial flock, communally displaying before dispersal over their territories. Thinner on the ground they may be, but they are there!

They are known to be mainly monogamous. The males share nest duties and incubation through the day. At least one male was known to have completed all the 'nidification' duties himself. A surplus of males suggests that this dotterel-like behaviour is more common than supposed. Pairings often last for years.

HEATH SPOTTED ORCHID
(Dactylorhiza maculata subspecies ericetorum)

Of the 28 species of native orchids which occur in Scotland, the Heath Spotted Orchid is probably the most common, occurring in a fairly wide range of habitats, particularly moorland. When in bloom the evenly scattered plants terminate in a distinctive short conical spike of pale to occasionally dark pink or white flowers, the broader than long lips of which are distinctly marked with a double loop of dark magenta or crimson broken lines and dots. The pointed leaves are covered, to various degrees, in dark purplish brown roundish spots.

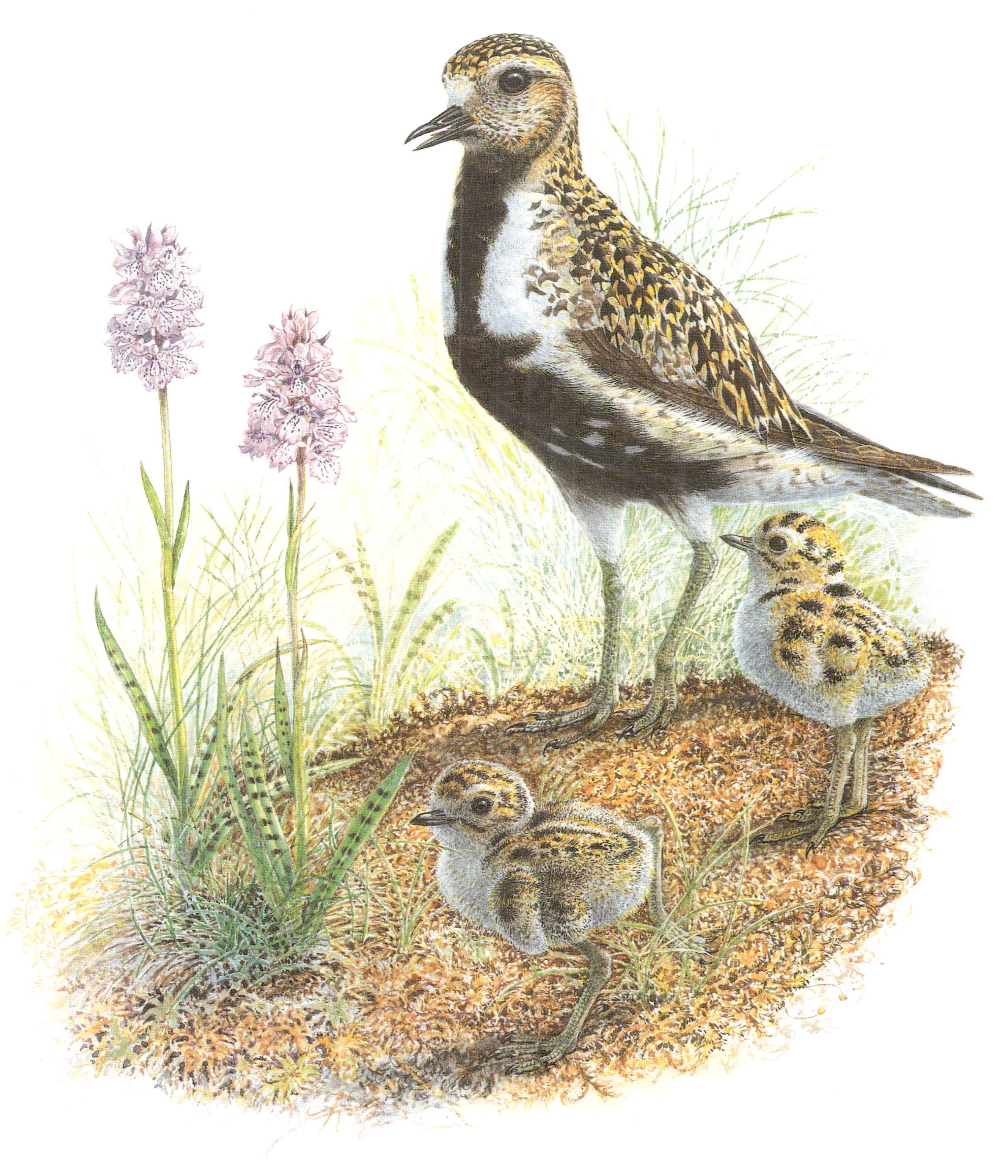

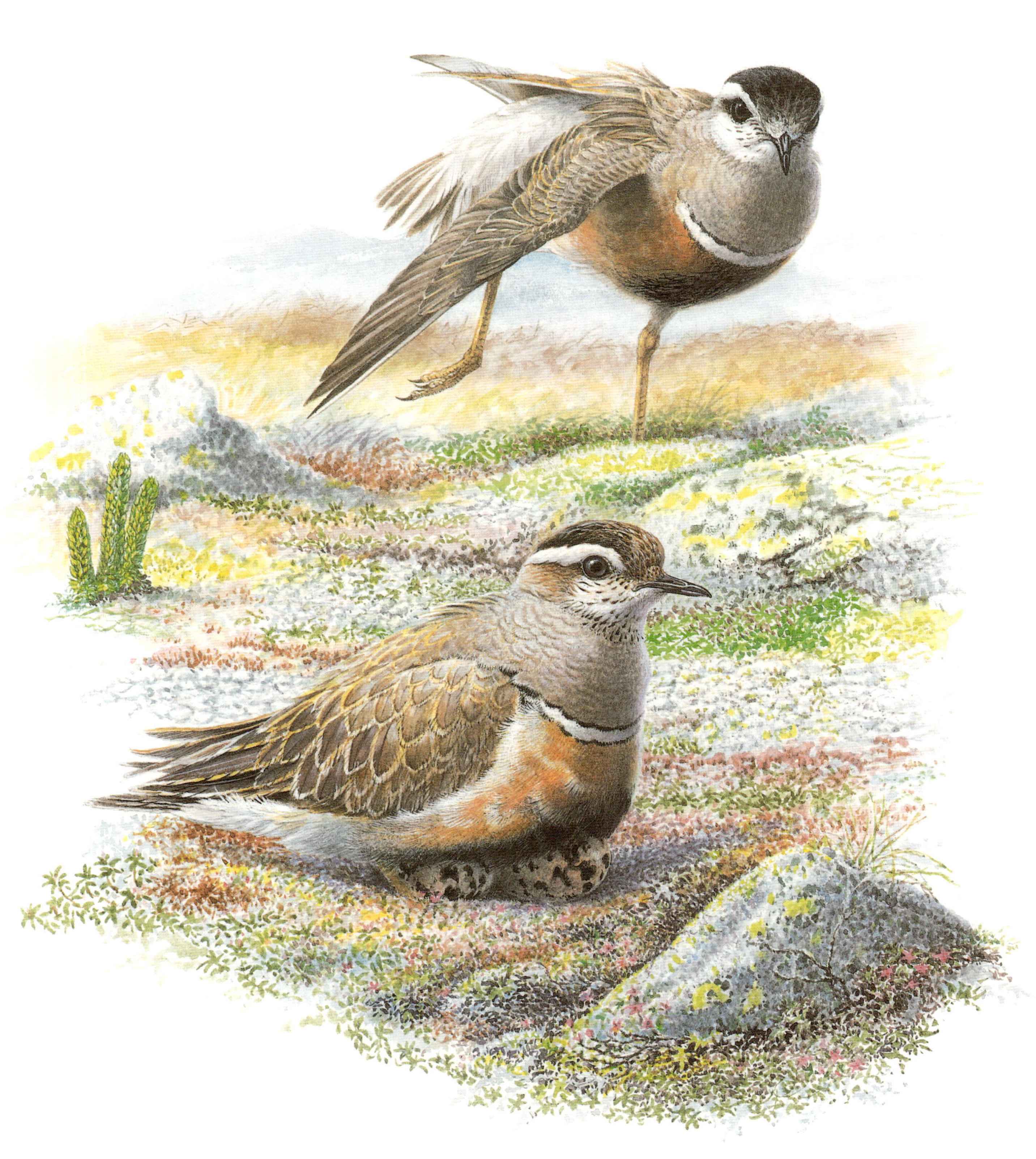
JAMES ALDER '96

When on migration, these beautiful plovers will allow close approach by a careful watcher. Although they are then slightly duller than during the breeding season, they are still a joy to see, usually in small 'trips' or groups. Their stance at rest is upright and delicate, and the high 'plover' forehead is characteristic. This contains a 'supra orbital' salt gland the size of which is related to the salinity of their habitat.

On the high plateaux of the Central Highlands of Scotland their favourite territories are flattish, open areas of dry grit and rock, with prostrate carpets of creeping azalia, club moss, rushes and short heather.

On arrival the females court the males, separating them from the flock by various wiles. The nest is but a shallow scrape among the gravel, sparsely lined, where the smooth pointed-oval eggs are laid. These are beautiful, buffish, blotched, spotted and streaked with rich browns.

The females, who are slightly larger and brighter than their partners, sometimes lay clutches of up to three eggs by different males, who they promptly leave to get on with incubation! Plovers usually lay four eggs, but a smaller clutch permits the smaller male to incubate and care for a smaller family!

This is a finely adjusted arrangement. Life on these exposed grounds is hazardous, the weather causes loss of young, while they are open to predation from falcons and foxes. The resultant high mortality is offset by this neat polyandrous system which produces the maximum numbers of young!

Incubation takes about 24 days, and the male is in vocal contact with the chicks before they hatch. On leaving the nest, the young are instantly active and are cared for by the male who defends them, not the territory. He indulges in the most flamboyant injury-feigning to distract predators.

Since the males carry the parental duties, the females flock in 'hen parties' and may leave the grounds early. Eventually, dotterel destinations are the winter quarters of Spain, the Middle East and North Africa. Formerly fairly common in Britain, their numbers here are limited to Central Scotland and a very few sites elsewhere.

The Dotterel's few common names accentuate the idea that they are 'dotty' – the ease with which they are caught, their famed tameness, the males 'willingness' to accept the female role, all strengthen the fable! I like particularly an ancient description '... this dotterel is a lytell fonde byrde for it helpeth in a manner to take itselfe.'

MOUNTAIN AZALEA *(Loiseleuria procumbens)*

FIR CLUBMOSS *(Huperzia selago)*

Exposed vegetation of mountaintops becomes dwarfed and wind-pruned, and the Mountain or Trailing Azalea (related to but not a *Rhododendron*) is a fine example. It has evolved a compact, leathery-leafed prostrate habit. So slow is its growth that a stem but one millimetre thick may have taken a decade or more to develop.

In Britain, Clubmosses also occur mostly in mountain habitats. Botanically known earlier as *Lycopodium* (from the Greek meaning wolf's foot) they are now divided into four genera in current classifications.

The Fir Clubmoss, depicted here and reminiscent of a miniature cactus, is now known by the scientific name *Huperzia* of which over 100 species occur worldwide. All the Clubmosses produce copious quantities of bright yellow pollen-like spores which in the past were used medicinally and in dyeing.

PLATE 34 PTARMIGAN *(Lagopus mutus)*

The Gaelic name is Tarmachan and should have remained so. Sibbald (1684) pre-fixed the name with a P and this was copied by Pennant (1768) into the ornithological literature. It is now in common use. In its many Gaelic spellings I see the idea of a tor – a high place or cairn, a heap of stones. The few common names, indicating the species insularity, all focus on 'mountain bird, 'cairn bird,' 'snow bird.' All are derived from the ptarmigan's harsh habitat, the highest and bleakest places that maintain alpine heath conditions and the heather, blaeberries, crowberries and dwarf birch upon which their survival depends.

The 'mountain grouse' is all white in winter except for its black tail, and in summer, via complex body moult, is mottled grey and brown. The white wings when partly exposed, help in the general cryptic pattern of the bird at rest against white-veined, grey-lichened granite. They are rarely driven from the high peaks of 3000 feet or more, except in the harshest conditions of deep freezing snow, when they may descend to lower grounds, overlapping those of Red Grouse.

Courtship begins early. The most conspicuous displays are by the males, who fly upwards abruptly then descend on bowed white wings, black tail spread, uttering a croaking call which is not easily heard. The voice is difficult to describe, a series of clicks and harsh 'karr' notes quite different from the 'go-beck-go-beck' of the Red Grouse. Because of their lonely habitat, they are fairly confiding with humans, but too many visitors and dogs have made some populations warier.

The eggs are glossy and oval, a fine cinnamon red, blotched and spotted brown, fading to yellow buff. These are laid in a shallow scrape, lightly lined with twigs, grass and fibres, made by both sexes and sheltered near a stone. Incubation – by the female only, takes 21 days and the young hatch synchronously, leaving the nest when dry. They feed at first on small insects, abundantly brought upon rising wind currents. The young, while still chicks, can fly well.

Both male and female indulge in amazing distraction strategies to lead predators away from their young.

BLAEBERRY *(Vaccinium myrtillus)*

Blaeberries are tough little shrubs with angular green stems and deciduous leaves that turn a bright reddish-yellow in autumn. They grow abundantly on acid soils under pines, along roadside banks or high on the open moor. Take time to look at the structure of the whitish-pink urn-shaped flowers. These are followed by dark blue-purple fruits, the colour staining the droppings of browsing foxes and birds, and the lips of children feasting during summer picnics!

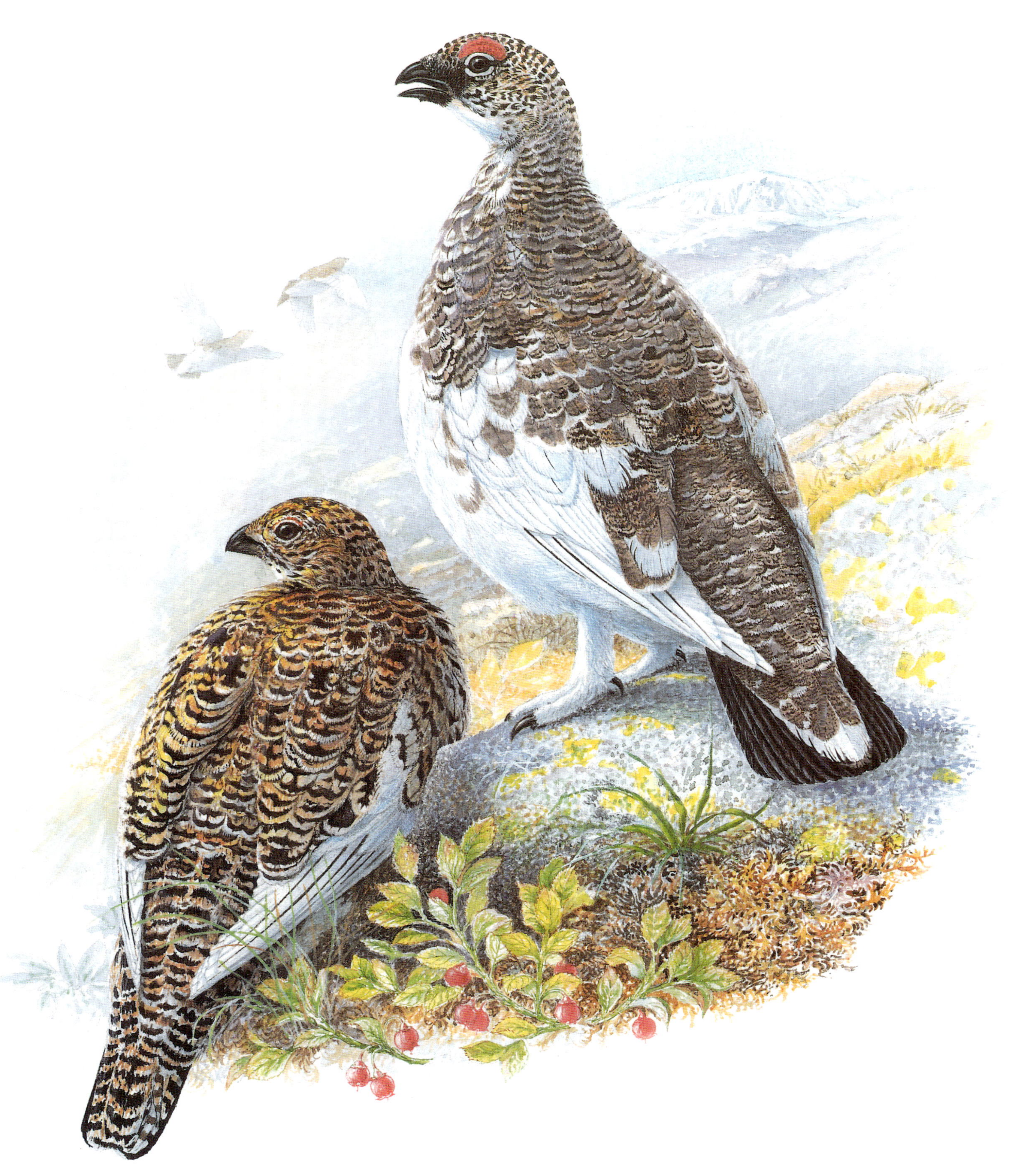

JAMES ALDER '96

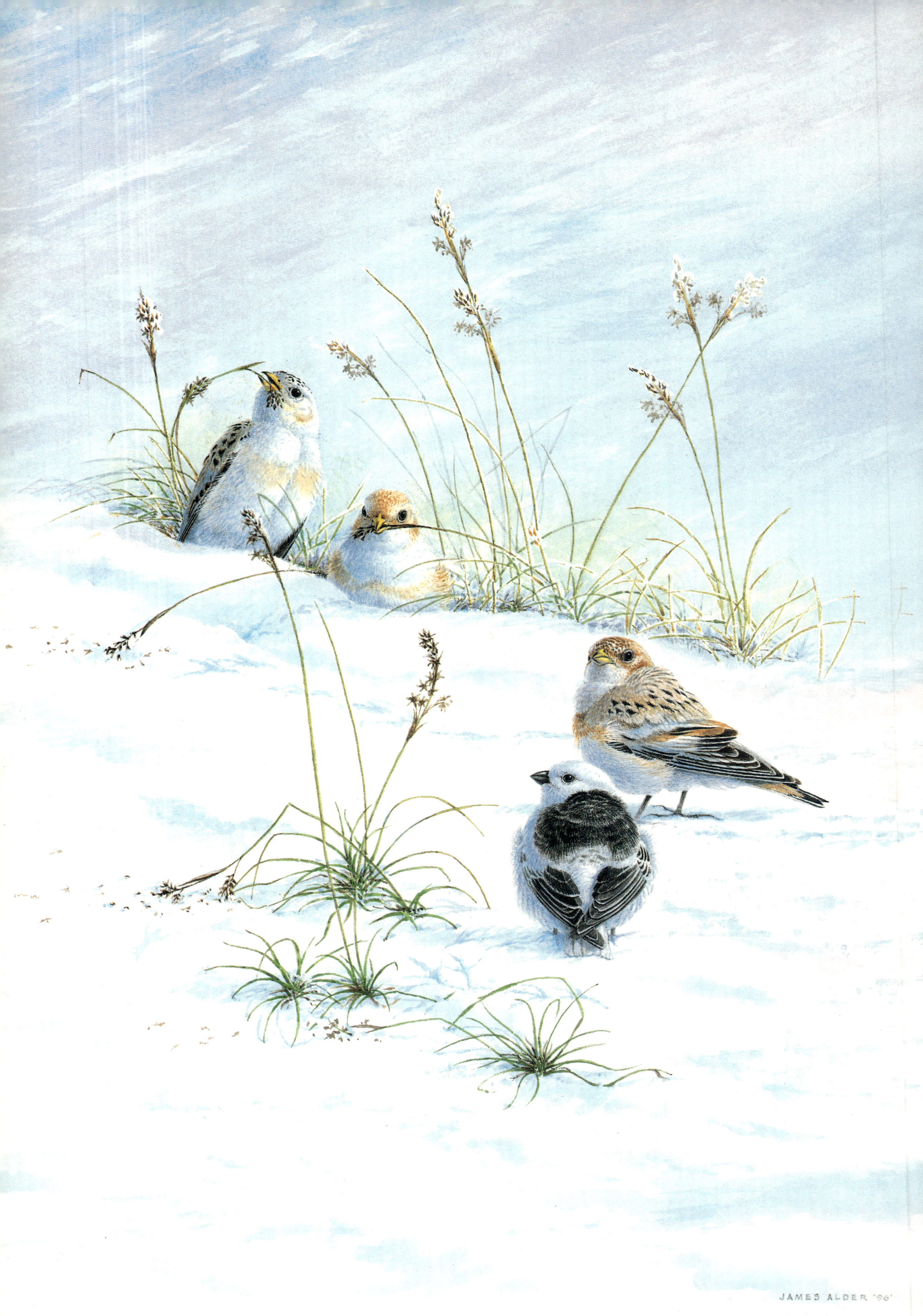
JAMES ALDER '96

SNOW BUNTING *(Plectrophenax nivalis)*

Distribution maps of this beautiful species show that they are the most northerly breeders among the passerines. With a circumpolar distribution, they are found in Norway, inland to the high snowfields, around the North Cape, where I have seen them, to the icy coasts of Russia, North into the Arctic to Spitzbergen and Franz Joseph Land. To the West they occupy Iceland, Greenland and North America.

Powerful fliers, autumn migrants from the latter regions may reach Britain via the Faeroes, when they scatter down the East coast as far South as Kent. In their winter flocks they are the most exquisite birds, particularly inviting superlatives as they 'drift' along sea-spumed beaches or huddle, with feathers ruffling, in flurries of snow.

Much loved, they have about 40 common names, most linking them to snow or their wild habitat. 'Snowflake' and 'mountain bunting' of Orkney and Shetland are characteristic, although over-sea-bird' of the Yorkshire coasts is less than poetic!

Their hardiness and migratory prowess are obvious adaptations to icy habitats; their uncommon presence in Britain shows this for we do not have the appropriate tundra conditions. Small breeding groups have been identified as coming from separate Iceland and Scandinavian populations. When they stay here to breed in Scotland it is likely that we have had a cold spell!

Their food is mainly seeds, although they are fond of flying insects which are raised upon warm air currents and deposited on snowdrifts. On these high screes the buntings wait for much of the snow to clear before staking out their territories.

The male performs his 'manikin' display to any female who is prepared to enter this territory. Upright in stance, his beautiful black and white wings spread and lowered, his tail fanned, he struts down his rocky 'catwalk' in excitement, or circles low in flight, or hangs in the breeze, wings vibrating, above her. Can this be imagined, at midnight in Arctic Norway against the backdrop of a glacier, as I have been privileged to see it?

SHEATHED SEDGE *(Carex vaginata)*
HEATH RUSH *(Juncus sqarrosus)*

Scottish mountain tops are inhospitable places for plants and those that manage to exist have evolved a prostrate, creeping habit, a cushion-like growth or, as in the case with grasses, sedges and rushes, tough wiry often tussock-forming leaves. Some rare species are restricted to a few alpine habitats but others such as the sheathed sedge and heath rush have adapted to the highland conditions and are locally abundant. At least the rush however may only survive vegetatively at over 2700 feet, and will seldom set seed above that level.

PEREGRINE *(Falco peregrinus)*

'Which is your favourite bird?' I am asked, and find it difficult to reply. All are so diverse in beauty and adaptation to their environs. On reflection, when fitness for purpose, wild beauty, proportion and breath-taking aerial mastery are the ingredients, I am bound to name the female peregrine. In this I am not alone: for thousands of years temples of stone and poem have been set up in praise of their envied powers.

The Egyptian god 'Horus' was a falcon, 'the lofty one,' whose all-seeing eye became an amulet for good. In the thirteenth century, Frederick II of Germany, a fanatically dedicated falconer, took 30 years to write his still authoritative text book 'De Arte Venandi cum Avibus' which glorified the 'sport of Kings.' Shakespeare captures our human moods vividly: 'in a towering passion'... 'her pride of place' ... 'she stoops to conquer.'... His subtle use of stoop, its hint of condescension towards the final deadly strike should not be overlooked!

A pair of falcons – the female is the larger – always defend their breeding territory and nest site vigorously, with wailing or screaming 'kak-kak-kak' sounds. They nest on ledge or cliff, a spartan fortress to which no concessions of added comfort are made.

The oval eggs are buff-cream, boldly marked rust and brown, usually three in number. The small male is undeterred by the female's power and takes his part in the long incubation, and the chicks hatch almost together. After hatching there is little or no nest competition between the siblings, unlike many other predatory species, probably because the cooperative and wide-ranging parents maintain a well-stocked larder.

After fledging the family remains together for many weeks, when the young are schooled and hardened before separating. Normally, on reaching independence the immature falcons don't breed until their second year. A 'pool' of potential mates is thus available for replacement when one of a breeding pair is lost. An incubating female, having lost her mate, got a new one who took over fostering duties without interruption. A male, losing his female, left and returned quickly with a new one!

A gamekeeper 'Kept his crows under control' by shooting the male of a pair at their nest, then waited for the new unsuspecting suitors to appear, finally shooting the female! He must have read the opera!

After independence, young birds disperse to coastal estuaries, cliffs and islands where winter-feeding is good among flocks of waders, ducks and gulls. Ancient bird catchers did fine trade in the netting of young falcons, 'haggards' (wild young things!) on passage. They were much preferred to 'eyases' taken from the nest, for they were stronger and fitter and already knew what hunting was all about!

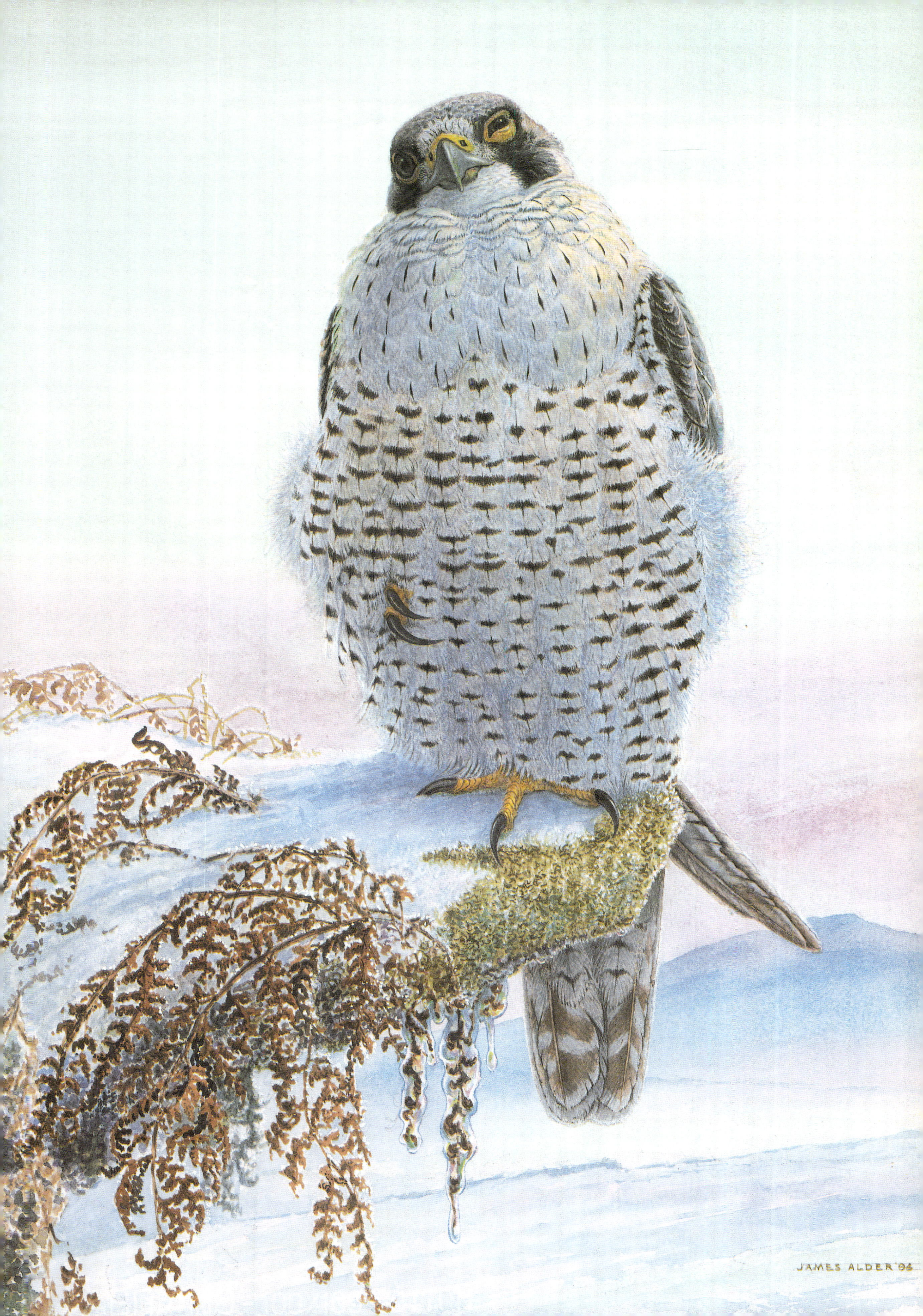
JAMES ALDER

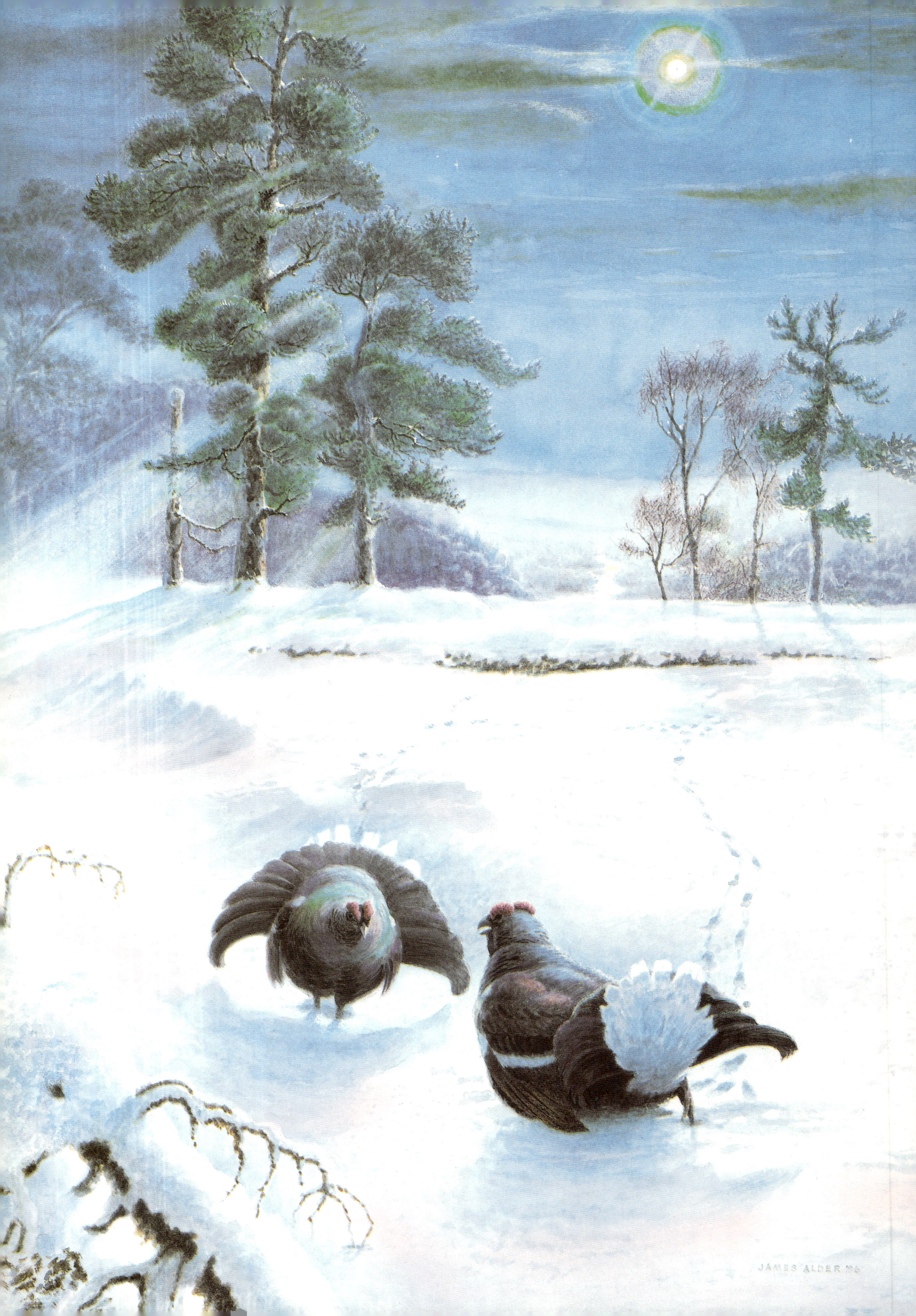
JAMES ALDER

The famous 'lek' of this fine grouse is a playground, from the Scandinavian 'leka,' to which the males resort to assert their authority over each other and compete for the female's favours. The club, which it surely is, is open all the year round, especially in spring and autumn.

I have heard the males wassailing across the moor, a far-carrying 'rrooo-oo-rroo', and hissing as they display their lyre-shaped tails and leap at each other repeatedly. There, in spring, they have a promiscuous mating system, the females choosing the males, apparently at random. But... there is a plan. Newcomer males are kept at the club's perimeters, only finding their way to the privileged core through age and experience. It all sounds very familiar! I wonder what the grouse expression for 'the drinks are on me' is...

Woodlands of various tree species and clearings of heath and shrubs are a desired habitat mixture. Formerly found in suitable environs in lowlands, the blackcock are now almost all relegated to upland regions and are not easily found, although a more sensitive balance of tree planting is helping them recover in some areas.

Their food is predominantly vegetarian, with the addition of some animal matter. The buds of heather and dwarf trees, the berries of cowberry, blackberry and bramble, seeds of grasses, birch, pine and juniper make a short list in a varied diet.

The demurely and cryptically patterned female makes a shallow scrape for a nest, with a light lining of moss and grass, and the mainly ochre-coloured eggs are about 6–10 in number. They hatch together, the precocious young leave the nest immediately and feed on insects with little help from the otherwise caring mother.

Blackgame roost together in small groups and use the trees as look-outs, often until after sunset to check the presence of danger. In very cold winters they may roost in deep snow, flying directly from the trees to the chosen spot to avoid making a trail of prints and scent, and change their position daily.

It is with great pleasure that I have just heard a report that blackgame are to receive special protection.

PLATE 38 BUZZARD *(Buteo buteo)*

The buzzard's cry is a far-carrying high-pitched 'mew', often made when it is soaring too high to see easily. In spring it is worthwhile to watch patiently if a pair are seen. Sky-dancing' is part of their ritual. Stalling followed by closed-wing dives for hundreds of feet, loops and slow rolls are an exhibition of surplus energy that announces their right to hold a territory and breed.

This begins in late March to April: each pair has the choice of several nest sites which are changed annually. The nest may be on a crag, cliff or tree where free flight is important. It is about a metre wide, made bulkily of branches and heather with a shallow cup of fresh green foliage.

The two to four eggs, once collected for their beauty, are white and boldly marked reddish, brown and grey. Incubation takes about 36 days, both sexes taking part. The young hatch at about 2 day intervals and, at different stages of development, are vulnerable to attack by their heavier siblings. Death and cannibalism may occur.

Fledging takes 50–55 days and a further 40–55 days takes the young to independence, during which long apprenticeship they learn their trade. The oldest ringed buzzard was 25 years.

Balmoral is eminently suitable for buzzards, with crags, stands of open pine, secluded mixed woods – and rabbits. Ridges and hilly slopes provide constant updraughts for free flight and I have heard and seen them soaring as I stood sketching in the Castle garden. In the South of England they nevertheless hunt over flat fields and may hover gracefully close to the ground like huge kestrels.

During the nineteenth century they were heavily persecuted by gamekeepers, perhaps even more by egg collectors. The war years 1914–1918 saw the pressures lifted and numbers peaked until the rabbit's decline due to myxomatosis in 1955–1956. The use of toxic chemicals brought on a further decline, but their ban again improved numbers. There are now strong populations in the South West of England, the Lakes, South West and North Scotland and a secure population in Northern Ireland. The total population may now be over 10,000 pairs, a credit to all-round common sense.

COWBERRY *(Vaccinium vitis-idaea)* HEATHER *(Calluna vulgaris)*

Two members of the heather family, *Ericaceae*, are depicted on this plate, heather itself and cowberry, a close relation of the blaeberry. Of the five Scottish species of *Vaccinium*, cowberry is possibly the most handsome with its glossy evergreen leaves, creeping habit and clusters of pink, bell-like flowers followed by shining scarlet berries. Depending on various factors heather can grow as a tiny shrub of a few inches or form a large bush two or more feet high. Its flowers vary through various shades of pinkish-purple to the rarer and 'lucky' white.

The transition of colours from the golden browns of autumn and winter, to the fresh greens of spring growth are but a foretaste of the moorland glories of late summer, when the subtle purples of the heather, the heady scent and the hum of bees foretell a harvest of honey.

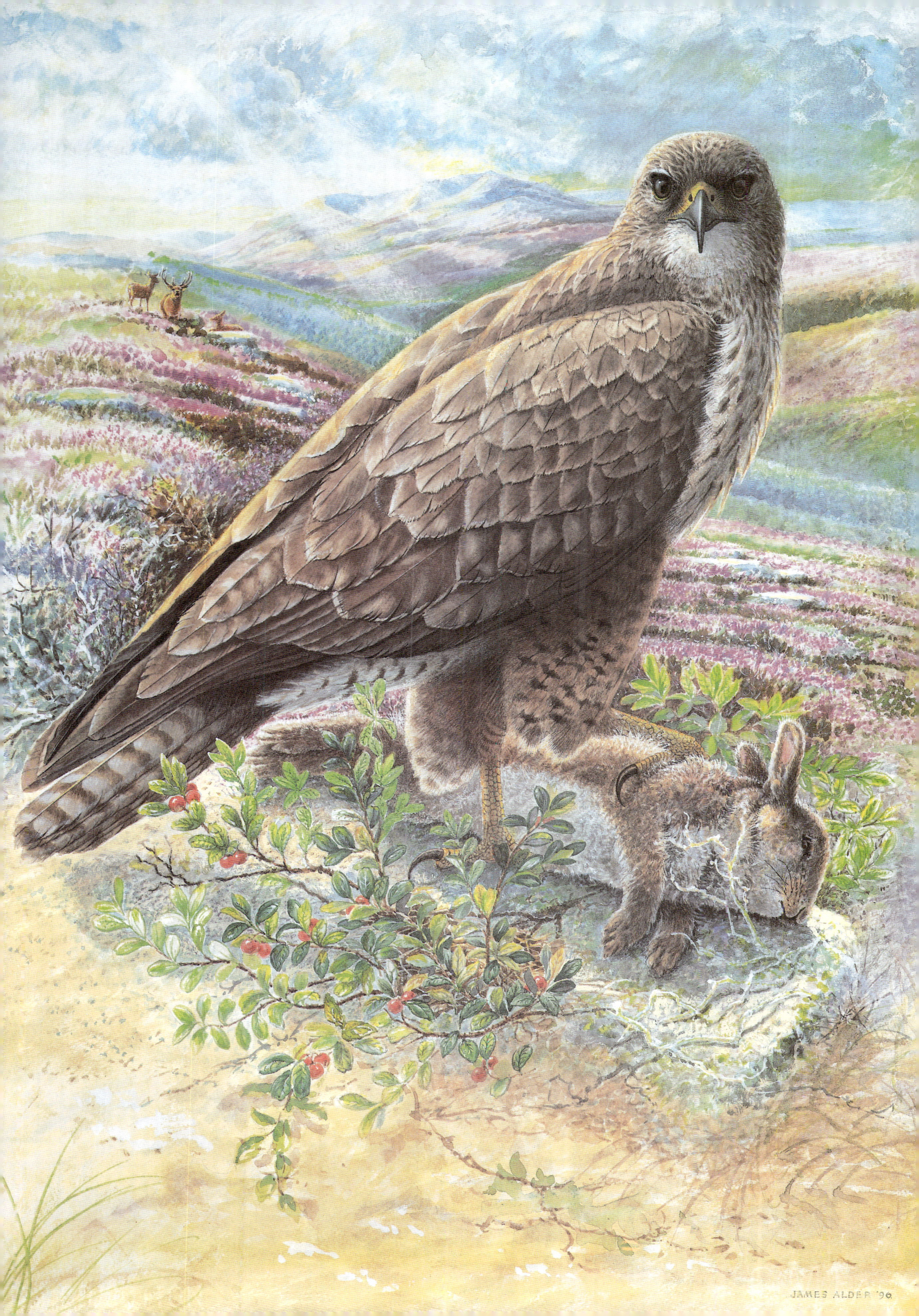
JAMES ALDER '90

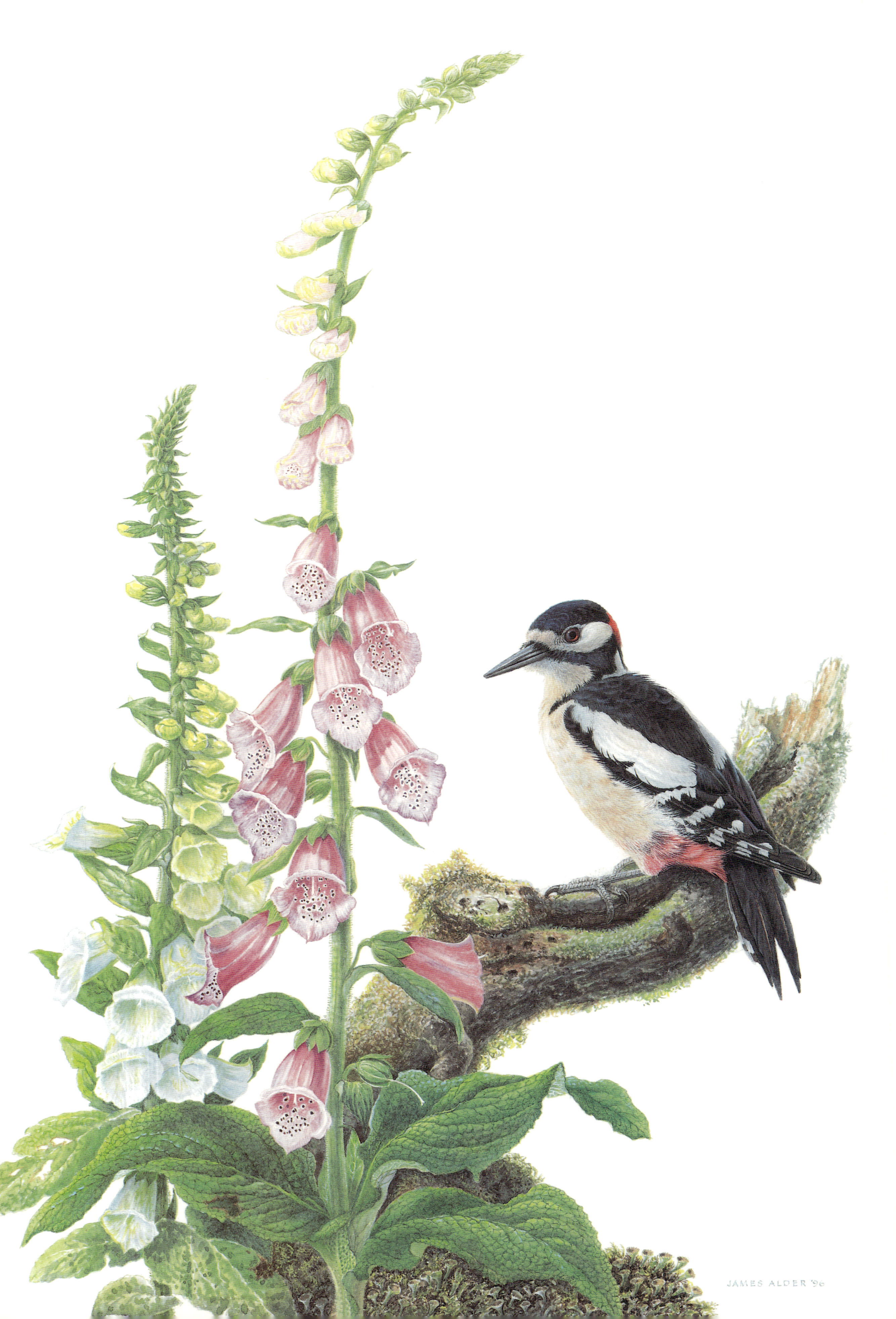
JAMES ALDER '96

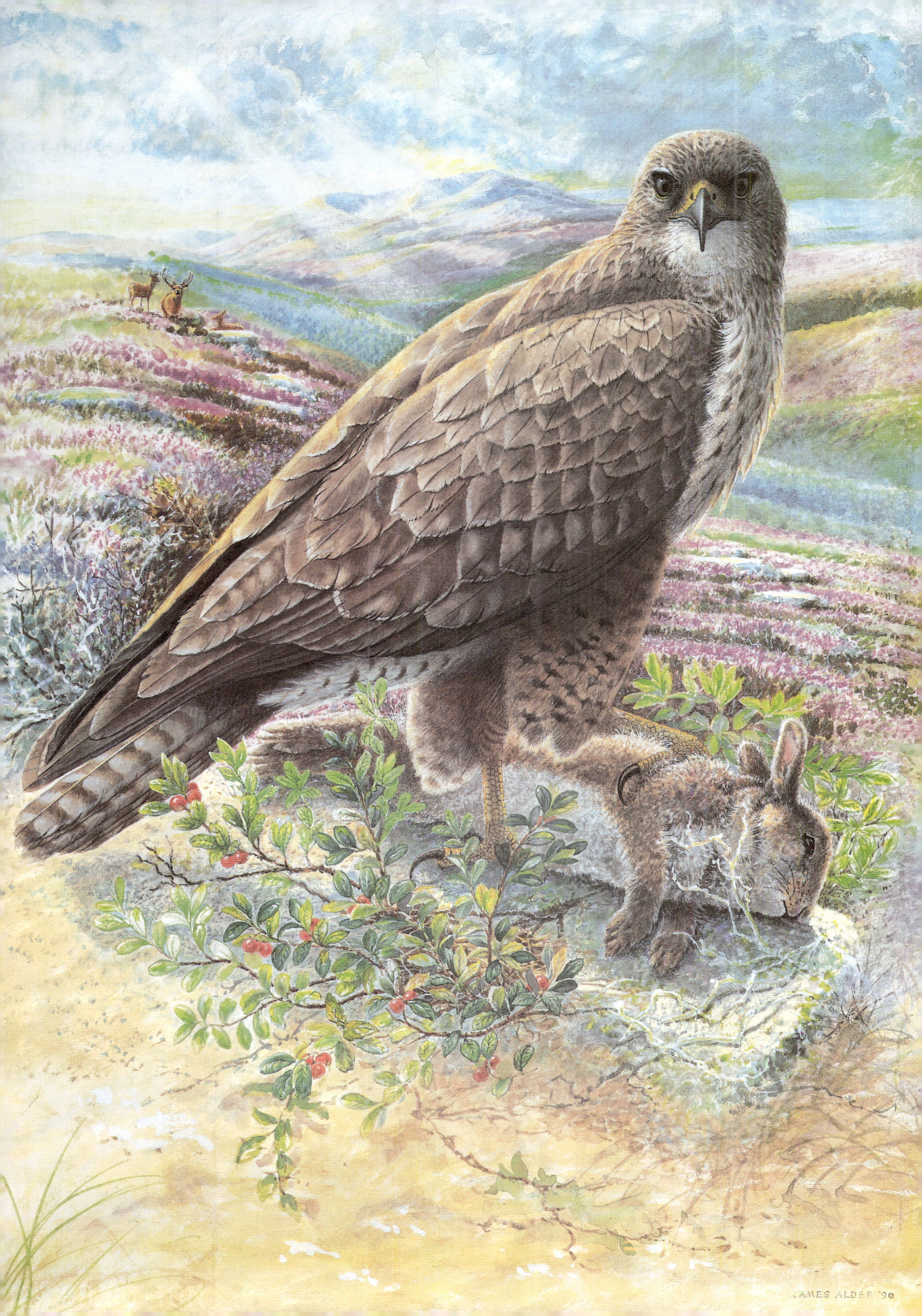
JAMES ALDER '96

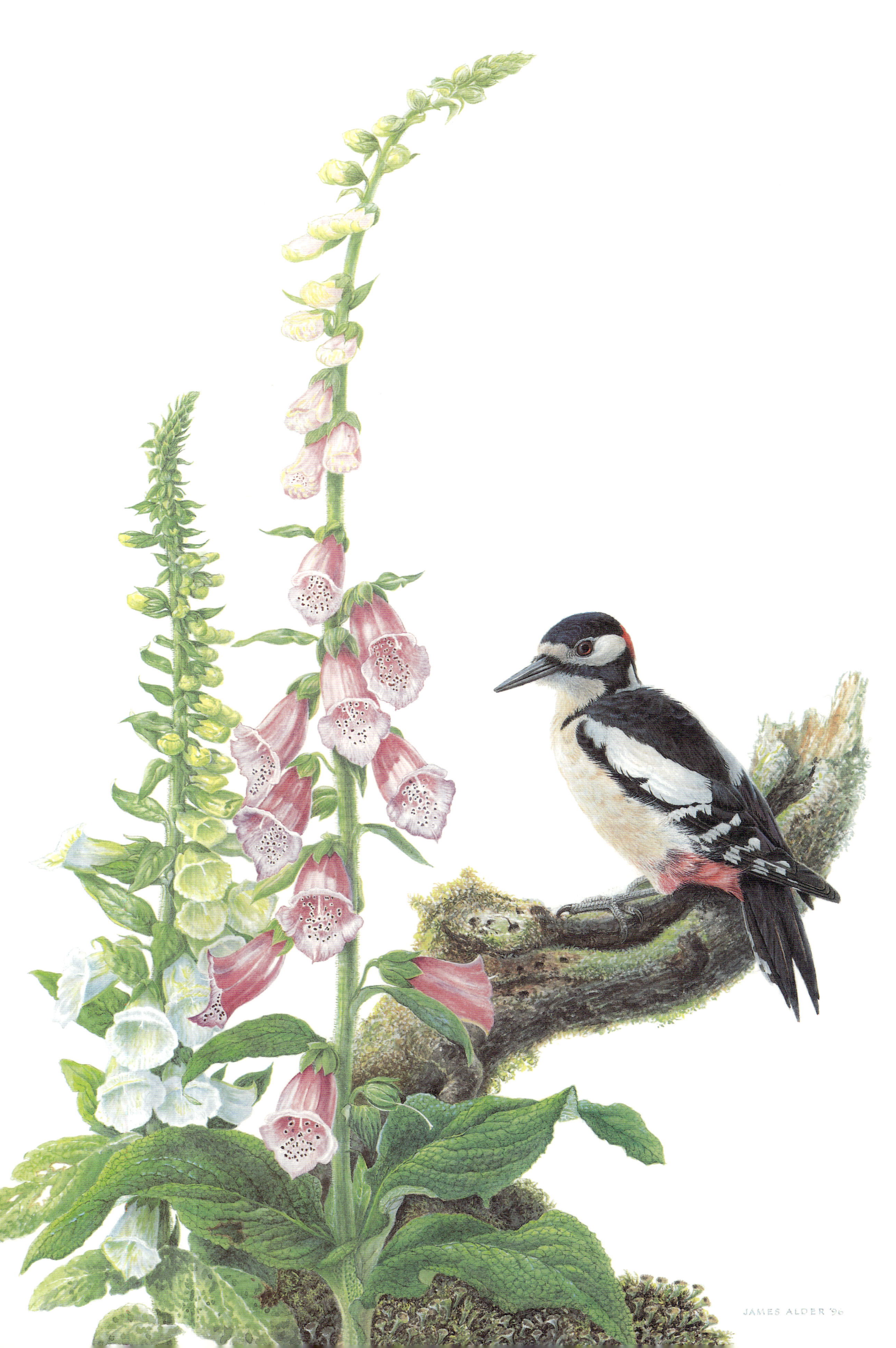
JAMES ALDER '96

On finding a 'pied woodpecker's' nest hole about 18 feet up in a tall birch tree, I was determined to photograph and study the bird. I used three larch poles from which to make a huge tripod, which I raised up leg-by-leg. I placed a ladder against it, and on top screwed a small platform on which to sit, with the quarter-plate camera between my legs. The woodpecker, which was accustomed to me as something neutral, threw caution away and fed her young so quickly that I had to chat her into posing. This occurred from sunrise for several mornings.

On his rounds each day, the local postman, seeing me from a distance and not knowing me, waved enthusiastically and spread the gossip that there was a madman who sat night and day on a tripod in a wood. My friend the farmer deliberately kept the truth to himself! One becomes a recluse, and learns a lot by gaining a sort of rapport with wild creatures...

The wood was a typical habitat, an open mixture of birch, pine and stunted oak with ferny undergrowth and fallen rotten branches where larvae abounded.

Woodpeckers are adapted to exploit an arboreal habitat in many ways – they are rarely found far from trees, and disappear where de-forestation occurs. This and other pressures such as starlings using their nest holes may have caused their disappearance from Scotland and Northern England in the early nineteenth century. Their return to these places at the end of the century coincides with afforestation programmes and the amelioration of the climate.

These woodpeckers are mainly insectivorous, finding food by hacking and chiselling the bark – not unexpectedly their head muscles and bones are beautifully adapted as shock absorbers. In tapping the wood they appear to be using its resonance to check the presence of unseen larvae! This activity is mainly limited to dead and rotting trees.

Nuts, often wedged in crevices as 'anvils', fruit, sunflower and seeds of cones, especially those of pine are high on the diet. On the Continent when such crops fail, these woodpeckers may 'erupt' to other countries, including Britain, and seem to anticipate the failure of these harvests.

In the woods this species will be known by their voice as brittle 'tchik-tchik', and their 'drumming' on favourite dead branches, when pairs or antagonists duet at a distance.

FOXGLOVE *(Digitalis purpurea)*

The Foxglove ('fairy folks glove') is one of our most beautiful herbaceous plants. It is found in open woodland and on road and riversides where the tall spikes of pendant flowers always arrest the eye as the sun catches the rosy or white bells. It is normally biennial: the flowering stems are produced in the second year from rosettes of large soft leaves. The drug digitalin, used to treat heart complaints, is extracted from the leaves.

CURLEW *(Numenius arquata)*

The graceful curlew, whose lovely scientific name, with reference to the elegantly curved beak, means 'new moon', remains from boyhood my symbol of freedom. I remember decorating two curlew eggs with painted curlews, presenting these to two little girls at Easter. The girls are now old ladies, and the eggs, still treasured, remain intact in their nests of cotton wool. They recall the excitement of crawling on elbows and stomach behind stone dykes to watch unseen the spring displays: the fluttering ascent, the heart-stopping pause and the long glide on bowed wings accompanied by the wild bubbling song.

At night I listened to their urgent, measured, echoing calls 'curlee-curlee' and wondered where they were going... 'shouting loud to warn their comrades of the way, lest darkling from the line they stray...' Then, finding for the first time the cold, flat, long grey estuaries of their search I heard those distant disembodied cries that insinuate the being of all birdmen.

Although curlews look overspecialised with their long curved beaks and gangly legs, they are remarkably adaptable. The long legs are not so much used for wading as to keep the beak high off the ground so that its arc can be used to best advantage! Can one imagine a curlew with short legs?

Natural selection will have made the radius of the arc exactly right for efficient probing at full depth into ooze where nutritious lugworms and shellfish abound: held higher the beak becomes delicate tweezers for picking shrimps, crabs and sandhoppers from the surface. On the high breeding grounds of spring and summer the beak is equally useful for probing into the matted bent or short heather for snails, insects, worms and small lizards – and, small birds eggs and young!

Curlews have held their numbers in traditional habitats, although they have mysteriously disappeared from some and appeared in others. They are mainly migratory, British birds moving South and West, while many Scandinavian migrants find their way to Britain. The oldest known curlew was 31 years, a remarkable achievement for a wild bird.

'Whaup', 'Wap' and 'Wylp' from the Scandinavian and imitative of the curlew's wilder yelping calls, are names heard mainly in Scotland and Northumberland.

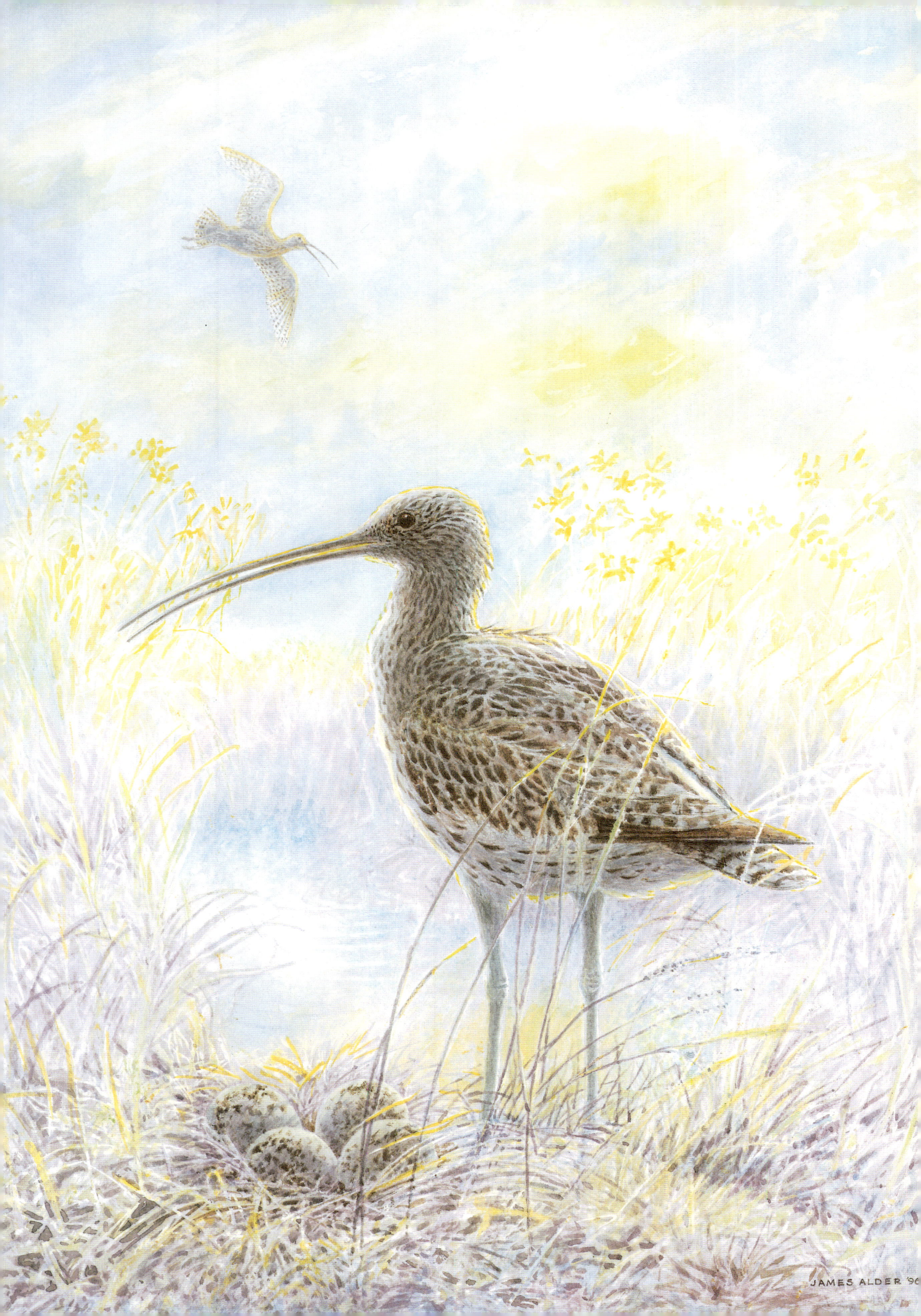
JAMES ALDER '96

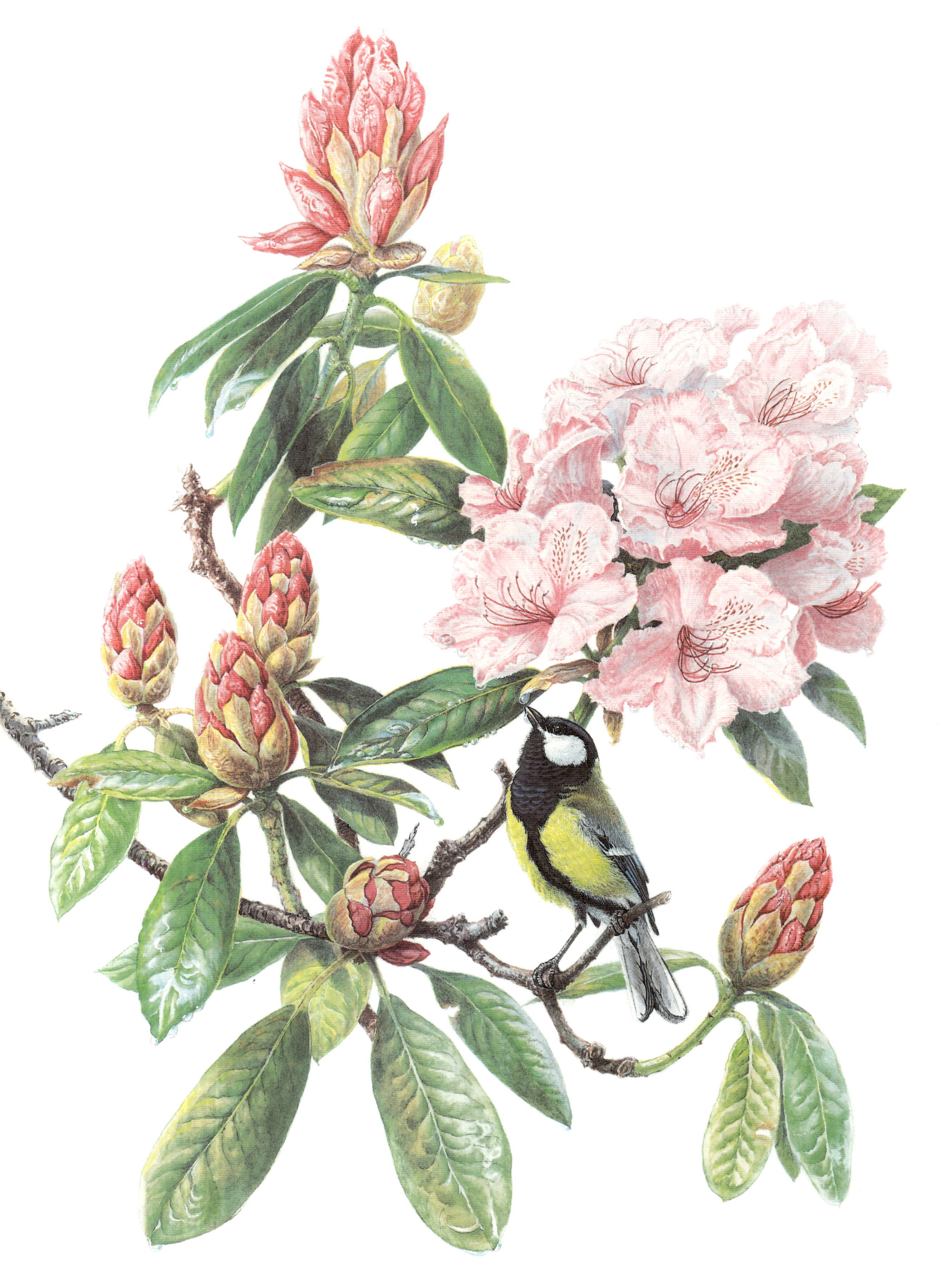
JAMES ALDER '96

GREAT TIT *(Parus major)*

Great Tits increased northwards into Scotland in the early nineteenth century, an expansion that continued until the 1980s. As with the great-spotted woodpeckers, afforestation, and a generally warmer climate, may be responsible, since the genus is closely adapted to the presence of trees. Where these abound, the species and its many varieties occupy the whole of the Palaearctic Region from Ireland to Japan, India and Indonesia.

If you were lucky enough to be with a party of ornithologists, say in South Eastern Asia, you might be pleased to see a 'British' great tit (*Parus major*). 'That's not a "major", your learned leader might say 'it's a green backed tit (*parus monticolus*)'. 'But they look identical' you may counter. 'No they're more brightly coloured' comes the reply. 'While the two species do occur in different regions, here their habitats do overlap, but they don't interbreed and hybridise. They must therefore regard each other as different and, remaining separate, must be named as different species.'

On that trip you would experience a simple example of speciation at work. If 'sympatric', living near each other in similar environs, the birds can be judged by their behaviour to be separate species or not. But if living widely apart ('allopatric') such judgements are difficult to make. Until proved otherwise, one form will be treated as a 'sub-species' of the originally named species. Had 'monticolus' been completely isolated from 'major' its name would have been a 'trinomial', *Parus major monticolus*. And you may not try to prove by caging them together that they are one species. Wild natural selection must be the true test.

The great tit's strident calls, 'teechu-teechu and a loud metallic 'tink-tink' are among the spring woodlands' welcome sounds. One of its name, 'saw-sharpener' is a good description of the call note.

Great and Blue tits are sympatric and compete for nest sites. As I write, they are quarrelling over a nest box, which has been occupied traditionally by the smaller blues The nest hole is too small for the great's comfort and it retires reluctantly. The oldest known great tit was 15 years old and a blue 12 years old, very great ages for small wild birds A tame injured cock bullfinch which I kept as a pet, lived for 15 years.

RHODODENDRON *'Pink Pearl'*

The influx of new Rhododendron species from the Himalayas in the second half of the nineteenth century soon led to the production of colourful hybrids. The hardy 'Pink Pearl' was introduced by John Waterer of Bagshot and won an award of merit in 1897. A gardening journal in 1905 states 'the finest self pink hardy Rhododendron in cultivation' and in 1923 'several years have elapsed since it first captivated the gardening world but it still stands in the front rank as one of the best rhododendrons.' Still available after over a century of popularity it is cited by Peter Cox as 'a very reliable commercial standard, probably the most famous hybrid of them all.'

PLATE 42 RING OUZEL *(Turdus torquatus)*

The decline in numbers of ring ouzels is attributable to the increase in numbers of the heavier blackbirds and their northerly spread, even to the lower harsher slopes of mountains, once the terrain of the ouzels. Happily, the ouzels are still to be found on the lower mountains of Balmoral, and I have heard the 'piper of the hills' singing in the mists of my native Northumbrian Cheviots.

Tucked against a turf or bush of heather, the nest is bulky, made of twigs and heather, roughly plastered with mud and finished with a deep lining of grass and roots: four pretty eggs are laid, pale blue, spotted red brown, purple and grey. The devoted pair take turns at incubation (male blackbirds, their cousins, hardly ever do) and the eggs hatch at about 14 days. The young fledge early and will bolt prematurely if disturbed. This 'explosion' of young has survival value.

The female may begin a second family, leaving the male to tend the first brood. In Scotland they are known to have nested near the golden eagle and peregrine, and I have recorded finding a nest and eggs below a peregrine's site in Northumberland. Ring ouzels are brave and they will attack possible predators such as buzzard, merlin, kestrel, sparrow hawk and short-eared owl, and I'm sure, will be cheeky enough to see off the peregrines. Records show that the young return to their natal environs to breed!

'The etymology of the ouzel's name is unknown,' says the book. But may we propose that osle, osel, owsell, ouzle, wezel and throstle, found throughout Britain, are an etymological 'cline' through history, all meaning a black or blackish bird. The beautiful sounds merle and merula mean blackbird, the ancient Somerset name 'mountain colley' means black, from coal: and the puzzling, ancient 'craigie-easlin' of Scotland is the 'burnt' bird of the crags? 'Throstle' for thrush is derived from the German 'drossel' which perhaps comes from 'dross' which means small or waste coal, or rust! We are well acquainted with coal in all its forms in Northumberland and I recall poor quality fuel being described as a 'load of dross.'

ROWAN *(Sorbus aucuparia)*

In 1776 the naturalist James Robertson travelling near Balmoral wrote in his journal 'I saw great numbers of the Ring Ouzel called here Etenchaker or Juniper eater. Juniper berries are said to be their principal food... in the winter they are said to feed on the berry of the Mountain Ash.' Known more commonly in Scotland as the rowan it is, with its brilliant red fruit, a striking autumn sight in Deeside. 'Ash' is a misnomer as, although the pinnate leaves are similar to those of the common ash, the two are not related, the rowan being closer to the white-beam or to the hawthorn.

Steeped in folklore, always as a tree of good omen, every cottage had its rowan. Now, as it is unlucky to fell them, a single specimen standing sentinel is often the only indication of a past dwelling.

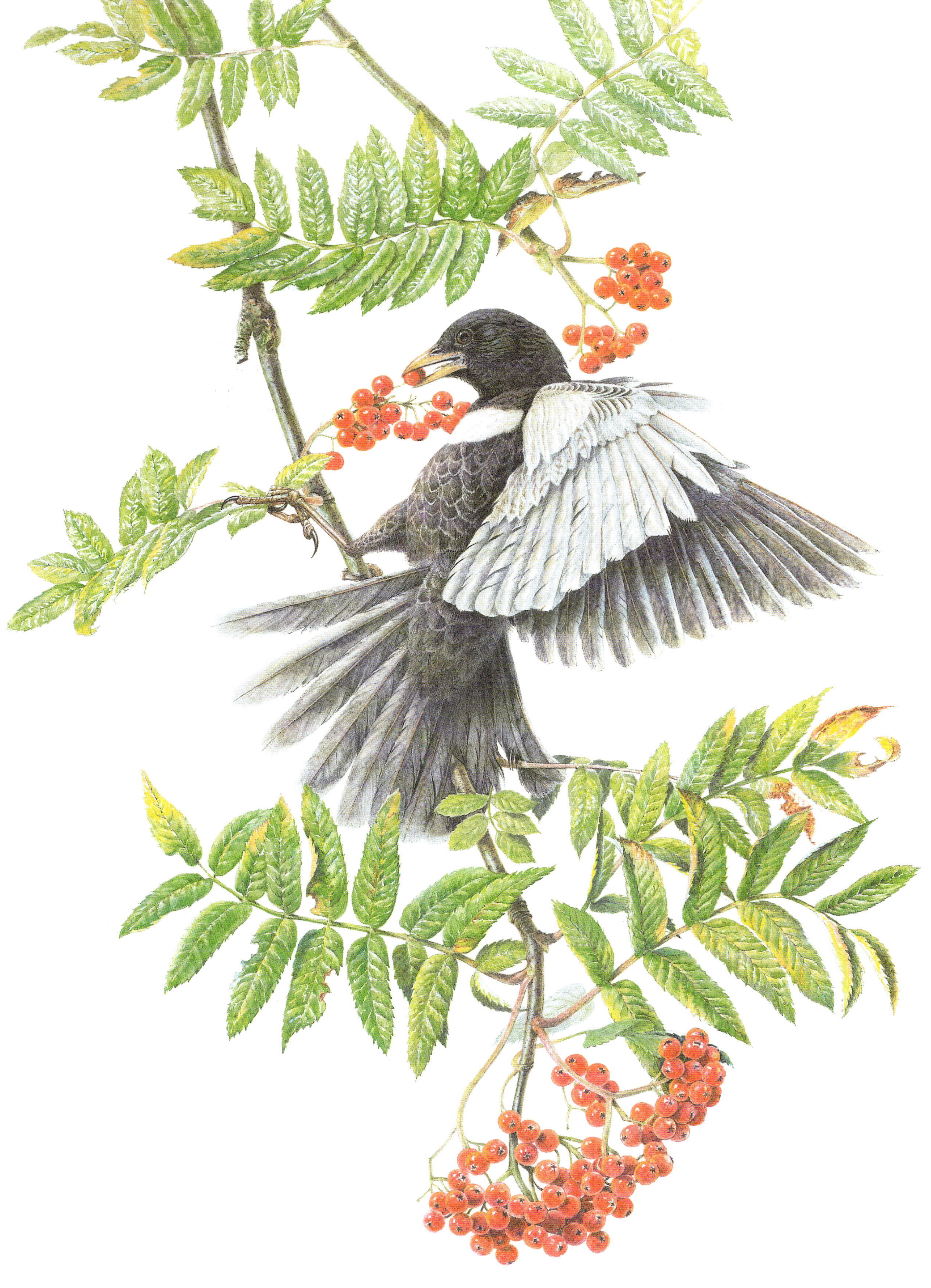
JAMES ALDER '96

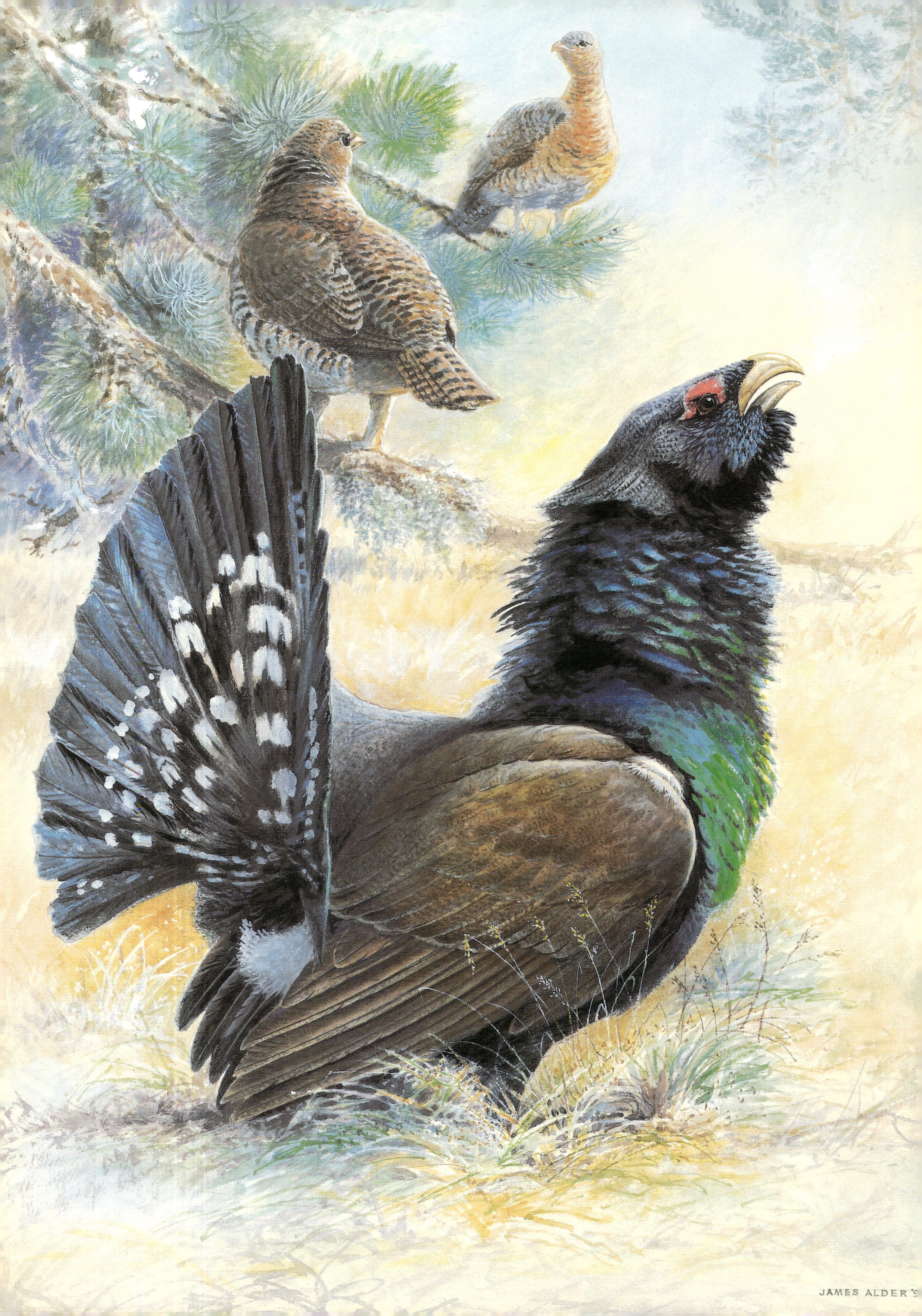
JAMES ALDER

CAPERCAILLIE *(Tetrao urogallus)* PLATE 43

Described as the 'world's largest grouse' the magnificent caper is as large as a turkey, a spectacular, powerful sight as on broad pinions it weaves with surprising agility between the ancient pines of the Balmoral forests. Formerly resident in the great woods of most of Britain, they became extinct in England in the seventeenth century, and later in the eighteenth, in Ireland and Scotland, due mainly to deforestation. It is recorded that the last indigenous Scottish birds were shot in Deeside in 1785.

All the present capers are descendants of birds reintroduced from Scandinavia. Many groups failed to spread – they were regarded as vermin because of their destruction of forest trees. When foresters began to tolerate their presence, they regained favour as sporting birds. Now there is growing concern for them as well… birds, simply lovely to have them around!

The remaining populations are located in the pine forests of Central to Northern Scotland, apart from the far North, where they are jealously protected and not easy to see.

The inspiration for my drawing was not achieved without travail: a stumbling, shin bruising tramp through a steep-sloping Black Forest at two in the morning in April. Then the remainder of the night sleeplessly in my sleeping bag, trying not to toboggan down a sleet-covered slope. The reward of dawn was heralded with singing chaffinches, a silhouetted squirrel woven into a tracery of twigs, and a pair of roe deer, wary but curious. And then, the 'horse of the woods' blowing steam in the cold bleak light as he strutted in the glade, courting indifferent females.

The habitat is arboreal: a large tract of woodland, mainly conifers, especially pine, with a mixture of broad-leafed trees and open glades, preferably carpeted with berried plants and heather. Here fresh pine needles, insects and berries provide a year-round diet.

The females, but half the size of the males, choose their partners at 'leks' in early spring. The nest is a shallow depression in thick cover on the ground, and the eight or so eggs are incubated by the female alone for 24–26 days. The young are nidifugous and are capable of flight at 2–3 weeks, although continuing to grow for another ten.

In Britain they are mainly sedentary. 'Capercaillie' is a corruption of the Gaelic name *capull coille*, 'great cock.' Their size promotes the idea of a 'horse-of-a-bird', helped perhaps by their capering and prancing in their arenas at dawn. 'Goat of the woods' is another name, from the Latin *capella*, a he-goat, showing how easy it is to invent a neat series of unrelated names!

PLATE 44 CROSSBILL *(Loxia scotica)*

In describing the Crossbills illustrated in the Queen Mother's book 'Birds and Flowers of the Castle of Mey,' I am sure that these were correctly identified as *Loxia curvirostra* from Scandinavia. Found in a small flock feeding on weed seeds on the shores of John o'Groat's, their tameness and unwillingness to fly showed the pressures of a long migratory flight.

The Scottish Crossbill is now only found with any degree of certainty in the Central Highlands, in the remains of the old Caledonian forest, and is non-migratory. The two species are so alike however that even with the birds in the hand, the most practised ornithologists must show care in identifying them where the northern visitors overlap with Scottish residents.

The main clue to identification lies in their food preferences, imposed upon them by their environment. The *curvirostra* birds come from the cold far north where spruce, the Christmas Tree, is King. The cones and their scales are soft, and the seeds easily extractable. The evolutionary result is that *curvirostra's* beak need not be too robust!

Scotica eats the seeds of pine. The cones are roundish with hard, often tightly-closed scales, and this crossbill is required to have a larger, stronger, more powerfully-muscled beak than its Scandinavian cousin to survive.

When failure of cone harvests occur in the northern forests *curvirostra* migrates for the winter, and it is then that it may encounter its Scottish cousin. It can just manage pine cones, but this would result in competition, and I am sure that they are helped on their way! The visitor seeks out seeding spruce, and sooner or later will find forests such as Kielder, on the Borders, where spruce is found in crop rotation. There they may settle and become resident.

Where they overlap it is possible that crossbreeding is attempted. However the *curvirostra* partner would be unable to fulfil its own needs and those of its growing chicks (nesting occurs as early as February when 'fuel' requirements are at a premium!) and the chicks would die. In these and other tiny but inexorable ways the species are adapted to their main food resources and are kept apart.

SCOTS PINE *(Pinus sylvestris)*

Scots pine seed provides an important food for red squirrels as well as for crossbills and it is interesting to learn of their co-existence from observations made by Summers and Proctor in the 1994 proceedings of a conference on scots pine. Squirrels feed where the pines are younger and grow more densely whereas crossbills feed among the older trees which are more evenly spaced. It seems that wider spaced trees give the birds better vantage to see and avoid predators such as sparrow hawks, while the squirrels are able to move around in the closer canopy without the necessity of travelling on the ground where they would be more vulnerable to foxes and other enemies.

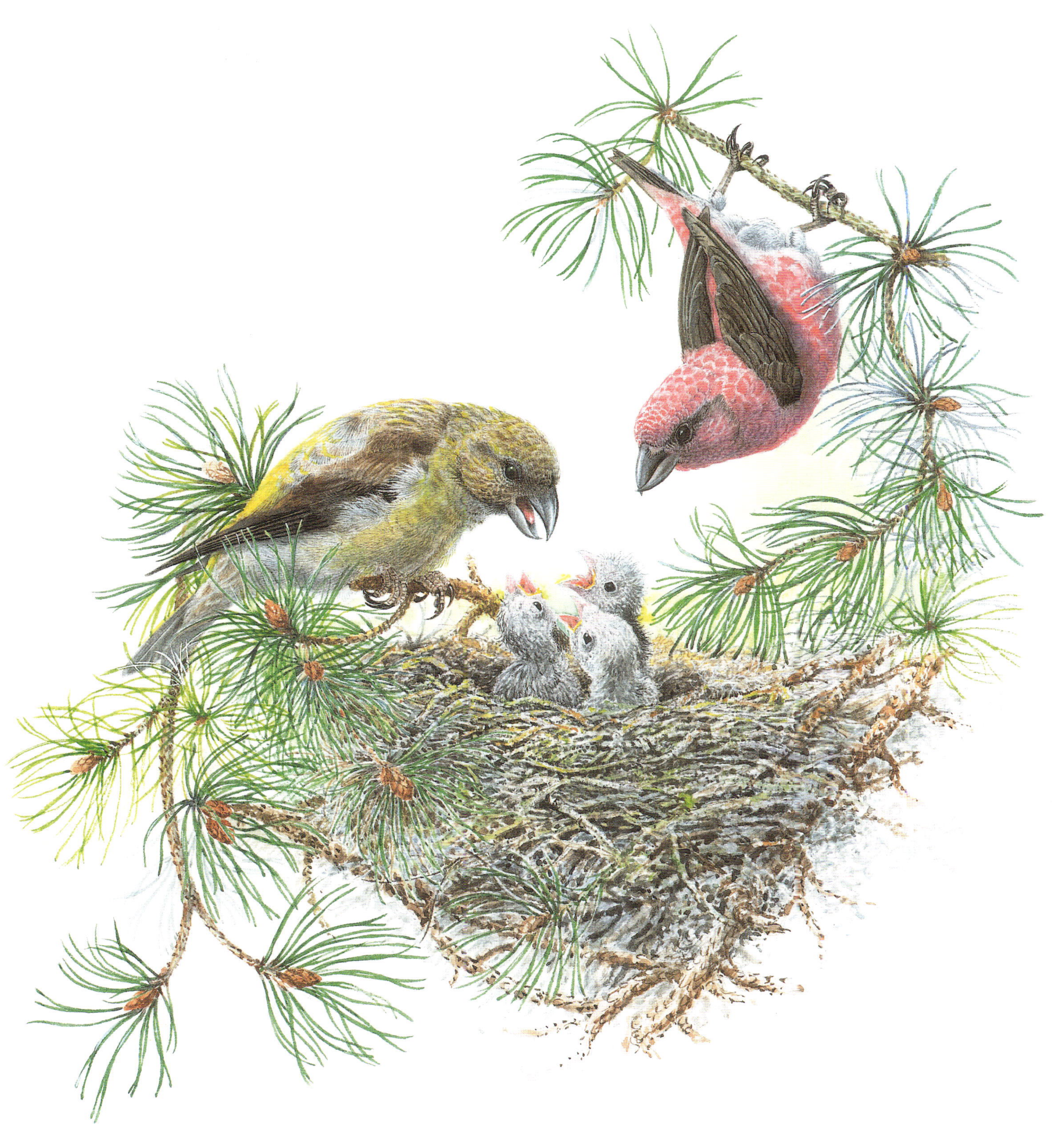
JAMES ALDER '96

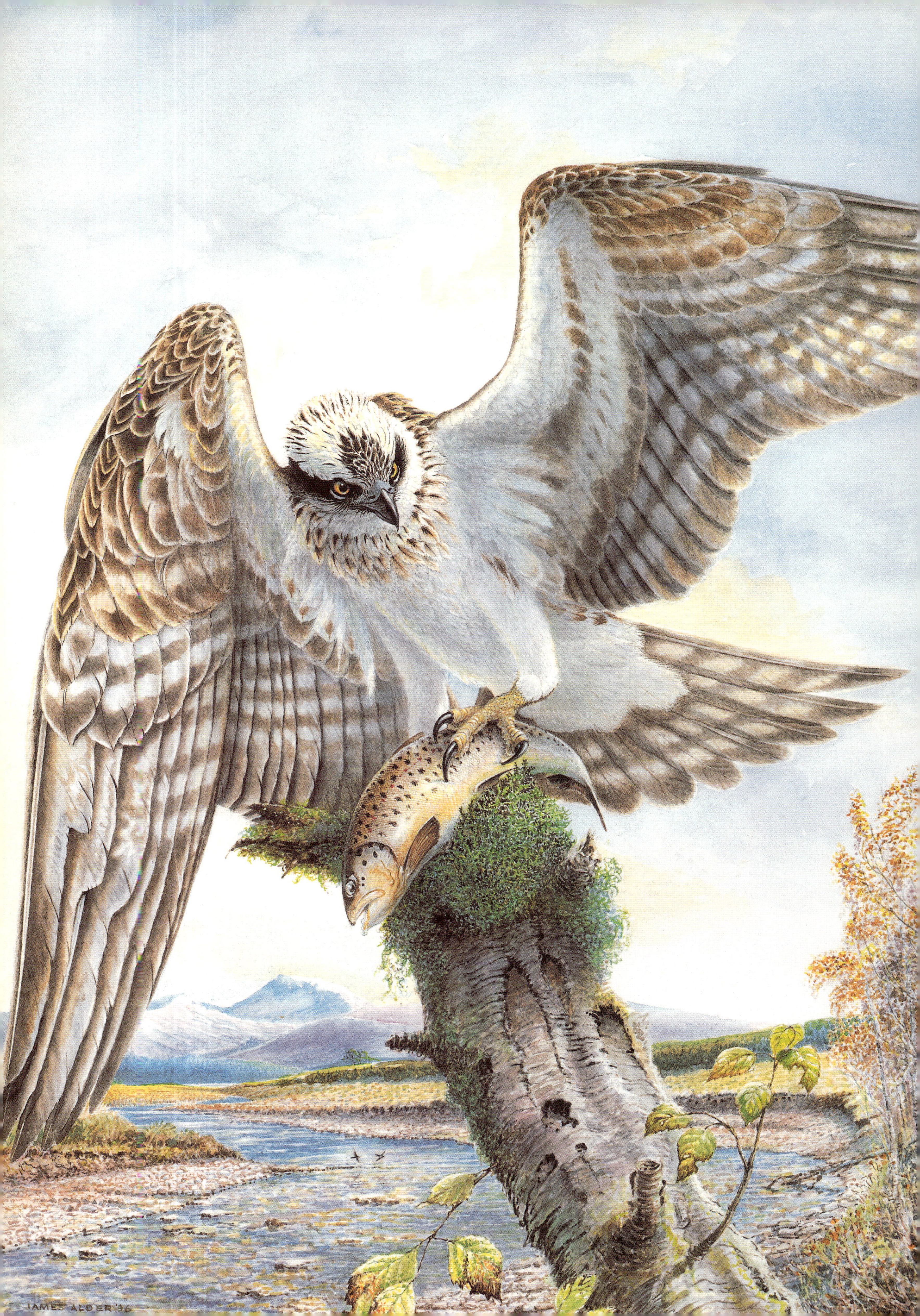
JAMES ALDER '96

The restoration of the osprey as a breeding species to Scotland in the early 50's was a triumph of organisation by the RSPB. It caused a sensation, and became an inspirational turning point for the reintroduction of other lost species. The late George Waterston, justly honoured with an OBE for his tireless work, described this with typical modesty as 'only meaning Ornithology Before Everything.'

Now, the magnificent species is firmly settled in many breeding sites in Scotland. Formerly living in quiet isolation, (I remember the whispering caution of approach to the first site) we now have the concept of 'entertainment ornithology.' One should have known! In the USA they regularly build on telegraph poles, electrical installations and almost any stable vertical structure near water that would hold the large nest.

Ospreys are almost cosmopolitan in their distribution, rarer in the Southern Hemisphere and not proved to breed there other than in Australia. As fish-eaters, they are highly specialised predators, whose food requirement is high protein fish, 21bs or more daily. For this they have evolved strong legs, powerful claws, barbed toe pads and strong wings.

Their hunting technique is thrilling. Circling at about 100 feet above loch, river or sea, they may hover briefly to sight their prey. The dive is a breath-taking plunge; the lift-off amidst flying spray with a heavy thrashing fish an exhibition of natural power. Surface-basking pike are a favourite food. Frozen water is out! In winter they are committed to a search for open water to fish and are confirmed migrants, able to cover great distances.

The bulky nest is made by both sexes, the female arranging material brought by the male. The eggs, beautiful in chocolate-brown and white, the desire of nineteenth century egg-collectors, are often three in number, incubation beginning at the first egg. The young hatch at intervals, resulting in differential growth and much bullying of the small by the large! Fledging takes a long time, up to 50 days or more, and 'visiting' males carrying fish are thought to be welcome! As with all raptors, they sky-dance in display early in the season, when they may symbolically carry fish or nest material. The oldest osprey was known to have lived for 32 years.

PLATE 46 TEAL *(Anas crecca)*

The beautiful teal are among the smallest ducks. They are therefore very agile, fast – and mighty migrants. In suitable habitats they are distributed throughout the northern regions of the Northern Hemisphere. In North America they are replaced by a 'sub-species,' the American Green-winged Teal (*Anser carolinensis*) which migrates annually between its breeding grounds and Central South America, a round trip of up to 10,000 miles. Sometimes they cross the Atlantic, possibly via Iceland to Britain where they are identified by their vertical, not horizontal white side-stripe.

Teal are a delight to watch, as individuals or grouped. A small flock is a spring (earlier 'sprynge') epitomised in their agile rocketing from land or water, when their erratic flight foils shooters.

'*Anas*' is said to be Latin for duck, and '*crecca*' is probably derived from the drake's call, a musical 'krick-krick.' The ducks quack softly like quiet mallards.

The English name is certainly derived from the reedy creeks and polders of coastal Holland, where wild fowl have collected in their hundreds of thousands and have wintered and bred there. 'Taling' or 'teling' meant any one of several species of small duck such as wigeon, garganey and gadwall. First recorded as 'teles' in 1314, the time of Edward II, they became a popular delicacy and were fattened in 'tealeries,' although they don't readily breed in captivity.

British teal are mainly sedentary, but their numbers may be swollen by thousands of immigrants from Iceland and Western Europe. Counts of mixed species, up to 35,000 have been noted in the Mersey Estuary, although recently numbers have fallen. Before drainage and land reclamation numbers must have been huge and a wonder for the ancient tidal hunters to gossip about.

In our youth my brother Harry and I 'tallied' birds for the British Trust for Ornithology, a necessary activity which is still pursued. Duck, waders on mud flats, pre-roosting starlings were counted by 'guesstimates,' and these were reported – a story about numbers! It is not too far-fetched, I suggest, that this is the origin of teal... a 'tale' of numbers of uncountable proportions.

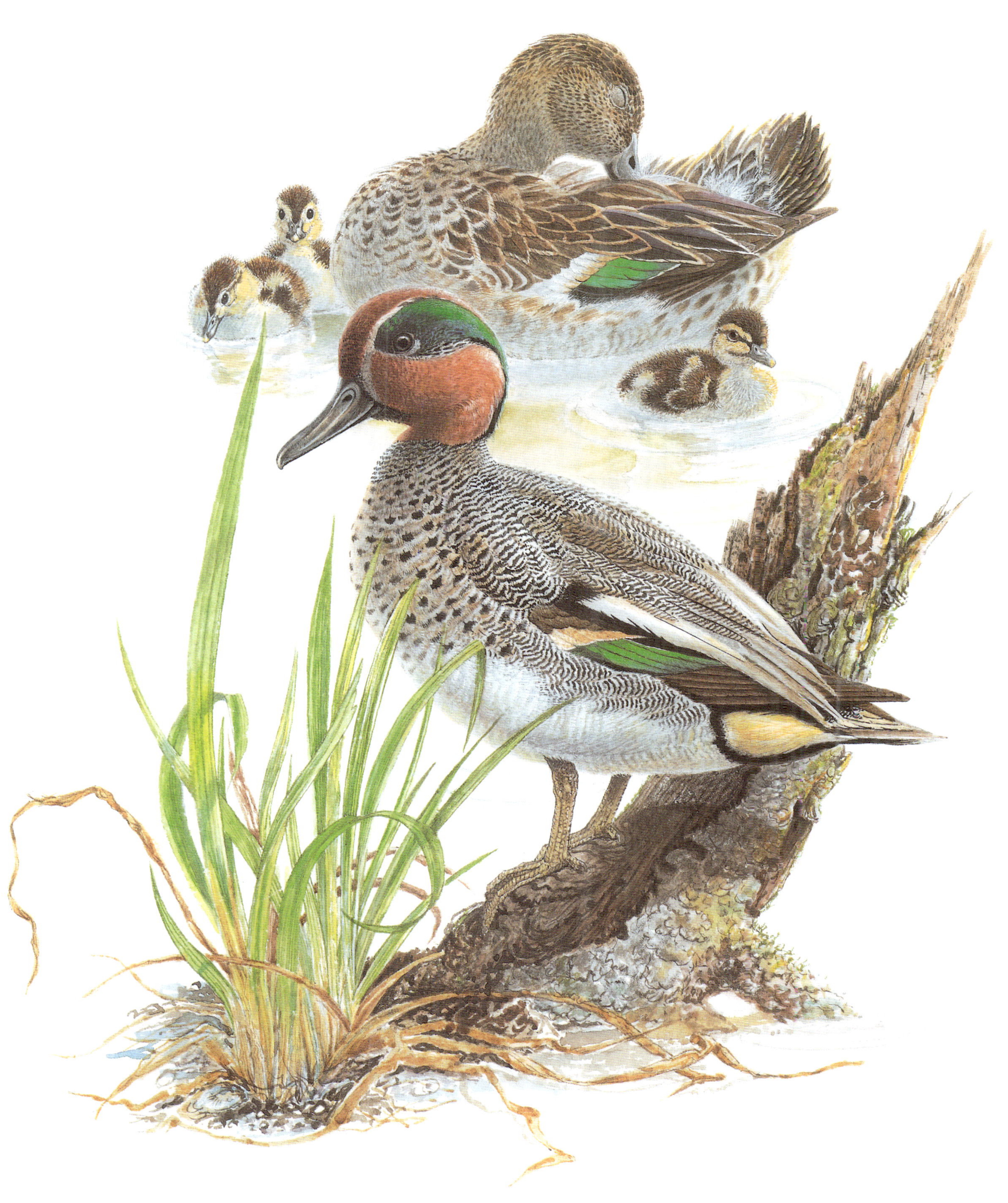
JAMES ALDER '96

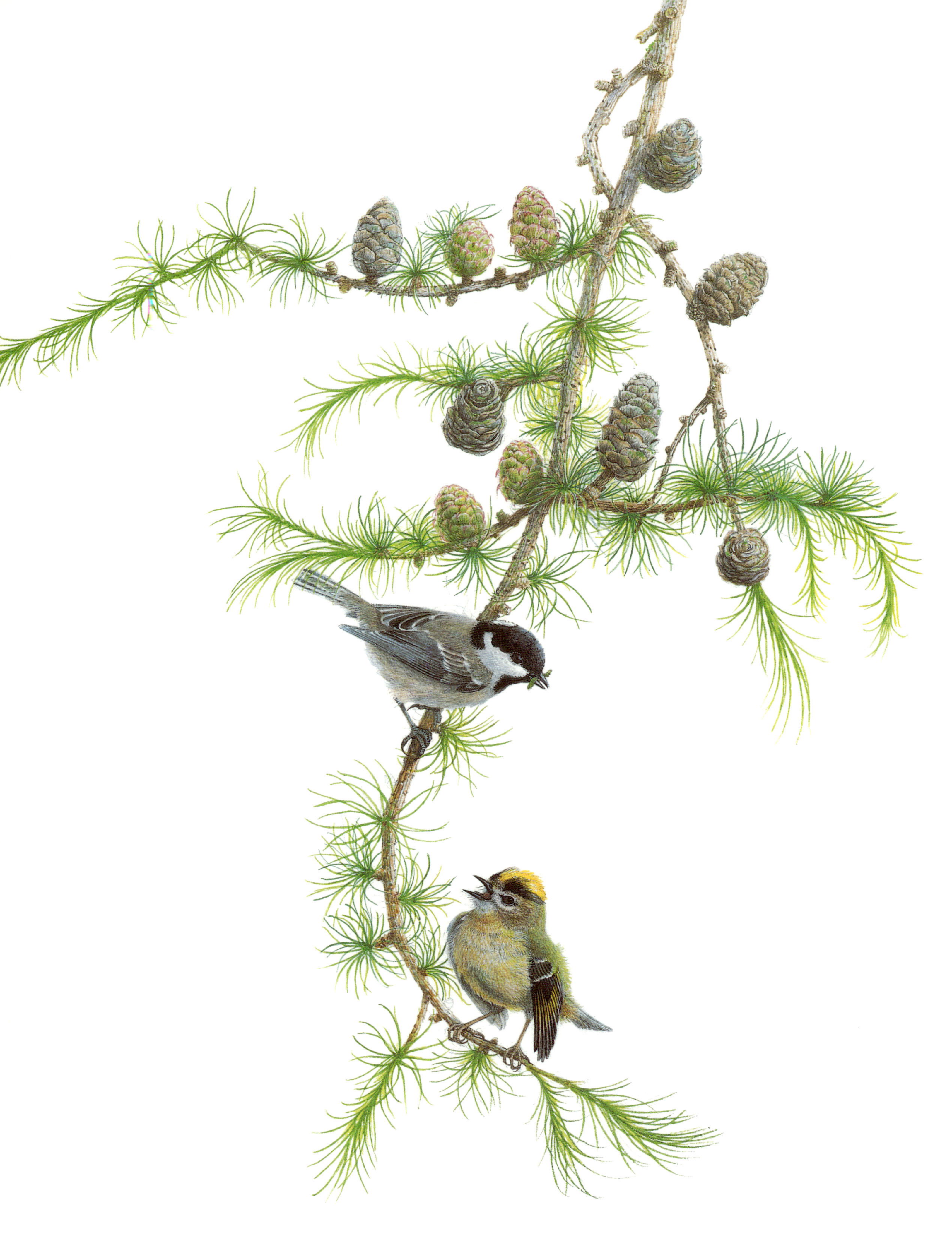
JAMES ALDER '96

COAL TIT *(Parus ater)* GOLDCREST *(Regulus regulus)* PLATE 47

Coal tits, among the smallest birds, weighing only 9gr. or so, are compact, neat little packages, short of tail, finely beaked, designed for rapid exploration of their favourite habitat, conifers. Their voice, a sweet high-pitched 'peet-suu, peet-suu' will be heard before you see them foraging through the needled twigs, rapidly fluttering and hovering as they search for spiders, aphids, caterpillars and insect eggs. Seeds of pine, larch and yew, rowan and alder are also among their diet, which they handle deftly with feet and beak. Watch carefully – you may observe that they store surplus food in little caches in holes, for later use. They too have learned to open milk bottles!

They habitually nest in holes near or on the ground for which they were laboriously named 'underground tits' in Surrey. They pair for life, in one case for six years. Staying together shares intelligence and, helps survival!

'Titmice' were, originally, in Northern climes 'titmose,' meaning small birds. Mice have nothing to do with it – that's a sixteenth century corruption. The name titmouse then required a plural, titmice, complicating things further. The scientific name *parus* is derived from the Greek, *paros*, and surely refers to the smallness of the genus. Two distinct languages have stated the obvious.

Goldcrests are even tinier than Coal Tits. Weighing only 6 gr. or so, the goldcrest is recognised as the smallest bird in the West Palaearctic region. Its smallness commits it to a constant search for food, when it shows a nervous energy that surpasses even that of the tit. Yet, despite the hazards of weight loss, Scandinavian goldcrests, after refuelling with 2 gr. of high energy food, will set off in autumn, to cross the North Sea where on the coasts of Northumberland I have seen them fall exhausted after a 400 mile flight!

They are widely distributed throughout Britain and Ireland, a calculation of about 1.5 million pairs is estimated and they are mainly resident, with cold weather dispersal to milder areas.

Keeping out the cold is vital. The nest, a globe-like elastic structure with a small open top, is not unlike a circular long-tailed tit's nest, and is made of the same materials, with plenty of spiders webs for roping the parts together. I have watched them building and their movements were identical to the long-tails.

The nest is richly feather-lined, these forming a springy, 'air-lock' to the open top. Ten or so eggs are laid, and are incubated by the female from the beginning, resulting in asynchronous hatching. The young lie in layers, each rising to the top when hungry! A second nest is made by the male, who also takes part in helping with everything.

DUNKELD LARCH *(Larix x eurolepis)*

The larch is not a British native but has become a widely planted forest tree. The first hybrids were discovered around the turn of the century and were it seems the result of a deliberate attempt at hybridisation by the Duke of Atholl. In 1885, at Dunkeld House, he had planted a number of Japanese larch close to the European. From the resulting plantations of seedlings exceptionally vigorous, and paler plants were selected.

The characters of the hybrid are for the most part intermediate between those of the parents but are most easily observed in the scales of the cone which have wavy margins, not straight as in the European and not clearly reflexed as in the Japanese. As with most hybrid plants the outstanding feature is the phenomenal rate of growth with five feet in the season being not exceptional.

SPOTTED FLYCATCHER *(Muscicapa striata)*

They are among Britain's most well-distributed species, although they are late arrivals, because they depend almost entirely on flying insects. Being tolerant of man they share the affection of country folk with the robin and the swallow, to which latter species they are closely related.

Like swallows they show the same confident sweeping flight, although in the smaller confines of woodland glades and larger gardens. Characteristically they have a distinct upright posture on post, twig or wire, from which they forage to catch flies, returning usually to the same observation post. Long pointed wings, lustrous eyes, a wide flattish gape and rictal bristles to contain their prey, declare their relationship to swallows. Mayflies, house flies, midges and moths are taken, although they will eat some plant food, honeysuckle, rowan and bramble.

These flycatchers build their nests on natural or artificial ledges, such as the fork of a tree, cross beams in a barn, open-fronted nests boxes, but always with a good fly-way. I have found one nesting in a small hole in an alder by a stream (it was not a pied flycatcher!) the nest being a cup of fine roots, twigs, dry grass, lined hair and feathers.

The eggs, usually 4–5, can be pale blue, greenish or buff, finely spotted, and take about 13 days to hatch, incubation being by the female along. Fledging takes about 12–16 days, both sexes actively feeding the young and they often have two broods.

Deforestation and the resulting drop in flying insect populations seem to be associated with a decrease in numbers of flycatchers everywhere, although as yet their numbers are not endangered. On warm summer days the glades and woods of Balmoral are full of flycatchers on passage.

As in Britain, they are solidly distributed throughout Europe and Eastern Russia, even to the far north where there are trees and flies. To winter they must therefore migrate on a broad front southwards, over the Mediterranean and the Sahara to the Equator and beyond to South Africa, a trip of up to 7000 miles. Most small migrants are required to make frequent stops for refuelling before continuing long-distance flights. Being swallow-like, flycatchers are opportunistic aerial predators of flies, and may be able to continue longer non-stop journeys.

Among about thirty common names are beam bird (South England), rafter bird, wall bird, wall robin, white robin and post bird.

HONEYSUCKLE
(Lonicera periclymenum)

The humble and fragrant honeysuckle or woodbine is native throughout Britain in a range of habitats. The tough stems twist and turn, climbing through other shrubs and trees or form a dense mass on their own. The young shoots are smooth, often with a purplish bloom while the flowers range from pale cream to deep pink and have long tubes pollinated by moths. Later in the year, the clusters of round red berries can persist for several months. Several garden forms, originating in Holland, vary in colour and size of flower, but it is the strong perfume, particularly in the evening, that is their true delight.

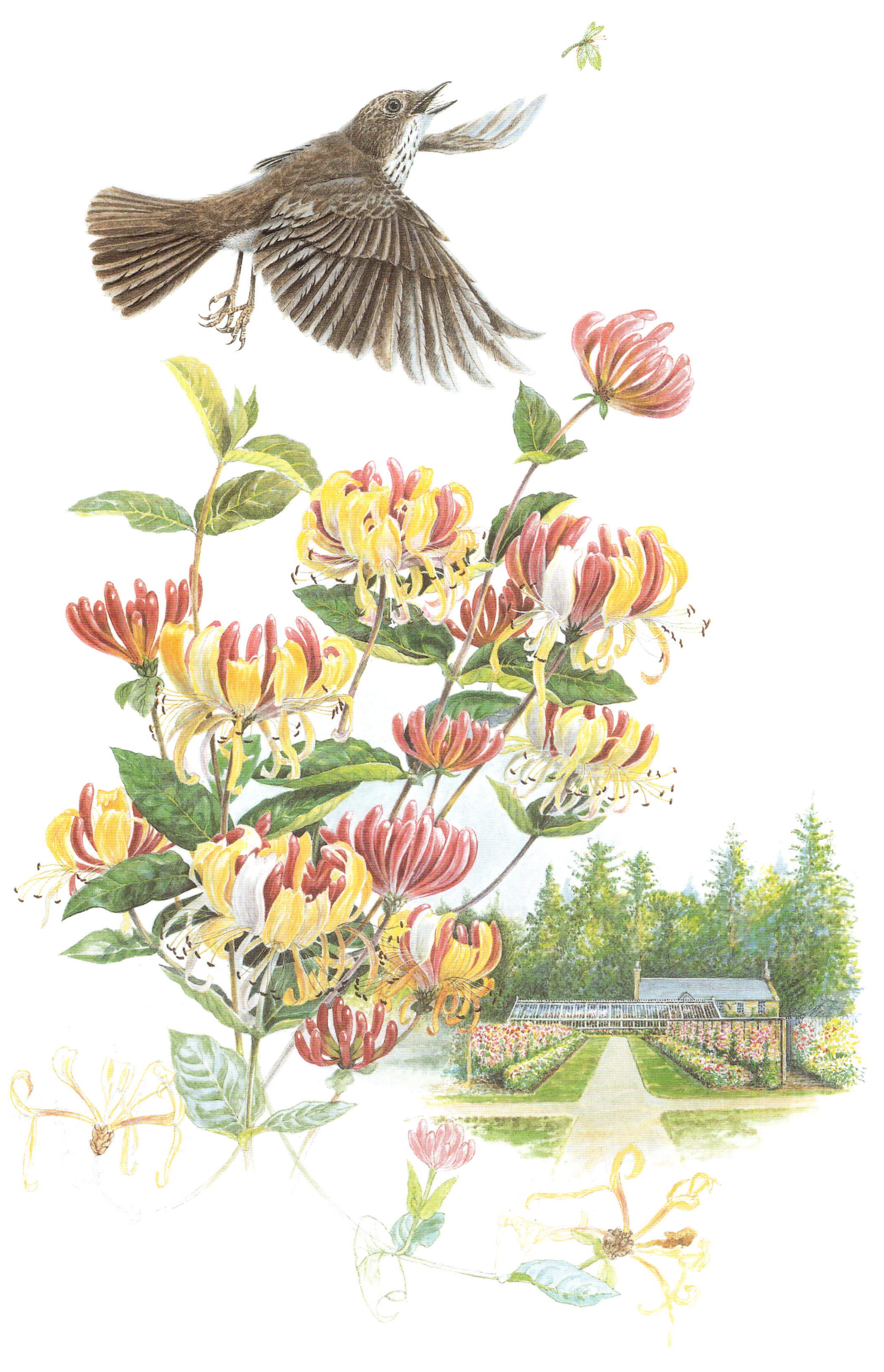
JAMES ALDER '96

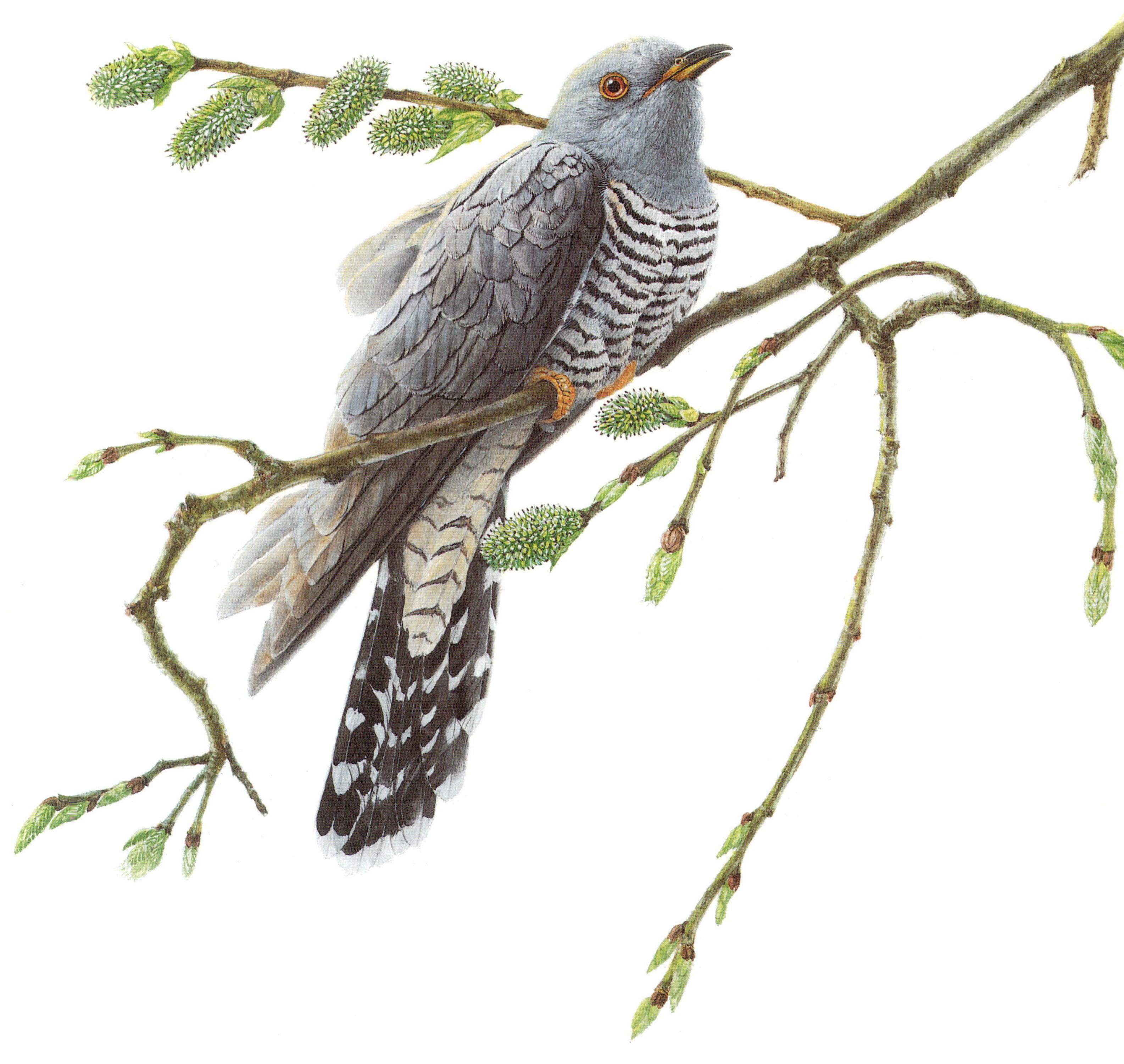

CUCKOO *(Cuculus canorus)*

My drawing is based on finding a newly-arrived cuckoo in spring. It was a very cold day, the bird was clearly exhausted and hungry and permitted examination from only 3 feet away. Its favourite food, hairy caterpillars and other insects, noxious to most birds but not to it, were not yet available.

The cuckoo's gizzard is specially adapted to deal with nasty insects, and the tough gizzard lining is periodically sloughed off and regurgitated. When I found one on the Hexhamshire fells, a strange bottle-necked semi-transparent object I was much puzzled. My friend the gamekeeper instantly recognised it!

Walking through the Glen of Gairnshiel near Balmoral, I was struck by the hawk-like appearance and flight of cuckoos. Their soaring 'raptor' flight and their habitual mobbing by small birds needs explaining. I suggest that they are fact-finding, stirring up the small birds to assess their numbers, and to observe their behaviour as future nest-builders and potential foster parents. Their laying of eggs in other bird's nests with precise timing must be a kind of family planning.

I unearthed a tattered diary of 62 years ago which recorded the hatching of a young cuckoo among a clutch of meadow pipits eggs. This pipit is a common resident of the fells and a favourite dupe of the cuckoo, and I insisted that my old friend Turnbull trudge along with me to see the miracle I was expecting...

With blind instinct and determination the chick wriggled below an egg, balancing it in an obviously special hollow in its back, and reaching backwards with strangely human-like arms and hands, it positioned the egg, pushed upwards and tipped the egg over the edge.

My old friend was not impressed. 'Little black devil' he said, and was even more upset when the cuckoo reached over the edge to check that the egg had fallen, before it slid down into the nest to rest a little before tackling the remaining three eggs. As always, I tried to educate my patient old friend that this was natural selection and evolution at work, and got a 'humph' for my pains

Cuckoos have been intensely studied and are fabled in literature. Despite this, they have few common names. The most familiar of natural calls hardly requires any other name to describe the bird. In English, Dutch, French, German, Spanish, Russian and Greek it is still a 'cuckoo.' Few others exist: 'Gowk' in Scotland describes the great orange gape, but I have no idea why in Wales it should be known as a 'Welsh ambassador!'

WILLOW *(Salix)*

The larger willows are usually found in damp places where they have been exploited by man for thousands of years. Wicker workers were mentioned in Braemar in lore and legend. As well as basket-making, willows have been used for fencing and chair-making, for charcoal, in tanning and dyeing and as a constituent of aspirin. Most willows hybridise freely and are notoriously difficult to name. Some flower in the spring before the leaves when the male and female catkins, which grow on separate plants, give rise to the familiar 'pussy willows' beloved of flower arrangers. Lochnagar is home to several north European dwarf willows which find their southern limit in corries on Scottish mountains.

THE GOLDEN EAGLE *(Aquila chrysaetos)*

Some forty years ago I was introduced to the Edinburgh stationery firm of Macniven and Cameron, of whom Waverley Cameron was its inventive Chairman. He saw that 'Notelets,' a decorated form of writing paper, could become popular and invited me to help design these and their boxes. At first all were floral and very successful, selling in Australia and USA. I suggested we portray birds. He had the same deep superstition about these as had my mother (also an Edinburgh Scot) 'They'll never sell,' he insisted.

When I pursued the matter further and offered him a stationery box with peacock designs he exploded 'They have the devil's eye!' I patiently waited for a year, when, showing him an eruption of bird books on the market, he reluctantly relented. 'But we'll try baby birds first' he cautioned. Eventually, in his way he became, through the promotion of millions of bird notelets, a promoter of Bird Protection!

Another famous Scot, the late George Waterston of Osprey fame (and incidentally from another great firm of Edinburgh Stationers) invited me to become involved in the publicity of The Royal Society for the Protection of Birds (RSPB), of whom the late Peter Conder was its fine Chairman. Both, as ex-prisoners of war, loved wilderness. We were soon friendly and George invited me, with the young Mike Everet and my son James, to ring golden eagles at the ten few known nest sites. On Morvern, that exquisite peninsula, he introduced me to my first, live, wild, golden eagle, which was ready to fly, and it did! It leapt from the huge untidy eyrie at the head of a narrowing ravine, and having no air space became tangled in dwarf birch. I caught it in my jacket with Mike's help and we ringed it ignominiously.

Whether our work helped in the total knowledge of eagle behaviour and distribution we may never know: but since then they have expanded their range in Britain, have nested in the Lowlands of Scotland and the Lake District, and are regularly seen here in Northumberland. And, seem to be secure in their tenure of Balmoral.

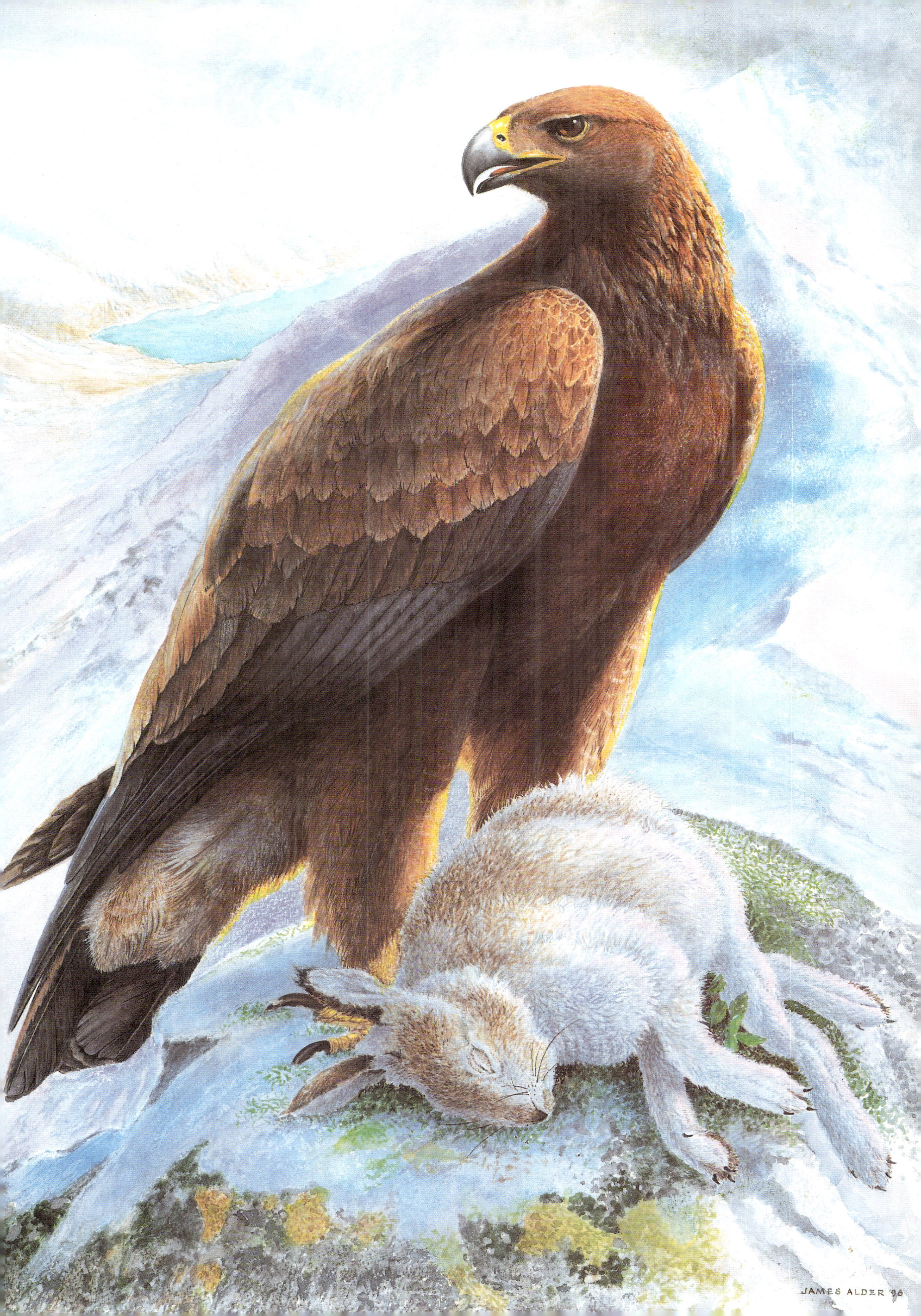
JAMES ALDER '96

ACKNOWLEDGEMENTS

I am indebted to Sir Robert Fellowes and Sir Kenneth Scott for their guidance, and to the Staff of Windsor, Buckingham Palace and Balmoral for their helpfulness.

To Mr Robin Janvrin I owe special thanks for prompt and efficient response to my many queries, and to Viscount Ridley for his thoughtful Preface and continued support in my 10-year project.

Alder, T. H.
Ball, Frank, Print Technologist
Conder, Peter, OBE, Director General, RSPB
Cook, Neil, Ranger, Balmoral
Crowthers, Malcolm, Photographer
Debremaeker, Monica & Martin, of Gairnshiel
Dobson, Forester, Balmoral
Hackett, Professor Brian & Elizabeth
Hamilton, Frank, Director, RSPB, Scotland
Leslie, Martin, LVO, Factor, Balmoral
Stewart, Max, Gamekeeper, Balmoral
Waterston, George, OBE, Director, RSPB, Scotland
Jennifer & Paddy Woods

Honouring my parents, who would have been pleased: and again my wife Lilian who drew on even further resources of patience in the four years of preparation of this second book.

BREEDING BIRDS ON BALMORAL ESTATE

Red-Throated Diver – *Gavia stellata*
Grey Heron – *Ardea cinerea*
Greylag Goose – *Anser anser*
Teal – *Anas crecca*
Mallard – *Anas platyrhynchos*
Goosander – *Mergus merganser*
Golden Eagle – *Aquila chrysaetos*
Buzzard – *Buteo buteo*
Sparrowhawk – *Accipiter nisus*
Kestrel – *Falco tinnunculos*
Merlin – *Falco columbarius* (irr.)
Peregrine – *Falco peregrinus*
Red Grouse – *Lagopus lagopus*
Ptarmigan – *Lagopus mutus*
Black Grouse – *Lyrurus tetrix*
Capercaillie – *Tetrao urogallus*
Pheasant – *Phasianus colchicus*
Grey Patridge – *Perdix perdix*
Moorhen – *Gallinula chloropus*
Coot – *Fulica atra*
Oystercatcher – *Haematopus ostralegus*
Dotterel – *Eudromias morinellus*
Golden Plover – *Pluvialis apricaria*
Lapwing – *Vanellus vanellus*
Dunlin – *Calidris alpina*
Snipe – *Gallinago gallinago*
Woodcock – *Scolopax rusticola*
Curlew – *Numenius arquata*
Redshank – *Tringa totanus*
Common Sandpiper – *Tringa hypoleucos*
Common Gull – *Larus canus*
Common Term – *Sterna hirundo*
Collared Dove – *Streptopelia decaocto*
Wood Pigeon – *Columba palumbus*
Cuckoo – *Cuculus canorus*
Tawny Owl – *Strix aluco*
Short-eared Owl – *Asio flammeus*
Swift – *Apus apus*
Great Spotted Woodpecker – *Dendrocopus major*
Green Woodpecker – *Picus viridus*
Skylark – *Alauda arvensis*
Sand Martin – *Riparia riparia*
Swallow – *Hirundo rustica*
House Martin – *Delichon urbica*
Tree Pipit – *Anthus trivialis*
Meadow Pipit – *Anthus pratensis*
Grey Wagtail – *Motacilla cinerea*
Pied Wagtail – *Motacilla alba*
Dipper – *Cinclus cinclus*
Wren – *Troglodytes troglodytes*
Dunnock – *Prunella modularis*
Robin – *Erithacus rubecula*
Redstart – *Phoenicurus phoenicurus*
Whinchat – *Saxicola rubetra*
Stonechat – *Saxicola torquata*
Wheatear – *Oenanthe oenanthe*
Ring Ouzel – *Turdus torquatus*
Blackbird – *Turdus merula*
Song Thrush – *Turdus philomelus*
Mistle Thrush – *Turdus viscivorus*
Wood Warbler – *Phylloscopus sibilatrix* (unconfirmed)
Chiffchaff – *Phylloscopos collybita*
Willow Warbler – *Phylloscopus trochilus*
Goldcrest – *Regulus regulus*
Firecrest – *Regulus ignicapillus* (irr.)
Spotted Flycatcher – *Muscicapa striata*
Coal Tit – *Parus ater*
Blue Tit – *Parus caeruleus*
Great Tit – *Parus major*
Long-tailed Tit – *Aegithalos caudatus*
Treecreeper – *Certhia familiaris*
Jay – *Garrulus glandarius*
Magpie – *Pica pica*
Jackdaw – *Corvus monedula*
Rook – *Corvus frugilegus*
Carrion/Hooded Crow – *Corvus corone*
Raven – *Corvus corax* (former)
Starling – *Sturnus vulgaris*
House Sparrow – *Passer domesticus*
Chaffinch – *Fringilla coelebs*
Greenfinch – *Carduelis chloris*
Goldfinch – *Carduelis carduelis*
Siskin – *Carduelis spinus*
Twite – *Carduelis flavirostris*
Redpoll – *Carduelis flammea*
Common Crossbill – *Loxia curvirostra*
Scottish Crossbill – *Loxia scotica*
Bullfinch – *Pyrrhula pyrrhula*
Snow Bunting – *Plectrophenax nivalis*
Yellowhammer – *Emberiza citrinella*

NON-BREEDING BIRDS

Black-Throated Diver – *Gavia arctica*
Great Northern Diver – *Gavia immer*
Little Grebe – *Tachybaptus ruficollis*
Cormorant – *Phalacrocorax carbo*
Whooper Swan – *Cygnus cygnus*
Pink-Footed Goose – *Anser brachyrhynchus*
Canada Goose – *Branta canadensis*
Wigeon – *Anas penelope*
Tufted Duck – *Aythya fuligula*
Goldeneye – *Bucephala clangula*
Red-Breasted Merganser – *Mergus serrator*
Osprey – *Pandion haliaetus*
Honey Buzzard – *Pernis apivorous* (occ.)
Rough-Legged Buzzard – *Buteo lagopus*
Hen Harrier – *Circus cyaneus*
Goshawk – *Accipiter gentilis*
Hobby – *Falco subbuteo*
Greenshank – *Tringa nebularia*
Black-Headed Gull – *Larus ridibundus*
Lesser Black-backed Gull – *Larus fuscus*
Herring Gull – *Larus argentatus*
Great Black-backed Gull – *Larus marinus*
Stock Dove – *Columba oenas*
Barn Owl – *Tyto alba*
Snowy Owl – *Nyctea scandiaca*
Kingfisher – *Alcedo atthis*
Waxwing – *Bombycilla garrulus*
Fieldfare – *Turdus pilaris*
Redwing – *Turdus iliacus*
Whitethroat – *Sylvia communis*
Blackcap – *Sylvia atricapilla*
Great Grey Strike – *Lanius excubitor*
Brambling – *Fringilla montifringilla*
Reed Bunting – *Emberiza schoeniclus*